WAR ON TWO FRONTS

WAR ON TWO FRONTS

An Infantry Commander's War in Iraq and the Pentagon

By

COLONEL CHRISTOPHER P. HUGHES

CASEMATE

Philadelphia and Newbury

Published in the United States of America in 2007 by
CASEMATE
1016 Warrior Road, Drexel Hill, PA 19026

and in Great Britain by
CASEMATE
17 Cheap Street, Newbury RG20 5DD

Copyright © Christopher P. Hughes 2007

ISBN 978-1-932033-81-6

Cataloging-in-publication data is available from the Library of Congress
and the British Library.

Printed and Bound in the United States of America

For a complete list of Casemate titles please contact

CASEMATE PUBLISHERS
Telephone (610) 853-9131, Fax (610) 853-9146
E-mail: casemate@casematepublishing.com
Website: www.casematepublishing.com

CASEMATE PUBLISHERS
Telephone (01635) 231091, Fax (01635) 41619
E-mail: casemate-uk@casematepublishing.co.uk
Website: www.casematepublishing.co.uk

THE VIEWS PRESENTED IN THIS MANUSCRIPT ARE THOSE OF THE
AUTHOR AND DO NOT NECESSARILY REPRESENT THE VIEWS OF THE
DEPARTMENT OF DEFENSE OR ITS COMPONENTS.

CONTENTS

Foreword *by Rick Atkinson*   vii
Preface   ix

PART I
THE 31ST INVASION OF ANCIENT MESPOTAMIA

1.   PREPARING FOR WAR   3
2.   THE BATTLE FOR NAJAF   37
3.   THE MOSQUE OF ALI   73
4.   AL HILLAH—THE BATTLE FOR BABYLON   123
5.   NORTHERN IRAQ   157
6.   CHANGING COMMAND IN COMBAT   189

PART II
A FOOTSTOOL AT THE SEAT OF POWER

7.   THE PENTAGON   203
8.   ON TO THE NATIONAL WAR COLLEGE   241
9.   THE GREATER WAR ON TERRORISM   255
10. THE WAY FORWARD   267

Appendix I: A Strategy for Leaving Iraq   281
Appendix II: Know Your Enemy   284
Acknowledgments   291
Notes   294
Index   297

In Memory of Master Sergeant Dan Maloney.
Dan was killed in a motorcycle accident two weeks before he
was to retire. We will all miss an exceptional NCO and person.
We take comfort and strength in the memory of our great
friend and comrade. His laughter and calm enthusiasm
will always be remembered.

This book is also dedicated to the men, women,
spouses, children, and veterans of 2-327th Infantry—No Slack.
May God always have a special place in his heart for the men of this
battalion and regiment who have done so much with so little and
asked for nothing other than never to be forgotten.

FOREWORD

By Rick Atkinson

Few literary forms are more enduring or compelling than the battle memoir. Thucydides was a young Athenian general whose *History of the Peloponnesian War* remains as vibrant and relevant as when he wrote it more than two millennia ago. The Welsh-born British adventurer, T.E. Lawrence, described his role in the Arab revolt against Turkish oppression in *The Seven Pillars of Wisdom*, a work that transcends its time. Among American military figures, *The Personal Memoirs of Gen. W.T. Sherman*, "written by himself," and *Personal Memoirs of U.S. Grant*, completed barely a week before the author died of throat cancer, immeasurably enrich our understanding of the Civil War. No textured history of World War II would be possible without the trove of memoirs that range from Dwight D. Eisenhower's *Crusade in Europe* to H.H. "Hap" Arnold's *Global Missions*, and from Mark W. Clark's *Calculated Risk* to Lucian K. Truscott, Jr.'s *Command Missions*.

Colonel Christopher Hughes' account of his battalion's role in the 2003 invasion of Iraq falls squarely within this tradition. The 2nd Battalion of the 327th Infantry Regiment, 101st Airborne Division, known as "*No Slack*," becomes a microcosm allowing us to see, through the lens of a single unit, the larger Army at this critical juncture in its history.

Colonel Hughes writes with clarity, candor and an abiding affection for his soldiers, even as he carries the story beyond the battlefields of Iraq for a glimpse of the inner workings of the Pentagon as invasion turned to occupation. He also writes convincingly about being "impressed, confused and frightened by the decision-making process" in Washington, DC.

As an embedded reporter in the 101st Airborne Division from the time *The Screaming Eagles* left Fort Campbell, Kentucky, to their occupation of southern Baghdad, I had the chance to see Chris Hughes on several occasions: at Camp Pennsylvania in Kuwait, shortly after a renegade soldier had attacked his officers with grenades and rifle fire; outside Najaf, as *No Slack* prepared to attack that vital city on the western fringe of the Euphrates Valley; and in the heart of Najaf, where his instinctive decision to avoid a confrontation with agitated Shiites remains one of the most memorable moments in the march to Baghdad. I found him to be thoughtful, professional and good-humored—a soldier's soldier. These qualities all emerge in *The War on Two Fronts*, and in taking time to tell his tale Colonel Hughes has made a valuable contribution to the growing literary compendium about our long war in Mesopotamia.

PREFACE

Arma virumque cano. (Of arms and the man, I sing.)
—Virgil, *The Aeneid*

After returning from Iraq in the summer of 2003, I found myself in the odd and uncomfortable position as reluctant public spokesperson on the war in Iraq and eventually the Global War on Terrorism.

After my return, local and national news agencies queried, requested and even harassed me for months in attempts to convince me to tell my story and the story of my battalion's role during the invasion of Iraq. Attempting to avoid them while dealing with the horror of battle, my personal guilt at leaving my men in harm's way, coming to terms with taking human life, and figuring out how to live the rest of my life as a father, husband and soldier, I wanted to avoid discussing something that civilians could not possibly understand or comprehend. Trying to answer even the simplest question from a friend or family member caused a flood of conflicting emotions that I could not explain nor physically endure—especially from my family.

Every time they asked me a question about Iraq, I was proud, embarrassed, ashamed, ecstatic, thankful and sad at the same time. While on leave after the war, I noticed my father's proud glow in his face and eyes as he kept a careful distance and intentionally avoided discussing the war. As he was a 23-year Air Force veteran of two wars, we both knew the secret horror of war but did not admit it to each other. He quietly respected my internal struggle and would not bother me like everyone else. I would have to be the one to bring it up.

As I spent my leave time running down the old and comfortable streets of my hometown, Red Oak, Iowa, I remembered how and where I grew up . . . I longed for the ignorance of my youth and slow-ly began to fully understand and appreciate my father's silence about the Korean and Vietnam Wars. I remembered the first time he finally broke down and told a war story, after years of silence, in 1995. After almost 35 years of trying to pull stories from my mother, grandfather and uncle, my father suddenly started telling a story one night to a group of my classmates from the Command and General Staff College staying at his house before a hunt the next morning.

When he started to tell his story I was in the other room. I slowly snuck into the kitchen and listened in shock while he discussed his 17th combat mission over North Korea to the mesmerized group of Army and Navy officers in the living room.

At the end of the story I entered the room. In disbelief, he handed me the picture that had hung on his wall for over 30 years, turning it over he showed me his citation for the Air Medal (Valor). Instinctively he straightened up and slowly began to read the citation aloud. When he finished he sheepishly looked up at me with tears in his eyes and said, "Now you understand. I couldn't explain it to you until now. I'm sorry."

As the phone rang at my father's house while I was on leave (or in hiding) after my return from Iraq, I looked at that picture on the wall and decided not to wait 30 years to talk about my experiences to the public and my family. Not to ingratiate, but to educate the public, ease my nightmares and placate the demons my soldiers and I will face for the rest of our lives. I told the man on the phone I would tell him our story.

Following this interview, I joined a select group of officers called the Army Initiatives Group in Washington, DC. In this capacity, I would have an opportunity to continue to fight for my soldiers in Iraq by providing sound advice to the senior leadership of the Army and the Department of Defense. Taking advantage of my short-lived fame in Iraq, I was also able to speak with authority in the nation's capital to newspapers, magazines, and thinktanks in hopes of further helping to educate and influence the outcome of the war and care for the men of "No Slack" still in Iraq.

As the insurgency began to gain momentum in the fall of 2003, I found myself in a unique position to participate in a number of initiatives and senior leader discussions key to finding innovative ways to confront the new war. On a "footstool at the seat of power" in the Pentagon, I was impressed, confused and frightened by the decision-making process in the most powerful city in the world.

Four years later and after dozens of interviews, speeches and articles, I have found that discussing what the battalion accomplished in Iraq and my experiences in the Pentagon have tamed the nightmares, caged the demons, and even given me some inner peace.

Writing this book is an attempt to help my former soldiers, who may still live with these demons, to understand and appreciate their decision to raise their right hand and voluntarily swear an oath to uphold and defend an ideal—the Constitution of the United States of America.

As their former commander, their welfare and peace of mind still remains one of my most sacred and honored responsibilities. This is their story from my perspective, and I pray that I have captured what they will hold most dear in their hearts and help them to accept and explain their experiences in Iraq. If the men of 2nd Battalion, 327th Infantry Regiment, known as *"No Slack,"* find solace in this book and begin to tell their stories to their families, friends and communities, then this book is a success.

As I first typed this note in the summer of 2005, the men of 2d Battalion, 327th Infantry Regiment were yet again crossing the berm into Iraq and returning to the great land of Mesopotamia to serve for a second year—and many *No Slack* veterans will return with other units across the Army. May God keep them safe, as they once again bring freedom to "The Cradle of Civilization."

Colonel Christopher P. Hughes,
Commander, Joint Task Force Bravo,
Soto Cano Air Base, Republic of Honduras,
30 April 2007

A DoD aerial view of the Iraqi city of Najaf showing sectors of assault
and the escarpment on the city's edge.

The town of Ash Shurah in northern Iraq, one of the objectives of
Operation Eindhoven.

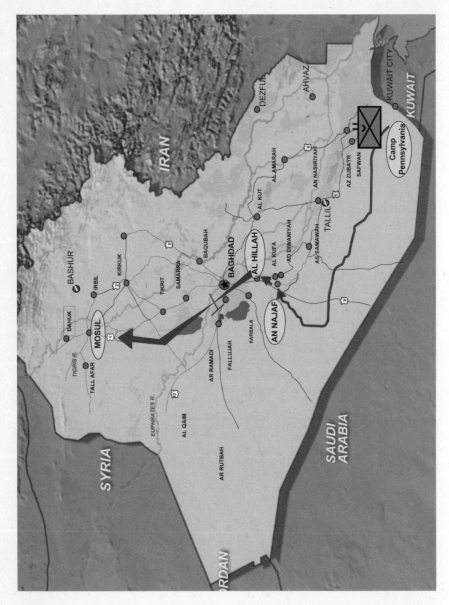

This map shows the progress of *No Slack* during the invasion of Iraq in
March–April 2003.

PART I
THE 31ST INVASION OF ANCIENT MESOPOTAMIA

1

PREPARING FOR WAR

"This is No Slack 6, I'm taking command."

FORT CAMPBELL, KENTUCKY

In a moment of weakness that came back and bit me square in the ass, I allowed the wives of my battalion, 2d Battalion of the 327th Infantry Regiment, access to the battalion area while their husbands prepared to deploy to war. It was akin to letting wives and girlfriends into the locker room hours before the Super Bowl, but my men were going off to something much more serious.

Under normal circumstances, Army families say their goodbyes at home, and most wives drop their husbands off at the edge of the battalion area in good order and then go about their own daily business.

However, going to war was not normal circumstances.

Therefore, when the wives of *No Slack* (my battalion's nickname) asked me for access to the battalion to say their final goodbyes before they entrusted their husband's lives to me, my resolve to keep my troops focused squarely on the job at hand weakened.

After all, they had promised to remain strong and not interfere with our out-loading. My gut told me it was the wrong thing to do, but it seemed a harmless concession at the time. Now, just hours before our departure, my battalion area was filled with painful, confused and heart-wrenching scenes of emotional hugging and kids crying.

It was a bad start.

A further distraction was that my own family was taking advantage of my decision. My wife Marguerite, daughter Ashley, and sons Patrick and Michael were all milling about, diverting my attention from the job at hand. In my twenty years as an Army officer, they had never once accompanied me to my office during a deployment, and most certainly not at 3:00 a.m. My normal pre-deployment routine was to say my goodbyes to my children the night before and briefly wake them in the morning to give them my last hug goodbye.

Marguerite and I would spend quality-time days before the deployment and then remain formal and business-like in the hours before and the morning of my departure. As the wife of the battalion commander, Marguerite was expected to keep a stiff upper lip and set an example for the other 380 wives and 213 children. In the Army, this was the traditional role of a senior wife—she bore the brunt of the demands, concerns and frustrations of the wives of junior soldiers on behalf of the Army. It was her expected place though not her job. It was by far the most difficult thing I'd ever asked of her in over twenty years of marriage.

Normally, Marguerite just dropped me off at my headquarters, and I would conduct my final checks—personal gear, maps, orders and memorandums. After which I would give someone the task of ensuring my personal stuff got on the right train, plane or bus.

When my personal chores were complete, I would take about 15 or 30 minutes alone, donning my commander's mask. The mask is one of the most valuable leadership tools an officer has. It is a facade leaders have used for centuries to deter or hide fear, check emotions, and present subordinates with an example they can count on during moments of great stress, such as war. Once the mask is donned, a commander walks alone and is held to a higher standard than his soldiers, peers or friends. It is often a lonely and difficult road of absolute responsibility, moral inconsistencies, religious quandary and the reality of dealing with death.

After twenty years of military service, I was comfortable wearing my mask, but this morning it did not fit right. Looking into the eyes of my soldiers' wives was making me feel more alone and anxious than ever before. The welfare of my men was always in the forefront of my mind, but the idea that this duty also extended to the continued well-being of their families was suddenly being driven home. It made me a bit uneasy. My own family's well-being was contributing to my unease.

Their presence had turned my routine upside down. I was finding it impossible to fit my commander's mask and monitor the progress of the battalion in the detached way I was accustomed to. The unexpected flood of personal emotions slowed my preparation, clouded my judgment, and hindered my ability to command at a time when I should have been more focused than ever before.

The fear in my son Patrick's eyes kept reminding me that I might never see him again; my daughter Ashley's precise and intellectual questions about the deployment process distracted my packing; and Marguerite's brave and proud looks were tearing me apart inside. Had we come this far in our lives and in my career to place myself in such a dangerous situation . . . was I an ignorant fool for dreaming of this moment for almost twenty years? Was I a bad father, husband—or person? Who in their right mind would dedicate their entire adult life to studying, training and planning to kill other human beings? Would God forgive me? How many of my men would die because of my faults and weaknesses as a man and as a commander? Had I done everything I could? How could I face the wife of a man killed under my command?

The flood of emotion was making me ill and weak in the knees.

I was snapped out of my reverie by my Executive Officer (XO), Major Peter Rooks, an exceptionally organized and competent officer, storming into my office with the battalion's senior ranking enlisted soldier, Command Sergeant Major (CSM) Richard Montcalm, in his wake to announce that a number of pissed-off wives from D Company were in the headquarters waiting area demanding to see me now. Montcalm was my senior enlisted advisor and responsible for the morale, appearance and discipline of the men. As my confidant, he was my eyes and ears—responsible for preventing me from forgetting my place and the welfare of the men. A matchless presence, Richard was a tinkerer—a gadget man who loved a mechanical challenge, a skill I would eventually learn to appreciate and leverage. Nevertheless, this kind of challenge was absolutely the last thing I needed, and as I glanced at my youngest son asleep on my office couch, I cursed myself for being so weak as to allow families to enter the battalion area as we were leaving for war. This unnecessary drama was a self-inflicted wound. I had no time for this kind of drama—no time!

"I'll be right back," I said to Marguerite as I left to deal with the upset wives. I knew what they were pissed about. The First Sergeant from Delta Company, First Sergeant (1SG) Steven Bratton, was a gruff, crusty old fart—an old Army sergeant who felt that wives were only authorized if the Army issued them to the soldier as part of his basic kit. The wives were lined up in my hallway and, as I expected, they were upset because Bratton had sent them packing because they were getting in the way and making it difficult to get pre-deployment tasks accomplished before the company's movement. Being the exceptional sergeant he was, Bratton had modified my rules to best support his mission. This was commendable, but I just wished he'd possessed a tiny modicum of tact. Instead, he had declared the wives camp followers, a nuisance, and had just run them off. I kept in mind that the collected spouses were tired and anguished, as I tried to explain that I had made a mistake letting them stay this long and that we now needed space to get our work done on time. After a bit, the wives settled down and reluctantly complied.

Back in my office, the drama continued as Patrick and Michael tried on my battle gear, Ashley worked at my desk, and Marguerite tried to be helpful while staying noninvasive. The dense cloud of emotions was more than I could take, and I desperately needed to get out of the office, clear my head and get my mask on. So I picked up my gear and told Marguerite I needed to go load my equipment on a truck in the battalion parking lot. Without a second thought, she told Patrick to help me with my bags. Before I could say no, Patrick swung my 120-lb deployment bag over his left shoulder and was heading for the door. My heart sank as I looked at him. Tall for his age, Patrick looked like any one of the 900 young men I was taking to war. Again, I was reminded that every soldier I would command in combat was someone else's child.

Patrick bore the heavy load well, and I noted how attentive he was to all that was going on around him. As I watched him throw my equipment bag onto the battalion bag pile, I could not help noticing how easily he blended in with the surrounding soldiers. He was almost 16, only two or three years younger than most of my young soldiers of the 101st Airborne Division. My mind drifted again and I wondered what he would do and become if I was killed. How would he react to the news, and what kind of man would he turn into? Would he step up and help his mother, or would he consider my death a foolish endeavor and curse me for placing myself in such a position?

I longed to hug him and tell him it would be fine and that I would be home soon, but that would be a lie and I could never lie to him. He had the ability to see right through me. I never sugarcoated what I did for a living. I wanted him to respect what I did, but I also made it clear that I didn't want him to follow in my shoes. I wanted him to be the first man in our family to reap the benefits and rights won for him on battlefields that his great-grandfather, grandfather and I have fought to protect since 1917. The men in my family had loved and defended their country, only asking for the opportunity to make a difference. I wanted a different path for him. But I am sure that this was a wish shared but not realized by each previous generation. Still, it was my strongest wish that I would be the last of the Hughes men to fight on some foreign battlefield.

After a three-hour ordeal of final roll calls and loading the buses that would take us to the airfield, I was happy to be getting away. The sun was rising and the faces of the wives were more visible. They reflected their solid support for the departing soldiers, but their eyes were also reddened from tears and worn from worry. I boarded last and quickly ordered the column to move. As the driver released the brake, I looked back at my family standing in a small clump in the morning haze. They bravely waved and Marguerite mouthed, "I love you." I waved back, swallowed hard and then forced myself to look ahead. My commander's mask was at last firmly in place.

THE *STITCH AND BITCH*

It was difficult to find ways to fill the idle time preceding the invasion once we shipped our equipment and awaited the final orders to deploy. Rumors, changes, politics and CNN all play a role in soldiers' lives before a deployment, for better or worse.

As warriors, my troops and I spent thousands of hours training, preparing, talking, drilling, learning, relearning and getting in the best physical shape of our lives. Consequently our spouses did the same, through the rituals of forming family readiness groups and attending records briefs and coffees. For the most part, all in our community did much to ease anxieties and keep everyone informed as much as possible, but mostly what the process did was drive the point home that we really knew nothing other than that we might be in combat soon.

And although we had lived this reality since 9/11 it was now becoming a reality—we were actually being issued our desert uniforms. Everyone knew that once we got our brown-mottled uniforms and boots we were going. No more guessing and rumors; it was now a fact in the eyes of all those involved, especially the wives.

I must admit in hindsight that I longed for the decision to finally issue the new desert uniforms to my battalion. My men were frustrated and needed to stop being told to stand by, get ready, or to be prepared—it was time to go! On the other hand, the gasp from the spouse when the uniforms actually came home that night was heard across Fort Campbell. They are actually going; the issue was decided. WAR!

This was a reaction I hadn't experienced since being at Fort Drum, preparing to invade Haiti with the 10th Mountain Division in 1994. During that mission I was already away from my family and did not witness the stress at the family level like I was seeing this time as the commander. The uniforms were akin to the enemy in Iraq, they represented the pending war and potential loss of life to the spouses...they hated them and I could see it in their eyes. The men ran around with them like a new toy; the women cursed them. In a day, after months of training and preparing the wives, I lost them with the dispatch of two sets of desert camouflage uniforms.

That night I was panicking, trying to figure out how I was going to get my patches sewn on my new uniforms. Normally this was a very simple process: buy the patches—US Army, Hughes, and my 101st Airborne patch—then take them to the tailor shop and pick them up the next day. The problem: 17,000 other soldiers from the 101st were all trying to do the same thing at the same time. How could we get through this hurdle, a hurdle as small as a mouse turd, but in the eyes of my soldiers and me the size of a small mountain? It was a matter of pride and history; we needed that 101st patch on our left shoulder so the world would know that *The Screaming Eagles* were coming!

That evening, after thinking about this new issue, mainly because everything else was done, I considered something I hadn't tried in seventeen years: I prepared to ask Marguerite to sew on my patches. Now this was a significant emotional event for me because I had asked Marguerite one other time to sew on a patch when I was a second lieutenant. At the time it seemed like a reasonable request because she was a hell of a fine seamstress and constantly made clothes for herself and others, a skill that continues to impress me today.

However, when she quickly complied with my request all those years ago, I discovered my paranoia with the appearance of my uniforms, and after numerous attempts and one of the first fights in our young marriage, we agreed that I would never ask her to sew or iron my uniforms ever again—they would forever be my responsibility and mine alone. So the thought of asking her to do this a second time was a bit intimidating; the last thing I needed was to start a uniform debate the week before deploying to combat.

The approach was simple. I complained about my inability to get my uniform sewn and asked for a needle and thread to do it myself. With her famously dismayed look she snatched the uniform from me and went into her sewing sanctuary. I paced outside the garage like an expectant father, vowing to accept the uniform no matter what it looked like; I still had time to take it to the tailor shop if she screwed it up, right?

When Marguerite emerged she handed me the uniform, and much to my surprise and relief it was perfect.

That night I watched her sew my other uniforms and hat. She was so serious and involved. The uniform became her link to me and the deployment . . . she was helping, she was accepting, it was relieving her stress. When she was done, I could see in her eyes that she had given me something that I could carry with me to Iraq and back and always remember she gave it to me. This inspired a thought: Seeing her enthusiasm, I asked if she thought the wives would consider setting up a sewing shop in the battalion classroom to do the same for all the men in the battalion. With a grin she said "yes."

Over the next seven days as we prepared to leave, the battalion classroom was transformed into a sewing shop, hundreds of uniforms piled in the corners with their name tags, rank and 101st patches pinned to them—piles of patches, dozens of busy wives and girlfriends, an occasional mother and father, and the kids of the battalion.

Not all could sew, but others could collect the minimal charge for thread and patches, stacking and tracking the uniforms through the makeshift assembly line. It wasn't perfect or even very efficient, and in some cases we lost uniforms altogether, but one thing did emerge— contentment and camaraderie.

It was working. The wives were bonding in a new way; they were helping, they were venting, and they were sharing their support in a way they had never done before. The emotions were high and the Chaplain realized the power of the forum, as did the commanders and I, as it became a source of community and easing the pain. It eventually became affectionately known as *The Stitch and Bitch*.

When the uniforms were finally done, the sewing room slowly returned to normal and it was finally time to go.

CAMP PENNSYLVANIA, KUWAIT

Camp Pennsylvania was named in honor of Flight 93, which crashed in a field outside of Shanksville, PA, on September 11, 2001. Forty-five miles west of Kuwait City in the shadow of the Iraqi border, the camp's name reminded every soldier of his or her purpose for being so far from home—to ensure that men like Todd Beamer and the other 41 courageous passengers of Flight 93 were never forgotten. For all of us, what we were doing was supposed to make sure terrorism would never again enter the United States. We were preparing to take the fight to the enemy.

Our movement from Kuwait City to Camp Pennsylvania was executed in the darkness of night with small 25-passenger busses. Soldiers were crammed in along with huge duffle bags, rucksacks, 50 lbs of combat gear apiece, their weapons and a non-English speaking driver. The ride across the Kuwaiti desert was a cross between a roller coaster and a mechanical bull ride. It was quickly obvious that the Kuwaitis did not spend a lot of money on road maintenance north of the capital. I did not know if they had better uses for their oil money or just wanted to make sure that a future Iraqi invasion of Kuwait would have a miserable trip. As the battalion commander, even I found myself precariously uncomfortable, wedged between my combat equipment, a straight-back bus seat, two large foot lockers and a very cold window pressing against my back. I was on the verge of a charley horse for well over three hours.

About an hour into the ride, my intelligence officer, Captain Chris Hennigan, a charismatic officer from Tullahoma, TN, and son of a multi-silver star recipient from Vietnam, Lieutenant Colonel (retired) Al Hennigan, suddenly jumped up and desperately fought through the crush of sleeping men, scrambling to the door of the bus. Yelling at the driver, who didn't speak English, Chris grabbed the door handle and pulled back violently, allowing freezing cold air and choking dust to rush into the bus without warning. He pulled himself to the door with both hands like he was going to jump, extending his body beyond its frame. Then he lurched forward in the dark and dust and began vomiting out the door.

My first reaction was sympathy. I was concerned he was going to lose his balance and fall out the rocking and pitching door of the still-moving bus. But as he slumped in the doorway, I suddenly remembered that vomiting was the first physical indicator of a chemical attack. We were only a few miles from the Iraqi border and instinct took over. I moved into defense mode. Were we under attack? Half awake, I quickly scrambled for my chemical mask, yelling to the men "Get your masks on, Goddamn it! Gas! Get your masks on!" This surprised everyone, even Chris. Everyone dove for their masks simultaneously in a mad scramble. Holding onto the door rail, Chris leaned back and looked at us. We looked like a bus full of drunken Twister players; our panicked rush almost caused the bus to run off the road.

Chris realized he had caused an overreaction and began to yell over the roar of the engine, "I'm OK! I'm OK—it's only motion sickness!" The jarring of the bus had made him sick. He closed the door and sat down on the dashboard looking at us. An odd silence fell over the bus. Looking down at the horrified and confused driver, Chris looked back at the rest of us in the confusion of bags, bodies and half-donned protective masks and began to laugh. Everyone joined in at the ludicrousness of the scene; everyone, that is, except me. I was too embarrassed.

Feeling a little stupid for overreacting, I kept my mask on to help with the smell of Chris' situation and to hide my embarrassment in the dark. My first decision in a combat zone and I was 0 for 1. But it

would be the first of many snap decisions I would have to make without fear of failure, trusting my instincts and training. Sometimes its
better to make a mistake and laugh at yourself then to be too afraid
of embarrassment to save your soldiers lives. Being popular and cool
in combat are not sound leadership traits! Luckily, as I tried to hide
my embarrassment, Chris stole everyone's attention back when he
realized he had lost his $120 sunglasses. They had slipped from his
forehead as he vomited out the door. In a fit of rage and disappointment, he managed to fill the next two hours with colorful swearing
that weaved common vulgarity with inspired prose in equal measure.
He was convinced that without his expensive sunglasses he would go
blind in the desert before the war even began.

As Hennigan's antics filled the dark and boring ride, I remembered his wedding in a small white church down a gravel road just
outside of Hopkinsville, KY. He and his young wife, Christie Clune,
had decided to move their April wedding to just days before the
January deployment. It was a small wedding led by my administrative
sergeant, Staff Sergeant (SSG) Reed. Reed was an ordained minister
when he was not in uniform and somehow found time to care for his
own local congregation as well as my soldiers. So it was only fitting
when Chris and Christie took their wedding vows that No Slack stood
firmly at their side on the eve of war. This was just one more act of
devotion and camaraderie that would reinforce to me that these were
not just my soldiers, they were my friends, my family and my brothers. I could not and would not fail them.

About an hour later, we pulled into a well-lit checkpoint on the
outskirts of Camp Pennsylvania. The checkpoint was the beginning of
an extensive set of control points and obstacles defending the entrance
to the camp. The camp itself was one of several massive installations
constructed in the deserts of northern Kuwait to receive the tens of
thousands of soldiers arriving daily. The access point consisted of a
series of sand berms, jersey barriers, barbed concertina wire, floodlights and armed guards. When we arrived, the temperature was in the
low-40s and I could see the breath of the soldiers at their guard posts.
I hoped the cold would encourage them to process us through quickly, but they kept to their methodical and laborious procedures.

Once we were finally inside the camp, there was clearly a well thought-out reception system. As I stepped off the bus, I was met by 1st Brigade's Command Sergeant Major (CSM) Bart Womack. Bart was an interesting character, to say the least. He was physically fit, unusually articulate and poised, and one of the most refined sergeants major I had ever met. Years after the war, I would sit mesmerized watching a TV series called "The E-Ring" where Bart would get his first break into Hollywood as an actor—a goal he would profess to me on occasion that I would brush off as idle talk between two warriors dreaming about retirement—and yet he attained fame. I looked hard to see Womack in the dark wearing his newly-issued cold weather gear; I hardly recognized him with his black knit cap pulled down to his desert goggles, black neck scarf, pull-over jacket and side arm strapped to his right thigh John Wayne-style. As expected, he summoned my first sergeants to give them some quick instructions then quickly ushered me to see Colonel Fredrick "Ben" Hodges, my brigade commander, who was actively greeting my soldiers as they stepped off the buses and found their gear. Seeing his smiling face helped ease the anxiety my soldiers were feeling, and mine.

Hodges had a knack for being at the right place at the right time. His meeting us in the middle of the night boosted morale and conveyed to the troops that he cared for them. He didn't do it for show; his feelings were genuine and it set him apart from other men I had worked for. Ben Hodges was a natural and truly caring leader. He would also prove to be an aggressive and extremely confident combat leader in the days and weeks to come. He graduated in the West Point Class of 1980, and I had known him for almost fifteen years.

When I was a young captain and new company commander, Ben had been the most senior company commander in our unit, the same brigade he would command in combat. In personal style, he was the epitome of what is stereotyped as the true southern gentleman. He had a quick wit and infectious laugh, which was always a calming influence in trying moments. His gentle nature hid a quick intellect and a huge capacity for decisive action. His only obvious eccentricity was a collection of rocks he had picked up from many of the world's great battlefields. His primary criterion for rock selection was that he had to be convinced it was an "eyewitness rock." In other words, the rock had to have been there to see the battle and not added later as part of a road or landfill. Later in the war, I saw him debate taking a rock from the site of the ancient city of Babylon. In what must have been a true test of will for him, he decided that taking a Babylonian rock was too much like stealing antiquities and he left empty-handed.

Camp Pennsylvania was little more than a large circle in the desert. It was over a mile in diameter, surrounded by huge earthen berms[1] and seven 50-foot tall guard towers manned by soldiers with machine guns. Inside the perimeter were seven separate battalion camps arranged around four massive white and red circus tents, three for feeding and one full of fitness weights to maintain our pre-deployment physical strength. There was a separate section where the brigade staff resided.

Exhausted and standing in the cold night air, I did not have much chat in me and Hodges pointed out our tent city homes, about a half mile or so east. I looked into the darkness and could just make out some dim lights in the distance. Without another word, I picked up my bags and began to walk toward the lights. Several hundred soldiers fell into line behind me and, in a walk that seemed endless, we reached the tents and finally bedded down. It was our first chance to get some rest at the end of our 42-hour trip.

Each heated tent had wooden floors, housed twenty soldiers, and provided just enough room for one to take acute notice that the other nineteen guys in the tent had not showered or taken off their boots in almost three days. Despite the crowding and the smell, they were quarters, and heated ones at that. We were very lucky to have them. The 3d Infantry Division soldiers who had occupied the camp prior to our arrival had been sent to live in the open desert with only what they could carry as creature comforts. My soldiers, long accustomed to sleeping wherever they laid their heads, were happy and settled in quickly. After months of training, preparing and worrying, we were finally here, only a few miles from Iraq and the struggle for our lives. I lay down, but couldn't sleep.

EMBEDDED REPORTERS

I woke early the next morning and put on my running clothes, planning to run around the inside perimeter of the camp and get the lay of the land. I tried not to wake anyone, but noticed that the brightly colored sleeping bags of our two embedded reporters, Stewart Ramsey and Garwin McLucky, were empty. I stuck my head out of the tent and got a rude introduction to the crisp cold air of Kuwait in March. I was greeted by the two missing reporters, who were stretching on a bench outside the tent.

"Up for a run, Colonel?" one of them asked.

Stewart and Garwin were a couple of wiry characters with heavy English accents from the Africa Bureau of *Skynews*. Stewart, "the talent," had a full head of dirty blond hair, a huge smile and a ruggedly tanned face that had seen too much stress, sun and rough living from reporting in some of the worst places on earth. Garwin, "the mule," was the behind-the-scenes guy who did virtually everything to make the team work and get the news to their viewers. Younger and much less worn than Stewart, Garwin was an exceptionally pleasant man who seemed to possess an inner glow and one of the most positive attitudes I had ever encountered. If I didn't know he was a cameraman, I would have thought he was a newly-ordained priest ready to save the world on his first mission. He would become one of my favorite people to visit on a daily basis to get a positive attitude boost—his was infectious.

It hadn't taken long for Stewart and Garwin to earn my respect back at Fort Campbell. The day they reported to our headquarters I made it clear that I wasn't thrilled having reporters following me around. I told them that I was blunt and normally unquotable because I felt political correctness was for bigots and people who lacked character. When this didn't seem to bother them, I decided to share an horrific 1994 experience I'd had with an Associated Press reporter in Haiti in order to gauge their willingness to stay with the battalion and endure my skeptical, suspicious and critical view of the media.

On September 19, 1994, the USS *Eisenhower* had dropped me off in Haiti. As a young captain, I was sent there with the 10th Mountain Division to take part in the removal of Haitian Lt. General Raoul Cedras and restore the presidency of Jean-Bertrand Aristide. Not long after my arrival I ran into an inquisitive man at Port au Prince International Airport. While awaiting the arrival of one of the battalions by air, the man and I struck up a conversation. When our conversation ended, I walked away thinking I had just met a nice guy to whom I'd merely explained the situation that was unfolding around him. Two weeks later, when his report hit the front page of *USA Today*, I was almost arrested for divulging classified information to the media.

The man was a reporter who had managed to use our conversation to corroborate a story he was investigating alleging that US commandos were planning to kidnap Cedras if former President Jimmy Carter's negotiating team failed to defuse the standoff in Haiti prior to the invasion. *USA Today*'s above-the-fold lead story started with "U.S. commandos were 'cocked and loaded' to kidnap [Raoul Cedras] as the invasion began, says Capt. Chris Hughes." As if that wasn't bad enough, the article went on to say that senior Pentagon officials had denied Captain Hughes' claims and would investigate the allegations. As a young captain with no access to any classified information of that nature, it was a ridiculous claim, yet there was my name on the front page of *USA Today*. At the time, the very thought that my name had come up at a Pentagon press conference made me sick to my stomach. How could I ever recover from such a stupid mistake?

Even though I was never charged and the allegations were deemed unfounded, it did not matter to anyone who knew about the case. During the following years, I would learn that once your name is in the media you are guilty, and if the charges are dropped, it must be part of a cover-up! For years, I lived with the shame and embarrassment of my inability to recognize I was being used by a reporter to create a false story in order to sell more papers. I made it very clear to Stewart and Garwin that I would not allow that to happen again, to my soldiers or me. The key to our relationship would be the truth. Unlike the Associated Press reporter in Haiti, who had simply shown up and drew false conclusions out of context, I expected Stewart and Garwin to be with the men, getting dirty, sweaty and maybe even bloody. Only then could they know, see and report the truth in its entirety. If they were willing to do that, I would give them unfettered access to the battalion and its missions. But if they ever compromised my men in anyway, I planned to shoot them myself.

When I first told Stewart and Garwin my Haiti story and it didn't cause either of them to draw a pen or notebook, I knew they were the right reporters for *No Slack*. We shook hands in agreement, and then I told them to report to physical training the next morning at six a.m. The next morning they were in my office ready to go, and for the next two months, they ran every day with the battalion until we crossed into Iraq.

THE REALITY OF PENDING WAR

The ten months leading up to our deployment to Kuwait was one of the most intensive training periods in my career. As a commander, I was given every resource I needed to train my battalion. It was an unprecedented bounty of time, ammo and resources. I was able to hone my force to a fine combat edge, but I remained uneasy about one major factor. No amount of time or money spent in the scrub pines of Fort Campbell would prepare my men for operating in a desert. I considered getting my guys into the open desert and making them comfortable with the vast distances, the effects of the sand on their weapons, their movement formations and survival skills as the most important training we would need in preparing for Iraq. Less than 50 of my men had ever been in a desert and of them only 38 had trained in one. Most of those, like me, had fought in mock battles at the Army's National Training Center in the Mojave Desert. Only twelve were Desert Storm veterans.

Once we hit the ground in Kuwait, every waking minute of the day was dedicated to training. No one knew when, or even if, we would attack Iraq, but I hoped we would not languish in the desert too long. During Desert Shield in 1991, the 101st had sat for six months in the open desert. After a while such prolonged waiting wears on the troops and dulls their edge. At Fort Campbell, the battalion conducted two multi-hour physical fitness sessions per day to make sure every soldier deployed in the best physical condition of their lives. We had shipped our equipment early so all we had left to do was run, lift weights and mentally prepare our families and ourselves. Now that we were 40 miles from the Iraqi border, I needed to sustain that fitness level and get the men ready for the desert without tearing them down physically and mentally. Every day that we waited to attack I was losing a bit of our unprecedented physical advantage over the enemy. On the other hand, every day we waited gained us a bit more desert training experience. We were losing our physical edge as we improved our desert war fighting advantage. The trade-off had to be finely balanced and I had to find ways to make the best of it without knowing how long I had to sustain either.

However, one residual advantage I hadn't anticipated was taking the men from good to exceptional when it came to field craft. Field craft is a term that is used to describe a soldier's ability to sustain himself or herself in the field without becoming sick and rendering them combat ineffective. Field hygiene is not a skill that American men join the Army with; it must be experienced and taught.

The men of the battalion, especially the junior officers, were constantly learning ways to make existence in the field tolerable and sustainable. How to deal with cuts, bug bites and the types of bugs that like to live with you, sand where you don't want it, and keeping your clothes clean. Most Americans don't experience extended periods of outdoor living, so anticipating not seeing a shower for the next 30–90 days during the invasion, we pushed hygiene more and more every day. The day that I realized we were prepared to attack was the day I found myself kneeling outside my tent with Majors Crider and Rooks talking about the weather with my hands in a small plastic tub, hand-washing my socks. Enough was enough—we needed to attack, and attack soon.

FRAGGING THE BRIGADE STAFF

Not too long after our arrival, the Scud attacks began. After the first two or three alarms, our reaction drills became as familiar as eating. Our greatest fear was Saddam's chemical Scuds. These missiles were capable of carrying payloads that could either cause blisters in the throat and lungs or destroy blood cells. In either case, the victim would die a painful and horrific death by convulsions, seizures and eventual suffocation in his own body fluids. Saddam's chances of hitting us in the middle of the desert with a high explosive Scud did not concern us much. The greater and more likely threat was a chemical warhead mounted on a Scud. If a chemical Scud hit close to the camp and released its deadly gasses in the cold night air, the agents would hug the ground and sneak into our tents, killing us long after the missile had landed in the desert. Our best defensive weapon, the Patriot Missile System, could destroy the Scud in flight, but the warhead was still likely to survive and detonate wherever it fell to earth. Because of this nasty and very real threat, the key element of every Scud drill was for each soldier to put on his chemical protective mask (gas mask) until the air was tested and declared clear.

By the middle of March, the drills were starting to take a toll on the men and our "give a shit" levels began to wane. Even I was growing weary of the constant drills that sometimes happened three and four times a night. The sirens would sound and we would grab our weapons, don our gas masks, and run to the bunkers to take cover. After 50 to 90 minutes, we would get the all-clear siren and return to our duties or sleep, only to be pulled away to execute the same process all over again. It became a leadership challenge to make sure soldiers did not adopt the "big desert, little me" attitude and start shrugging off the alerts.

On the 19th of March, 2003 the real story became the invasion into Iraq and not these silly Scud attacks in Kuwait that had little or no affect on the Coalition invasion force postured to invade. The sense of urgency from the Scud drills faded to noise once the inevitable happened and the tanks of the 3d Infantry Division (3ID) rolled forward. Everyone wanted to be with them. In all honesty, most of us feared that the Iraqi's might surrender in less than three days and we would miss it like a bunch of rats scurrying around in the desert, dodging ghost Scuds four times a day.

I, too, feared I would miss another war, but this one was different. It wasn't a small Caribbean island, a trapped invasion force in Kuwait, or some Mickey Mouse police force flexing its muscle—this was the remnants of the fourth largest ground Army in the world that had chemical and biological weapons, and we were in the process of driving a stake in its heart—Baghdad. We were attacking where so many had attacked before and failed. This was Mesopotamia, and no one conquers Mesopotamia for long!

On the night of March 22, 2003, our lackadaisical regard for the Scud drills abruptly ended in one moment of confusion, dread and disbelief.

Master Sergeant Newsome shook me awake to the sounds of the muffled sirens of yet another Scud drill. Confused at the commotion and Sergeant Newsome's concern, I realized I had my earplugs in and had slept through most of the drill. I jumped up in my army shorts, pulled on my jacket, grabbed my weapon, and ran out of the tent with my gas mask dragging in the sand behind me. I was a sorry sight.

In the moonlight I could see other stragglers working their way to the bunkers as I squeezed my way into the confined space. I normally sat at the end so I could stick my head out and search the black, starry skies for any signs of a Scud. This night I was joined by a young soldier from my command post with a radio, Specialist Griffin (Griff). Griffin was my Executive Officer's (XO's) driver and my radio operator when I moved by foot. He had obviously gotten the job because he was smarter than most and didn't really fit the stereotype of a steely eyed infantrymen. Griff was too short, too round, and too smart to be a line dog, and we all knew it. It was his claim to fame and I admired him for it. His wit and constant sarcasm were reason enough to have him around, but they paled in the light of his ability to make a radio sing and a vehicle move when the situation warranted it.

Specialist Griffin stuck his head in the bunker and called out my name. Spotting me, he pushed into the crowded bunker and sat down next to me in the cold sand. "Sir, Major Rooks told me to find you and never let you be without the radio." As I sat there half asleep in the sand, I realized that Pete Rooks had once again proven himself an exceptional XO. It was his job to help me command and to think of what I did not or could not. Pete had essentially ordered Griffin to follow me around to ensure I was within arm's reach of a radio at all times. Griffin constantly monitored the radio to let me know when I had calls from my command post or from Colonel Hodges.

As I sat in the cold sand chastising myself for not thinking about a radio, Griffin suddenly grabbed my shoulder and yelled, "Sergeant Major Womack is screaming on the radio that the brigade command post is under attack!"

"What?" I pulled off my gas mask, grabbed the radio from Griffin, and heard Womack screaming my call sign into the radio, "*No Slack 6*, this is *Bastogne*-7.[2] We're fuckin' under attack—grenades and small arms! Get some Goddamn help up here now!"

Immediately I turned to my Command Sergeant Major Montcalm. "Brigade's under attack; you take everyone in this bunker and get up there and help Womack. I'm going to the battalion headquarters and control the brigade from there." I looked back at the dozens of shocked and confused men in the bunker. "I don't give a shit who's in this bunker; they now belong to you Monty—go kick some ass!" I grabbed Griff by the shoulder and ran across the compound toward my command post, yelling "all clear" along the way, calling for my company commanders and telling the men in the bunkers to get behind the barricades and form a defense perimeter: "We're under attack." As I neared the command post, I could hear shooting and explosions coming from the brigade headquarters. I stopped and looked in time to see the flash of an explosion. "Shit—come on Griff!"

Once in the command post, I realized I couldn't command from inside a tent so I grabbed everyone and everything I would need to fight the battalion from outside, in sight of the perimeter. As I envisioned a battle within and around Camp Pennsylvania, I was horrified about our chances of killing each other with "friendly fire." Without any knowledge of the position or nature of the enemy attacking force, the likelihood of friendly fire skyrocketed.

The company commanders were positioning their men along the barrier that surrounded our tent areas and establishing fields of fire. The commanders ran to my location as I gave them orders to close the perimeter, go to nightvision goggles and scopes, turn off all the lights within the compound and get accountability of all their men. I ordered Captain Steve Thomas, my A Company commander, to send out a patrol to our guard towers to ensure the perimeter was still secure and that the guards were alive. This information would help us determine the direction of the attack. I then got back on the brigade radio and tried to contact Colonel Ben Hodges: "*Bastogne*-6 this is *No Slack* 6 . . . *Bastogne*-6 this is *No Slack*-6 . . . *Bastogne*-6 this is *No Slack*-6." I heard nothing but static and dead air.

Then it happened. My training kicked in and I found myself energetically moving into action. "All stations this net, this is *No Slack*-6. I'm taking command . . . standby for orders, over." One by one the other battalions began to report in and await my orders. No discussion, no debate; just as we'd trained.

My boss was wounded or dead and I had to rally over 6,000 men and women to defeat an unknown enemy threat within Camp Pennsylvania. The orders I had just given my company commanders were sensible and more than adequate for the rest of the brigade, so I ordered the other five battalions to do the same. But I emphasized the need to take any and all precautions not to engage each other: "This is a leader intensive order gentlemen; we must clearly identify our own forces and separate them from the enemy. Let's find these bastards and kill them." Once the other battalions acknowledged my orders, I continued to call brigade . . . still no reply from *Bastogne-6*.

One by one my commanders and later my sister battalions began to report in. No enemy contact, all personnel and key equipment accounted for and the perimeter was secure. It was positive but confusing information . . . how did the enemy get in the camp? The perimeter appeared to be intact; all the guard towers were reporting no enemy contact, and the berms showed no signs of ground infiltration. How did they get in and, worse, where did they go?

As I tried to figure it out, my engineer platoon leader First Lieutenant Evangelist and his platoon sergeant, Sergeant First Class Kumm ran up to my position and asked to speak to me privately. Evangelist and Kumm were easily the most interesting command team in the battalion. Evangelist was an academic and almost pious officer who was always calm and deep in his thoughts and actions. Kumm was the epitome of the World War II sergeant depicted in the movies. He wore his emotions on his sleeve and I could always expect him to provide me the unvarnished truth on any topic, especially when I was the topic. I enjoyed his candor. So when I heard their concern it made my heart skip a beat as we stepped into the moon shadow of one of the concrete barriers around our perimeter.

"Sir, we think it's one of our men—Sergeant Akbar," said Lieutenant Evangelist. It only took a couple of seconds for their words to sink in. I didn't like it, but it appeared to be the only possible explanation. There was no way the Iraqis had managed to cross the border and get this far south; there was no way that any contractor or Kuwaiti national knew where my boss and his staff slept. The only possible explanation was someone on the inside. "Sir, we think Akbar is the one who attacked the brigade command post."

"Who the hell is Akbar and why would he attack Colonel Hodges?"

Sergeant Kumm began to explain. "He's one of our men and, well, he's a Muslim and he's been acting funny lately. We just went out to our vehicles to check the soldiers on guard and, well, they weren't there. Sergeant Akbar was the sergeant of the guard. The other guards are here with us; they told us that Akbar released them a couple of hours ago to get some sleep. When we went out to check on Akbar, he was gone. Sir, we found four empty grenade canisters in the front seat of the hummer and on the ground. We also noticed some of the incendiary grenade boxes were missing, and we found a gas mask on the driver's side seat. Sir, we think it's Akbar!"

I stood there in disbelief. I didn't know Sergeant Akbar, but I did know his tent was only yards from mine. Nevertheless, that didn't matter now. I needed to use the only clue I had to the mystery of who attacked us. In all honesty, I had the only reasonable one at this point. As I walked back to the radio, I contemplated how to craft my words as I was about to tell the brigade to be on the lookout for one of their own.

When I picked up the radio, Pete had already established contact with Major Pat Frank, the brigade's senior operations officer. Frank told me that they had eighteen casualties at brigade headquarters. He also reported that Montcalm had arrived and secured the area with *No Slack* infantry he had assembled from the bunker. I was informed that ground and air medical evacuation was en route to take away the wounded.

According to Frank, the scene was chaotic but organized. The brigade staffers had two Kuwaiti linguists in custody and were questioning them as possible suspects, while Montcalm was sending out patrols to look for possible suspects in the brigade sleeping area. Frank recommended that we stay in our security posture to see if we could notice anyone moving within the perimeter. I concurred with his recommendations and told him and the brigade intelligence officer, Major Kyle Warren, that I had reason to believe that one of our soldiers was the culprit.

I then made a radio call to the entire brigade. Once I had everyone's attention on the radio I told them to be on the lookout for

Sergeant Hassan Akbar from 2d Platoon, B Company, 2d of the 326th Engineer Battalion. As our most likely lead, it was my opinion that Sergeant Akbar was armed and dangerous. He was disgruntled and was a danger to himself and anyone who may come in contact with him, and I wanted him detained for questioning.

When the battalion had completed securing our compound and accounting for our equipment, I called Pete Rooks over and told him I needed to get to the brigade headquarters. I needed to determine Colonel Hodges' status and, as the acting brigade commander, I would need to organize the staff.

"Pete, you're in command. I hope that this is just temporary, but I know you're up to it. I will get back with you in the morning when I know more. Good luck!"

When we finished discussing the transition, Specialist Griffin told me that Colonel Hodges was on the radio asking for me. Relieved, I grabbed the mike and barked, "*Bastogne*-6, this is *No Slack*-6. Are you all right?"

A familiar voice finally made its way over the airwaves. "Hey Chris, I got knocked on my ass, but I'm OK. But I need you up here."

"Roger sir, I'm on my way."

Still not knowing for sure if we had a renegade soldier roaming the camp or a small Iraqi force, I decided to move to the brigade command post, taking an armed detail from my scout platoon with me. As we worked our way across the camp, I could see and hear the entire brigade searching their areas, challenging moving personnel and sending patrols to the outer berm as we continued toward the headquarters.

The fear that some nervous soldier would trigger a huge friendly-fire fight made me increasingly nervous as we neared the brigade headquarters. Then, suddenly from my right, a missile launched from the ground with a flash, and a bang rang out as the rocket motor kicked in to climb into the night sky. One of the young scouts with me yelled "RPG!"[3] and most of the men dropped to the ground.

Alarmed that they were about to start shooting, I barked, "That's no RPG—it's a Patriot missile! Fuck! We've got no place to hide," as I thought it was firing at a Scud. With nowhere to take cover, all we could do was watch the rocket plume of the Patriot climb and strike its intended target in the perfectly clear night sky. The explosion was loud, but there was no flash of light to give away the location of the hit. And then I saw the flashing wing and tail lights of an airplane.

"Holy shit! That Patriot shot that Scud right out from under that plane." How was that possible? I suddenly saw the wreckage of whatever it hit falling toward us. "Here it comes—run!" We ran all the way to the brigade command post as the wreckage landed in the desert behind us. We had no idea at the time that the Patriot had accidentally shot down a British Tornado jet fighter-bomber with a crew of two over Camp Pennsylvania that night. It was just one more thing adding to the casualty count and confusion of the night.

When I walked into the brigade area, the generator lights were illuminating the entire compound. I stood in the middle of the lighted area with my security detail and suddenly noticed two armed men standing over an American soldier lying face down in the sand next to the brigade Scud bunker with his hands cuffed behind his back.

I walked up to Major Kyle Warren, the brigade intelligence officer, who was always serious and reserved and who was clearly in charge, to let him know I was in his area and needed to find Colonel Hodges. Kyle quickly informed me that they had caught Sergeant Akbar, the soldier lieing in the sand. He then pointed out Colonel Hodges, who was surrounded by the embedded reporters in a blur of cameras and lights. I was happy to see we had control of Akbar, but I was horrified to see my boss standing in front of the video cameras with a bloody t-shirt, blood-soaked pants and his right arm in a sling.

I was furious as I walked over to the circus to pull him from the scene. He was clearly in shock and I felt the reporters were taking advantage of his weakened condition to make a more dramatic story. This would cause a riot back home if the wives saw him bloody and haggard like this on CNN. I tried to pull him away, but he insisted he was fine. Sharp and alert, he didn't want the enemy to think this incident would prevent us from attacking. Colonel Hodges was concerned about how the enemy would react to this incident, while I was concerned about how the wives would react. I guess that's why he was the brigade commander and I was not. He was right, and once again he had taught me a valuable lesson in leadership.

I left him talking to the media and presenting a good front for the enemy. My next order of business was to check the status of the medical evacuation and get a security assessment from Montcalm. Command Sergeant Major Montcalm was sure the perpetrator was Akbar because they had caught him in the Scud bunker during the Patriot missile attack. When Major Warren had entered the bunker during the drill, he had noticed a soldier without a gas mask and asked him his name. When the soldier identified himself as Sergeant Akbar, Warren and two of the sergeants in the bunker wrestled him to the ground. They found a grenade inside his gas mask carrier, and his weapon had been recently fired. Eventually, they discovered that Akbar was also wounded from one of the grenades he had thrown.

I walked through the tent where the attacks had occurred, and the amount of devastation and blood was overwhelming. The least critical casualties were on stretchers awaiting evacuation. I had a chance to talk to two of them before they boarded helicopters and ambulances. As I surveyed the area, one thing became clear—we were lucky, damn lucky, that the men attacked were not sleeping on cots. Because we had not received enough cots for everyone to sleep on, Colonel Hodges had forbidden anyone, including the officers on his staff, to use the ones we had. A classic case of leadership that inadvertently ensured that the brigade staff was sleeping on the floor and not elevated on cots. A difference of eight to fifteen inches had made the difference between life and death. Since a grenade's blast rises at a 15-degree angle, most of the eighteen wounded received only fragmentation wounds in their feet. Sleeping on the floor allowed the blast to miss their vital organs, significantly reducing the lethality of the attack for most of the staff. Despite that blessing, we still lost two good officers, and we would be going to war missing a dozen men who had been wounded.

Prior to taking command of *No Slack*, I had worked on the Joint Staff Antiterrorism Directorate in Washington, DC. I surveyed the crime scene with the eye of an infantrymen and the scrutiny of an antiterrorist expert, quickly realizing that this act was more diabolical and premeditated than would be expected from a simple combat engineer. The attack was precise, perfectly timed and obviously well rehearsed. This was a deliberate attack planned by a well-trained and motivated individual.

To identify the sleeping tents of the primary brigade staff, over a mile from his daily duties and in a sector of the camp Sergeant Akbar would have no logical reason to visit, would take time and patience. This would require Akbar to locate and stalk brigade staff members through lengthy and daily reconnaissance missions far from his place of duty and billet. He would then have to case their tents, identify access and escape routes, and determine any risks that might prevent him from accomplishing his attack. For example, he noticed that the floodlights outside the tents might expose him during his attack— something he must have determined during a night reconnaissance. Therefore, on the night of the attack he had located the generator and disabled it. Next, he would have to gather the tools and weapons he would need to kill as many officers as possible. To do this he would need access to his platoon's ammunition supply in their combat vehicles. During the night of the attack, he managed to be in charge of the security team guarding the ammunition. This access and his command authority made it possible for him to have complete access to the tools he needed, and it provided him the perfect alibi for not being accounted for during the attack.

The matter haunted me that evening and still haunts me today. If this was a man who simply wanted to disrupt the brigade and prevent it from attacking Muslims, why did he go to such extremes to attack the brigade staff across the camp when my staff and I were less than twenty yards from his tent? Was Akbar just a disgruntled Muslim soldier or was he a recruited and trained Islamic terrorist?

His reconnaissance skills, ability to stalk and track the brigade staff, and politically target the center of gravity for leadership within the brigade led me to believe Akbar was a trained terrorist. My staff and I were not strategically important enough for him to attack. He walked by me every day, yet sought out and found the brigade commander and his staff. This was not a random act; it was a deliberate terrorist attack and, in my heart, I believe he'd been trained. My experience taught me that there was more to this than a disgruntled Muslim soldier.

In any case, the damage was done, and as the sun rose, Colonel Hodges finally agreed to go to the hospital and have his wounds tended to. As I walked with the colonel to his hummer, he assured me he would be back before we attacked: "Don't worry Chris, I will be back before you know it. Take care of the brigade."[4]

* * * *

Jim Lacey was a war correspondent for *Time* magazine embedded with our brigade in the 101st Airborne Division during Operation Iraqi Freedom, and has contributed several of his articles from our campaign to this book. A New York-based writer, Jim now writes for *National Review Online* and is author of the recent book *Takedown: The 3rd Infantry Division's Twenty-One Day Assault on Baghdad.*

NOTE FROM JIM LACEY: The loss of that night was brought home to me over a year later when I received a letter from a sister of one of that night's fatal casualties. Below is my reply. I call attention to this for three reasons. The first is to remind readers far removed from events of the terrible toll war inflicts upon not only those who serve but also loved ones left behind. Second, I think it is important for those not in the military to get some idea of the caring and self sacrifice I witnessed repeatedly among American soldiers during the war. Finally, I want to call attention to the fact that none of the men killed or wounded that night have ever been awarded their Purple Hearts. Because the military never classified the attack as a terrorist incident, their deaths and wounds were not deemed worthy of the award.

Dear Ms. Hall,

Time magazine has just forwarded me your letter and I am going to respond as best I can.

First though, I am deeply sorry for the terrible loss you and your family have suffered. No one has the words that can even begin to ease the kind of pain your family feels over so terrible a loss. But maybe my impressions will help you understand that night and something about your brother.

I spoke to Gregory a few times while we were in Kuwait. He was attached to the 1st Brigade and I was there as an embedded journalist with the unit. I suppose we talked to

each other because we were both strangers to the other soldiers in the unit. From what I remember, we talked about
some technical stuff and how a war with Iraq would be
fought. When he did talk about personal things it was usually about his sons. I am sorry that I do not remember their
names, but it was apparent that they were his biggest concern and what he missed most about being away.

Anyway, I suppose he was a naturally easy-going guy,
because he soon had a number of new friends in the Brigade
and was spending a lot of time on his official duties. So, I
talked to him less as the war got closer.

On the night of the grenade attack, I had gone to bed
just a few minutes before it happened, in the tent directly
beside your brother's. When I stepped out of my tent, the
area was one of utter confusion that was being rapidly sorted
out by officers and sergeants on the scene.

At first, everyone assumed that terrorists had attacked
from outside the camp and that they were still in the area.
The fact that the grenade thrower shot two soldiers as they
exited their tents reinforced this impression and convinced us
all that there was still considerable danger. Disregarding that
danger, dozens of soldiers rushed to help those injured.

Despite the risk, one young medic ran several hundred
yards in the pitch black to get his medical bag, from a vehicle
packed for the invasion, and raced back with it. Others
immediately entered the tents and began taking out the
wounded. What I saw the rest of that night is still something
that humbles me every time I think about it. Two Majors
were left unhurt by the grenades. One of them took the job
of restoring order to the chaos all around and the other one
went to the Operations tent to coordinate with the outside.

The one who stayed on the scene put up a security
perimeter to make sure no further harm would come to anyone and also organized the search for the attacker. He was
greatly assisted in doing this by two captains. It was these
captains who organized the assistance being given to the
wounded and made sure that those worst hurt got the most

intensive care and were taken out to the hospital first. It was
not until later that I realized that both of these captains were
soaked in their own blood. They had both been wounded,
but refused all help or to be evacuated until they were sure
that everyone worse off than they were properly taken care
of.

The Major who went to the Operations tent immediately
ordered medical evacuation helicopters and alerted the nearby hospital trauma center. I was never sure of the exact timing, but I doubt more then 15 minutes passed between the
attack and when helicopters arrived to rush the injured away.
I also know that they landed within yards of the incident,
despite a continuing threat, in order to ensure that no time
was lost getting the wounded to a hospital.

I was not at the hospital, but I later spoke to people who
were. I discussed your brother with them and without going
into details I can assure you that the efforts made by the doctors and surgeons were truly heroic. He was in the hands of
some of the finest surgeons in a center as well equipped as
the best in the United States. They did everything possible to
save Greg's life. I saw one of the surgeons much later and he
was still upset that it was beyond his (or anyone's) ability to
save him.

I am totally satisfied that there was nothing more that
could have been done.

Now, comes the hardest part of this letter.

Before undertaking my journalist job that night I did help
carry out some of the wounded, including your brother.
When I placed him on the ground outside of the tent I was
immediately shoved aside by a trained medic who began trying to save his life. It was obvious that he was very seriously
wounded. Before another minute had gone by a second
medic was working on him. Two other soldiers had placed
themselves nearby to help protect him from further harm.

I stayed close by for a long while watching everything
going on around me. Your brother was initially in some
shock from his wounds, but seemed to come around a bit as

he was being worked on. I saw one of the medics give him morphine and that looked like it had an immediate effect. I hope it helps to know that because of this your brother was not in any pain that night. In fact, he may not have known how badly wounded he was. He began to push the medics away and though I could not hear what he was saying I could hear the medics reply, "No, sir we have to take care of you," and "Everyone is being taken care of. Let us work on you." This went on for some time. It was clear to me that your brother was trying to get the medics to go help the other wounded men.

He could not see that all of the other wounded were being taken care of and it struck me as both incredibly noble and very brave that he was putting the welfare of others before his own. I doubt there will ever be a time that the image of such selfless courage will ever leave me or that I will not be overcome by the memory of it.

It was easily seen that your brother was in very serious condition so nothing he said deterred those who were working on him. He was and remained their first priority until he was evacuated. One of the wounded captains at the scene made the decision that your brother would be on the first helicopter out. Again, I was only able to hear one side of the conversation, but as they were carrying him to the helicopter he was asking if everyone else had already been evacuated.

I also heard one of the medics tell him, "We'll get your pictures." Here I have to guess, but the only thing that makes sense was that he was worried about pictures of family members (probably his sons) that were left in the tent. He had already been told that they had to move him because the tents were in danger of catching fire. Anyway, it was clear that his only thoughts as he was placed on the helicopter were for those around him who might be in worse condition and of his family.

The unit chaplain later told me that he was surprised by how many people wanted to talk to him about your brother. What surprised him was that he had made such a big impact on so many people in so short a time.

I have spoken to family members of others that were seriously injured that night. All of them seemed to be truly bothered by the fact that it was another soldier who did this, and many commented that it would have been easier to understand if it was a terrorist attack. If you also feel the same way let me state my own personal opinion. The man who did this was not an American soldier. He was a radical Islamist that had been trained in his faith in one of the most radical madrasas (religious schools, often funded by hate-filled extremists) in Los Angeles. I am convinced that he infiltrated the U.S. army for the purposes of carrying out a terrorist attack. He was no more a fellow soldier then a Nazi in WWII who infiltrated an American unit to blow up a supply dump. We are now fighting an enemy that attacks out of the shadows. Worming their way into the military to conduct their savage attacks is just one of their methods. There is no doubt in my mind that the man who killed your brother was not a soldier and was in fact a terrorist.

I am not sure you really needed to know all that I have written, but I did as you asked and put myself in your shoes. I would want to know every detail of that night and I hope knowing all of this does not cause you too much renewed pain. As I said, he left us concerned only about helping those around him and his family.

I hope one day the ache of loss will go away for you and that you will be able to smile when you remember your brother. When you think the time is right I hope that you can share some of my impressions with his sons. They can do a lot worse then to grow up as brave, strong and loving as he was

I hope your pain ends soon. Greg was a special man and I will remember him for a long time to come.

Yours,
Jim Lacey

* * * *

As I returned to the brigade command post, I decided to speak to the surviving members of the staff to help begin the healing process and get the brigade back into the war. When I returned to the command post, a radio operator told me I had a phone call. The voice at the other end told me that Captain Christopher Seifert had died on arrival at the field hospital; three others were in critical condition; and the rest were in stable but guarded condition. I was surprised that Chris was dead . . . I hadn't realized he was so severely wounded. I had gotten to know Chris during the weeks and months before the deployment, not as well as one would wish in hindsight, but I did know he was a smart and formal officer who had a gift for providing me the kind of intelligence I needed to focus the battalion during a fight. But more importantly, he was a young husband and father. I struggled to remember his family's names, finally asking one of the other staff officers who reminded me: Terri and Ben. It was all I could do to maintain my composure as I said a personal prayer for his soul and the safety of his family. His death was so senseless and wrong. What had we missed; what had we failed to train; why would Akbar do this?

I had to shake this off. I told one of the battle captains to have the staff assemble in the intelligence section of the command post where we could have some privacy. When I walked into the tent it hit me that I didn't know this staff. The assembled group constituted the C-Team of the brigade staff—junior sergeants and officers still blood-stained and in shock from the attack. I looked into their red and teary eyes and decided to be harder than they expected. If I treated them like children, it would take hours or even days to get the brigade back into the war. As it was, the war had already begun and we would be following the 3d Infantry Division through the border defenses and into Iraq at any time. If Hodges didn't return with most of the senior brigade staff from the hospital, it was up to me and this group of young kids to take this 6,000 man brigade combat team into battle. I needed them and their minds. There was no time to coddle them.

"Ok folks, here's the score. We have seventeen wounded and one dead. Chris Seifert died this morning before he arrived at the field hospital, and I don't expect Air Liaison Officer Major Gregory Stone to survive." Greg would die three days later of multiple wounds on March 25, 2003, leaving behind a fiancée and his 7-year-old son Alex. "This is what you have trained for; we all knew something like this could happen. It will happen again." I let that sink in for a few moments before continuing. "I need each of you to step up and prepare this brigade to attack. You have 30 minutes to mourn the loss of our comrades and consult with each other—in this tent and only in this tent. Once you leave, I need your game faces on. This brigade will attack within the next 48 hours and we will not let this act of cowardice stop us. Your 30 minutes starts now."

When I went back into the main command post area, I noticed a couple of officers who had refused to let the medical personnel examine them as they evacuated their friends and comrades. One of them was Captain Mario Roberts. Mario had been my communications officer until he was promoted and moved to brigade six months before our deployment to Kuwait. He was an exceptional officer and man. As I contemplated my next move and reviewed the meeting schedule for the day, I noticed Mario limping to his desk. He looked dazed and slightly confused. I asked him if he was okay and he assured me he was. I told him to take off his boots. When he did, I found his socks covered in blood and sand. As he refused to leave his post, I had the medics treat him at his desk. He was not going to leave his duty post and I was not going to make him.

Mario epitomized the spirit and camaraderie of the brigade staff that night. As the hours and days passed, the primary staff members started to return to the command post by catching rides from the different hospitals and aid stations they had evacuated to. In one case, a young captain was found walking toward the brigade still dressed in his hospital gown after going AWOL from the hospital to rejoin us before we crossed into Iraq. Colonel Hodges later said he was tempted to send him back to the hospital, but since he himself was going to war with two pieces of shrapnel in his arm, it did not seem right to order a junior officer out of the fight. So rather than order him back to the hospital, he took in the image of the limping captain in combat boots and an open-backed hospital gown and warmly greeted him: "Welcome back! I see you have returned in full martial splendor."

The brigade staff's strong sense of duty and willingness to sacrifice inspired the rest of us as we steeled ourselves for what was to lie ahead.

I, too, felt a new sense of energy and invulnerability when Colonel Hodges, fresh from the hospital, jumped from his hummer with a cigar-choked grin yelling "Waddya say we go kick some Iraqi ass?" I think the only person more relieved to see Ben Hodges return than I was Major Pete Rooks. Pete wasn't any happier about leading the battalion than I was about leading the brigade.[5]

The following article by Jim Lacey outlines some of my own impressions at the time about how the 1st Brigade recovered from the shock of this terrorist incident.

* * * *

CAMP PENNSYLVANIA RETURNS TO DUTY
Jim Lacey reports as the 101st Airborne remembers a comrade killed in Sunday's grenade attack

By JIM LACEY

Tue Oct 18 16:28:03 2005. Just after dawn Monday the soldiers of the 1st Brigade, 101st Airborne Division mustered at Brigade Headquarters for a memorial service commemorating the life of an officer killed in a grenade attack the night before. A half dozen chaplains and fellow officers spoke a few words; there were a few tears and finally a 21-gun salute.

After the attack on the leadership of the 1st Brigade—for which one of its members has been arrested—I gave a number of interviews about the events of that night. There were a few recurring questions. How it would affect the unit's morale? Would it delay operations? And was this an indication of disgruntled soldiers in the 1st Brigade? At the time, I speculated that neither morale nor operations would be much affected and that whatever motives the suspect had it was definitely not part of a bigger problem with the leadership. However, this was really only speculation. I needed a day or two to prove myself right.

On the day after the attack, I spoke to over two dozen young soldiers from throughout the Brigade. Without a single exception, they all expressed genuine relief at learning that the Brigade commander, Colonel Hodges, had returned from the hospital. Hardly the reaction of soldiers who had taken a dislike to their commander.

The clincher on that question came later in the evening. As I returned from a trip to one of the other units at the camp, I discovered that the Brigade headquarters area had been surrounded by a platoon of heavily armed infantrymen. I asked a nearby first sergeant if Col. Hodges had asked for the added security during the night and was told, "I don't think the colonel knows. These soldiers volunteered to come do this." I wonder if any of the veterans reading this ever heard of soldiers volunteering to stand guard all night before?

Col. Hodges brought an end to the guard the next day saying, "I do not subscribe to the theory that the attacker had an accomplice and I do not want to give any of our fine soldiers the impression that we don't trust them." He learned about the guard when he was challenged for a password while returning to his own tent late in the evening. One officer jokingly asked Col. Hodges how he got past the guard without a password, and received the reply, "I tried to overwhelm him with the sheer force of my personality. When that failed, he eventually saw the logic of letting me into my tent so he could guard me properly."

As an observer, I can say with conviction that morale here is high, the soldiers overwhelmingly trust their leaders, and the 1st Brigade of the 101st Airborne Division is ready to begin combat operations.

One last thing I mentioned in many of my interviews: the admiration I felt while watching an Army major take charge of a chaotic situation, and for two captains who, despite bleeding from their own wounds, refused medical treatment for hours while they ensured the area was secured and that all of the seriously injured soldiers had been treated and evacuated.

At the time I was not allowed to name them, but that restriction has been lifted and all of you should know who they are. The major was Kyle Warren and the captains were Townly Hendrick and Tony Jones. In a night that had a lot of heroes, these three stood out.

2

THE BATTLE FOR NAJAF

"What time are you going to attack?"

OVER THE BERM

Once Colonel Hodges officially relieved me, I returned to *No Slack* and found the battalion prepared for combat. As expected, Major Pete Rooks had once again worked hard in my absence to get the battalion ready for its next rendezvous with destiny. He was not alone and another officer who was instrumental in making sure we were ready to move was Major James Crider, my battalion operations officer. Jim was a cool and methodical officer who commanded the respect of the staff and company commanders. His leadership style and persona complemented his soft-spoken demeanor and ability to always understand the big picture. He was the natural complement to Pete Rook's energy and attention to detail. Their combined strengths rounded out one of the best command teams I had seen in twenty years of military service. I was blessed to be on their team.

In the days leading up the this moment, President Bush had given the order to attack on March 19, and our brothers in the 3rd Infantry Division, 1st Marine Expeditionary Force and the British contingent had rolled their heavy tanks north, making short order of the pitiful Iraqi defenses along the Kuwaiti border. In all the commotion with our preparation, last minute decisions, changes in plans and the constant struggle to get all our gear from the port, I would lose track of time. To keep me up to date, Specialist Bowers would yell at me, "Sir, you've got to check this out!" I would pause and stick my head in my hummer that was now backed up to my tent. Bowers would be pointing at

the computer screen in my vehicle, my brand new Blue Force Tracker
(BFT). This newest toy was designed to give me perfect situational
awareness of my force and the forces around me by tracking everything on a computerized map. It was impressive, and at this early
phase it acted as a medium for the men to see the advance of the armor
assault to our front.

After returnng to the battalion command post, Pete and Jim gave
me a quick operational update and then hurried me outside to inspect
the soldiers as they continued preparing for our assault. Jim simply
told me that the attack would be through the western desert of Iraq to
one of the three operational bases that our 3d Brigade was in the
process of establishing as we spoke.

I was still uncomfortable attacking at this point because I had been
forced to relinquish a platoon's worth of anti-tank missile systems to
another battalion in 2d Brigade because their ship hadn't arrived, and
I still had most of Alpha Company guarding munitions storage facilities near Kuwait City. But the order was to move with what we had
and the rest would catch up—a "rolling start" as we were eventually
told. We had to keep the pressure on the Iraqis and move with what
we had, trusting the logistical systems to catch up. Despite the logic of
the concept, it was a tough sell to my Alpha Company commander,
Captain Steven Thomas. Steve was my oldest and most mature commander, having served as an enlisted man for many years. He was
calm and understanding with the order to remain behind, but I could
see the anguish in his eyes as I'm sure he could see in mine. It was a
hard right having his men guard the ammunition supply point, and we
both hated the order.

The 3d Brigade of the 101st Division went into Iraq with the 3d
Infantry Division to establish multiple bases in the Anbar region of
Iraq. Their key task was to establish refueling points for the lift helicopters and the division's famous gunships—the AH-64 Apache attack
helicopters. At this point in the war, the Apaches were the most valuable asset in the division, and as they waited for the infantry of the
101st to move forward they were helping the armor units that had
gone in before us.

The 3d Brigade infantry was securing bases well forward that
would give these critical assets a place to refuel and rearm much clos-

er to the front than if they had to return to Kuwait after each mission. It was a perilous job and left a lot of good infantrymen exposed and unsupported in the Iraqi desert, but the 101st Airborne was needed to secure these bases in order to keep the Apaches safe and in position to kill enemy tanks and convoys for the 3ID.

More and more I found myself sitting in my hummer staring at the computer screen trying to imagine what the men and women of the brigades and battalions in front of us were seeing and feeling. I wasn't afraid, but I was concerned because I had spent my whole life preparing for this moment and had no idea what I should be feeling. I really didn't know what to expect.

As the hour of our attack approached, we continued waiting for the trucks promised from division. To carry my battalion north, I would need at least fifteen trucks to augment the vehicles I already owned. Division headquarters ended up providing us with only five. Forced to prioritize and leave forces behind, I decided to take the risk and load the trucks like Hannibal's Elephants. Men and equipment were strapped down to every nook and cranny. Despite our best efforts, I was still forced to leave Alpha Company and elements of the battalion headquarters behind with Major Rooks. They would join us in Iraq by helicopter in less than a week . . . we hoped. At 8:24 a.m. on March 24, 2003, the men of *No Slack* and the *Bastogne* Brigade Combat Team crossed the Kuwait defensive berm into Iraq.

THE RIDE FROM HELL

Once the lead elements of the battalion were through the berm, we stopped on the far side to build combat power before we began our push north. As we waited, the men of *No Slack* stared at the first casualties of the Iraq war. Near our positions were the corpses of Iraqi security guards who had fallen victim to 3d Infantry Division's onslaught.

The meager Iraqi defenses along the Kuwaiti border had not even been a speed bump to the 3d ID soldiers and had been crushed quickly. Bodies were strewn across the road leading to the guard towers and the surrounding field. I was glad to see the bodies, not because I was looking forward to the deaths that lay ahead but because of the lesson the sight provided. Most of my men had never seen death up close, and these corpses provided my junior leaders a non-hostile situation to witness and discuss death. Such an opportunity would help me to begin the hardening process, a process that was necessary before we reached Baghdad. In Haiti I had learned that the more comfortable a man is with death the less likely he is to stop and look out of curiosity or guilt during a fight, thereby lessening his chances of being shot. We didn't kill these particular men, but those feelings of remorse were present. I needed to expose my men to this last mile of their training, which was something I couldn't provide at Fort Campbell. We stayed there long enough to quiet their nervous enthusiasm and to dampen their ignorant beliefs about the glory of war. Reality finally set in for all of us just a few meters north of the Iraqi border.

Fortunately, *No Slack* was following 1-327th and the brigade command team along the route north, so I had time to study my maps, review orders, think my way through each battle scenario imaginable and review the only two books I thought I needed in Iraq: *Sun Tzu, The Art of War* by Samuel Griffith, and *Origins of Terrorism* by Walter Reich.

It also gave me time to finally experiment with this new technological innovation in my vehicle called the Blue Force Tracker. BFT was a computer terminal mounted on a swivel arm in the front seat of my hummer. It was a satellite communications system that displayed maps of Iraq overlaid with active computer icons from every unit in the coalition. It allowed me to monitor any enemy contact with coalition forces anywhere in Iraq, track the progress of units on my right and left, read about lessons on how the Iraqis were fighting, and send emails to other commanders.

For the first time in my career, I wasn't forced to completely focus on navigating, constantly cross-checking myself with others on the move and tracking our progress on a map with varying degrees of accuracy. With this new technology, I was able to download maps and satellite imagery of Iraq while simultaneously tracking my computer symbol on a map as it moved across the desert, watching the units to my front, scrolling up to see the 3d Infantry's advance north, and the status of the 1st Marine Expeditionary Force (1MEF) to our east. I could also exchange emails with Colonel Hodges and was often able to do this when I couldn't reach him on the radio. It was a huge leap in battlefield technology. Not only did it ensure we knew where we were but it also freed me from the tyrannical drudgery of map and compass reading, giving me more time to think. It was, indeed, a commander's dream come true.

For months prior to our deployment, I had used every spare moment to prepare my officers and men for the attack on the Iraqi homeland, a predominantly Arab country with over 4,000 years of history shrouded in the mysteries of rising and falling empires and the convulsions of repeated invasions, occupations, foreign exploitations and conquests.

The American-led Coalition was in the process of becoming the 31st conquering army to enter ancient Mesopotamia, placing *No Slack* on the cusp of a historical event with monumental global security implications. Unlike 1991's Gulf War, we were not attacking with an overwhelming force. In fact, the Coalition was severely outnumbered and this time we were attacking them on their home ground where they had had years to get ready for us. I doubted the lessons of Desert Storm would be of much use. This time, my leaders would have to be bold, innovative and unafraid of risk. Beating Iraq in 2003 would be a thinking man's game; we would have to find nonstandard solutions to whip the Ba'athists.

It takes time to build innovative leaders who are willing and able to take risk with minimal guidance. One of the best examples of the training we conducted to instill the trust required to take risks was a leader training exercise we conducted in Nashville, TN before deploying. Our "invasion" of Nashville was designed to replicate the conditions we might find in Baghdad. As luck would have it, Nashville's residential and industrial zoning is strikingly similar to Baghdad's. Even Nashville's prominent natural surroundings mimic Baghdad's, to include the Cumberland River that bisects the Nashville area just as the Tigris River divides Baghdad.

The senior sergeants, officers of the battalion and I drove to the outskirts of Nashville and discussed how we thought the Iraqis would defend the city. After discussing their defense, we worked together to figure out how to penetrate to its core—the decisive points of the city, the various tactics we could use and where, identifying hazards and potential choke points, and recounting the numerous humanitarian situations we could find ourselves in as we progressed from residential areas to industrial zones to the inner city. Driving to each location and walking the neighborhoods, factories and downtown areas of Nashville, *No Slack*'s leaders fine-tuned their battle drills, modified casualty and prisoner evacuation processes, and discussed caring for civilians on the battlefield.

On one street corner in an inner city neighborhood, the subject of using civilians as human shields surfaced in the discussions. There were veterans of Somalia in the battalion leadership who wanted to know what I expected when they came to this fictitious Iraqi intersection and found the *Fedayeen* hiding behind a wall of women and children. Preparing to answer the question, I scanned the group of leaders to find our battalion Chaplain, Captain Scott Brown. He smiled at me and raised an eyebrow. But I didn't hesitate with my response.

"If you find yourself in this situation, I want you to shoot through the wall of civilians and kill the enemy. Minimize collateral damage if you can, but if you don't do this the enemy will believe their tactic works and will continue to use it against us . . . word will pass from street to street and neighborhood to neighborhood for the *Fedayeen* to use human shields against us because we will hesitate. If you shoot through the civilians during your first encounter, that lesson will also pass through the Iraqi grapevine and they will not use the tactic again. As I see it, men, if you fight through it the first time, you will save Iraqi civilians in the long run, protect your men, and accomplish your mission."

There was a cold silence amongst the leaders, a few serious smiles and head nods, and my approaching chaplain.

"Chaplain," I said to Scott, "anything to add?"

"Yes sir, the colonel is right; there are no noncombatants in a fight like this. Yes, there are women and children, but they are participants and you must consider that they may be willing participants in the fight. You may actually save lives by taking some upfront."

I turned to look at Scott and then back at the reaction of my leaders. The logic was sound, but the topic was an open sore that would tug at the hearts and personal faith of my leaders for the duration of the war.

Those who did not know Chaplain Brown may have been surprised at such an answer from the battalion's spiritual guide. However, I found it entirely in keeping with what I knew about him. He was not the kind of Chaplain to wrap himself in false pieties or try to give some nonsense answer like, "One should always try and distinguish innocents from others and avoid shooting if any innocent could be endangered by it." He was totally grounded in the real world and knew these men would soon be making life-or-death decisions, and needed more then platitudes. Brown knew that if we killed the first human shield we came across it could save thousands later on. His answer was the most humane and human solution available and he did not hesitate to state it.

The reason for this remarkable candor is probably rooted in the fact that he flew attack helicopters in the first Gulf War and was faced with his own life-or-death decisions. His experience in heavy combat led him to leave the Army to find some spiritual answers. When he finished divinity school, his love for soldiers brought him back as a Chaplain in order to help those who will face these kinds of decisions in the future. Because of his break in service, he was very close to my own age and he soon became a close confident and a rock I could lean on when necessary.

Jim Lacey likes to tell the story of one of our embedded journalists (Mark Strassman of CBS) asking Brown if he thought it was right for the Chaplains to be doing so many baptisms on the eve of war (or as First Sergeant Bratton said, "Heathens trying to get right with the Lord before they have to meet him."). Strassman thought that they were taking advantage of young men in who were in a weakened emotional state. Brown gave him a short explanation on why it was a good thing to be doing, but Strassman remained unconvinced and said, "It still does not seem right."

Brown was about to reply, but instead got up and began to walk away. Strassman hurriedly assured Brown that he was not trying to offend him. Brown smiled and said, "You did not offend me; I am just going to my tent to pray that you burn in hell." Strassman looked a bit concerned as Brown walked off smiling.

Besides terrain walks of areas I thought resembled parts of Iraq we might find ourselves in, I also never missed a chance to impart the mil-

itary wisdom of the ages to my battalion leaders. It was no secret that
I was a passionate student of the great 5th century B.C. strategist Sun
Tzu, as I quoted him constantly. I especially kept in mind his dictum:

> *For, to win one hundred victories in one hundred battles*
> *is not the acme of skill. To subdue the enemy without fighting*
> *is the acme of skill.*

I was convinced we could put this piece of wisdom to good use in
Iraq, defeating the enemy's military with a minimum of force. Of
course, it was never a smart idea to underestimate an enemy's willingness to fight, particularly when defending their homeland. However, I
was certain that after eleven years of UN sanctions the Iraqi military
was devastated and incapable of defending the regime. They were
going to find it next to impossible to face off with the Coalition's air
and ground assault. I based my opinion on opportunities I'd had to see
the remnants of the Soviet military while visiting Russia in 1994, the
forces of the former Republic of Yugoslavia in 1993, the Haitian army
in 1994 and countless other armies across the globe.

These experiences were always lurking in the recesses of my mind
and I considered them often while preparing my men to fight in Iraq.
The lessons I tried to impart to my leaders was that while national
intelligence reports usually get the numbers of tanks, planes and men
right, their assessment of an enemy's ability to fight were normally
wrong in terms of logistics, tactics and leadership. Moreover, no one
can truly gauge the morale of an army with a satellite or CNN. Finally,
economic sanctions wreak havoc on a country, wrecking its economy
and infrastructure, and starving its citizens.

I told them that when invading a country that is under UN sanctions, it is best to be prepared for sub-human living conditions and a
hardened enemy. Considering these self-proclaimed truisms, I surmised that the Iraqi Special Republican Guard (SRG) would fight the
Coalition's armor spearhead to the death, but that their regular army
and the irregular "Saddam *Fedayeen*" would avoid direct contact with
the Coalition in order to attack our flanks and rear. To do this, they
would use guerrilla hit-and-run tactics and do their best to avoid facing us in a straight-up fight.

I was sure that the SRG would be wrecked by the 3d ID long before *No Slack* got to Baghdad, because I assumed they were fanatical enough to face the Coalition on even terms. When it came to fighting the massed armor of the 3d ID, there would be nothing fair about it and the SRG would die at the time and place of General Franks' choosing.

I didn't think *No Slack* would be involved in that initial fight. Our fights would concentrate on their regular army and *Fedayeen* short of Baghdad, a force that would be isolated by the 3d ID's rapid advance from their central command in the capital. I needed to take advantage of their isolation to defeat them. From experience, I knew that isolated Iraqi units soon lost all initiative and withered. I made defeating their regular army and *Fedayeen* my cause—not destroying them. Destroying meant to kill them all, and this made no sense if we wanted to quickly rebuild Iraq and turn it over to someone who knew what to do and how to do it.

Defeating them would steal their will to resist but leave a force in being to help us stabilize and rebuild the country when hostilities ended. I did not foresee that Amb. Paul Bremer would later sweep the Iraqi Army away with the stroke of a pen. At the time, I hoped to outsmart and outmaneuver them in order to eventually help them.

Although I was mentally prepared to kill them to the last man, my experience in Haiti and the lessons from the Panama invasion were ingrained in my mind. We had to have a strong host nation force to maintain the peace after the war, like the police force we vetted and sustained in Haiti. Host nation police or military forces were the single most important pillar in our exit strategy. I didn't intend or desire to kill one more Iraqi soldier than was absolutely necessary—I was planning to put them to work rebuilding Iraq. To me, this was the essence of "Regime Change."

To work this resetting of the stage, I realized I would have to ruthlessly and swiftly kill those who would not capitulate, while giving those who wanted to quit the fight an honorable way out. The fight would be ruthless in the sense that I would bring all the instruments of power at my disposal against the Iraqi military without pause or hesitation, and would constantly hit them with different forms of maneuver and firepower simultaneously. Infantry, artillery, mortars, tanks, attack helicopters and close air support—a synchronized dance of death and destruction that batters a man's senses and destroys his resolve to resist when faced with General (retired) Colin Powell's definition of overwhelming combat power. Every first fight we had with the Iraqis had to be so devastating to them that they would lose their will to resist, yet realize their defeat was a result of the failed régime that they chose or were forced to support. My intent was idealistic, yes, but possible according to the great warriors in history and my mentors: Sun Tzu, Clausewitz, and Lieutenant Colonel (retired) Albert Clark Welch. It was from LTC Welch, former commander of the 1-8th Infantry Regiment, 4th Infantry Division, that I received a piece of advice I have never forgotten:

> "Always do what is right, Chris, realizing that the right path
> is always the hardest road to walk and mostly unpopular
> to those you lead. . . . Always do what is right"

I wanted the Iraqis to quit easily but retain some pride, which would be important when we rebuilt the force. I considered it crucial that we allow them to retain their honor, a core value among Arabs. And these were Iraqi Arabs, proud that no one had successfully occupied their lands in recorded history, so we needed to recognize this key cultural factor. The Iraqis and Mesopotamians had successfully defeated European and Asian occupations for over five millennia—not with superior armies or generalship, but through their ability to endure hardship, embrace their faith, and wait-out the politics and resolve of other nations and states.

We did not want to make the mistake of becoming occupiers and thus force them to resist us for generations. Rather, it was in our best interest to be partners with a new Iraqi army and do everything possible to retain and capitalize on their sense of honor and self-respect. We did this in Haiti when rebuilding their police forces in 1994. It was crucial to preserve what we could of Iraq's army, infrastructure, institutions and culture, even as we systematically destroyed the regime. Thirty armies had preceded us and failed to consider these factors, and all had failed to successfully occupy "The Cradle of Civilization."

THE GOLDEN DOME OF ALI

We had been traveling for four tortuous days along mostly dirt roads that vanished under the sands with amazing regularity. Fatigue became almost mind-numbing and every soldier was suffering muscle cramps as they stoically endured sardine conditions in overcrowded trucks. Besides being cold and hungry, many of them spent most of the ride soaked through after sudden cloudbursts caught them in the back of open trucks.

Sometimes these cloudbursts would strike during a sandstorm and it would literally rain mud on the exposed troops. At one point along the route, someone said this was like the desert in the movie *Lawrence of Arabia*.[6] It was covered with sand dunes, dust devils, Bedouins and small-dilapidated villages of lost and desperate Iraqi Shi'a who were banished from greater Iraq for alleged crimes against Saddam. Word that the brigade was setting up fighting positions west of the city of Najaf (which lies on the Euphrates 100 miles south of Baghdad), only a few miles distant, could not have come soon enough.

It felt good to finally stop and stretch our legs. The assembly area was nothing more than a couple hundred trucks and thousands of men casually arranged into a huge diamond formation in the middle of the desert. It was still littered with destroyed Iraqi vehicles that had ventured out of An Najaf to try their luck against the 3d Infantry Division. There was a two-lane highway to our east and the continuous flow of ammunition, fuel and supply trucks moving north along that road were a constant reminder that the 3d ID was to our north and getting ready to take on the Republican Guard. All around us the flash and bang of outgoing artillery told us that the enemy was close, very close.

It was late in the day, but there was still enough daylight to find the brigade command post and mark a trail so I could find it in the darkness. An early recon of the command post would allow me to get an informal update from the brigade staff, and also give me a chance to write down the timeline so I could sketch out some personal planning and possibly see Colonel Hodges.

When I entered the Tactical Operations Center (TOC) with my

operations officer, Jim Crider, I learned that the brigade had received another change in orders. Major Pat Frank, the brigade operations officer, gave me a quick update, telling me that the brigade was being sent to relieve the 2d Brigade of the 3d Infantry Division outside the city of Najaf. *No Slack* would relieve one of their tank battalions and block enemy forces from leaving the city from the west. When I gathered the information I needed, I left Jim with Pat to discuss the details. This would help Jim get an early start on planning while I gave my company commanders a heads-up so they could start their own preparations.

When I returned to my makeshift command post, I had a chance to see the whole battalion together for the first time in three days. I took the opportunity to walk the line of trucks and talk to the men. They were in good spirits and very glad to be off the trucks. Their eagerness to get into the fight was palpable. It is hard to explain the feeling, a kind of nervous enthusiasm mixed with fear that is both volatile and possibly debilitating if not harnessed. We were on the verge of testing the battalion's mettle under fire.

As I walked and talked to the men, my personal anxieties eased; they were ready. Intuition and experience told me to trust my junior leaders and focus on my personal tasks as their commander. The men of *No Slack* were ready to see the beast. But was I ready to open the door to its cage?

When I returned to my hummer, I pulled out my Wal-Mart camping cot in an attempt to get some horizontal sleep before the brigade operations order. What sleep I stole in my hummer over the last four days had been anything but horizontal or restful. As I was setting up my cot and trying to transition into sleep mode, a short man of Arab descent approached. Mr. Kadhim al-Waeli from St. Louis, MO walked up and introduced himself. He was an Iraqi national who had fled after the failed Shi'a uprising against Saddam Hussein in 1991. After working his way through numerous refugee camps, Kadhim had ended up in the United States and become an American citizen. My sleep would have to wait.

For nearly ten years Kadhim had worked his way from one odd job to the next in search of the American dream. He had gone from dishwasher to waiter to college student to political consultant, the latter a position he lost when he decided to join the "Bush War" in Iraq. The Iraqi National Congress (INC), in collaboration with the Department of Defense, coordinated the recruitment of an Iraqi Dissident Force, which would participate in the possible invasion of Iraq. Kadhim was one of those dissidents.

After volunteering to fight with the Iraqi force, Kadhim was secretly deployed to Tazar, Hungary for training. The original plan for these Iraqi dissidents called for 600 Iraqi men, but when it came time to train the force only 65 Iraqis had answered the call. Although the numbers were disappointing, these Iraqi-Americans were still trained and organized into the Free Iraqi Forces (FIF). According to Kadhim, the Department of Defense, seeing little practical battlefield use for them, decided to deploy the FIF as cultural and linguistic advisors to American commanders. No matter whose idea it was, it was one of the smartest initiatives of the war. Over time, Kadhim al-Waeli became the most effective combat system at my disposal.

The brigade command post was crowded, dirty and dark. My staff was preparing the formal operations order for the next day's operations. At the time, I did not realize it would be the last detailed order the staff would present during the invasion. From this point forward, events moved too rapidly to accommodate lengthy staff processes. At the end of the operations order, Major Crider and I stepped out of the tent and into the darkness. Our eyes adjusted quickly as we watched a horrific barrage of American missile artillery firing toward Iraqi defenses in the Karbala Gap to our north. Plumes of smoke and flame indicating rockets, carrying thousands of baseball-sized cluster bombs that would explode on impact every two to three feet over a one-mile square, raced north. As we stood in the darkness, watching in disbelief, someone muttered "poor bastards."

On the way back to our assembly area, I noticed my watch was missing. Under normal circumstances, this is a minor inconvenience, but for a commander in combat it's devastating. Time is a weapon and without a watch, it cannot be controlled. Fortunately, I always carried a backup in my rucksack, but it was my only backup. It bothered me that I was only 96 hours into the war before I needed to use a backup item. I would waste valuable time the next morning searching for the watch in the desert because I wasn't comfortable working without a backup, not knowing when or if I could find another one. It was a truism in the Army that if you only had one of anything God would punish you and take it away.

As I searched, there was time to consider all the other items the battalion would consume once the fighting began—most importantly, my men. The thought caused me to call off my futile search and spend my remaining time walking the line of vehicles talking to my soldiers. I drew strength from their courage and high morale, especially from men like Sergeant First Class Daniel Maloney and First Sergeant Ronald Gregg. They were two of my most trusted leaders and I considered their counsel and friendship absolutely essential to success. Their constant concern for their men and their positive attitudes helped me routinely articulate purpose to the men. Both had an uncanny ability to advise me with a nod, a look or a smile. When they occasionally pulled me aside to make a recommendation, I listened with great attention. As I stood with First Sergeant Gregg looking at his men in the moonlight, he leaned over to me and said, "The boys are ready, sir." I did not need to see his face to know he was grinning from ear to ear.

As the sun was rising, my command team drove east to the outskirts of Najaf in order to coordinate with Colonel David Perkins, commander of 2d Brigade, 3rd Infantry Division. For three days, Perkins' brigade had repelled continuous ground attacks from Iraqi regular army and *Fedayeen* forces fighting out of Najaf, attempting to disrupt the flow of Coalition forces up Highway 8 to Baghdad. Some of the worst fighting had taken place in the sector *No Slack* would occupy in less than 24 hours.

When we reached Perkins' command post, his staff told us he was forward watching a fight at a road intersection nicknamed Check Point Charlie on the southern edge of Najaf. From our vantage point at his command post, we could see and hear his tanks engaging the enemy. His executive officer gave Lieutenant Colonel Marcus De Oliveira, the commander of my sister battalion, 1st Battalion, 327th Infantry Regiment, and me a quick rundown of the brigade's activities over the last three days as we awaited Perkins' return.

As we waited, Marcus and I made small talk about the road march in the desert and the size of Perkins' brigade along the road to Najaf.

It was a good stress reliever to be with a fellow commander with the same pressures and sense of presence on the battlefield. Marcus was a nominally coarse yet passionate man with extensive ranger experience. He was a true warrior and I drew strength from him, yet often wondered if his demanding style was a strength or hindrance. Leaders are as different in style as they are in size, shape, and color. Marcus and I were very different but thrived on each other's company and advice. I trusted him with my life and I'm sure he trusted me with his.

The wait gave me another chance to talk to Kadhim, now a permanent member of my command team, in an attempt to understand these *Fedayeen* Forces and their role within the Iraqi military. Before we left Kuwait, at the operations conference the night before, we got the impression these guys were a bunch of loosely-organized thugs who bullied the Iraqi population and spied for the regime on disloyal Iraqi citizens.

But from the extent of the devastation and their obviously fanatical response to the presence of Perkins' brigade, these guys were much more organized and well-trained than previously believed. Kadhim quickly explained the role of the *Fedayeen* and their purpose in Najaf, but more importantly, he told me for the first time about the importance of the city of An Najaf itself. From the moment we got in my hummer until we got back to the assembly area, Kadhim began to rant and rave about Najaf, with its Mosque of Ali, its importance to the Hajj and the Ali Cemetery.

"Najaf is the Holiest City in all of Shi'a Islam. God lives on that hill," he told me. "To be here is to be closer to God." I looked at Kadhim and then back to the fighting to our front. The more I listened to Kadhim and witnessed the carnage of the fighting around Najaf, the more convinced I was that Najaf would play a major role in the defeat of Saddam and his regime. But how could my single battalion make a difference?

Moments later, as Colonel Perkins rumbled up in his armored personnel carrier (APC), I was struck by his quiet bravado and apparent willingness to get close to a fight. What was even more surprising, at least for me, was that he was an armor officer.

Most armor officers I had served with in my career were content with using radios and binoculars when gathering information up close and personal. Dave Perkins was in a league of his own. A from-the-front leader, he immediately impressed me. His instructions to us were quick and precise, and I was soon moving north to find 2nd Battalion, 70th Armor Regiment, commanded by Lieutenant Colonel Jeffery Ingram, to relieve his battalion west of Najaf. Armed with his location and radio frequency, Jim Crider, Kadhim and I went looking for 2-70 Armor.[7]

* * * *

JIM LACEY: The following story from *Time* magazine covers my memories of meeting with Colonel Perkins that day.

"WE ARE SLAUGHTERING THEM"
On the Road to Death at Najaf

By JIM LACEY

The 2nd Brigade of the 3rd Infantry Division planned to halt west of Najaf, about 100 miles south of Baghdad; it also planned on facing some resistance from local irregulars. What it didn't expect was a rush-hour-like Iraqi attack, the road dense with enemy trucks bearing down on the brigade. "My headquarters had just rolled into the objective area when ten pickup trucks loaded with men firing machine guns and RPG-7s came racing down the road," recalls Colonel David Perkins, commander of the 2nd Brigade. "My lead tanks blew up the first three vehicles, but the rest kept coming."

For hours, the Iraqis continued this furious drag race—floor it and fire—whipping down the road from Najaf into the waiting guns of the 2nd Brigade's M1 Abrams tanks. The M1s obliterated them. Says Perkins: "I didn't expect this many of them, but all that meant was we used up more ammo. And I have plenty of that, especially if it means not fighting these guys in Baghdad."

Iraqi irregulars have tried everything to get at 2nd Brigade soldiers. When two Bradley fighting vehicles got stuck in the mud, dozens of irregulars, armed with a machine gun, TOW missiles and a chain-firing cannon, tried to crawl up to them.

Another group attempted to paddle across the Euphrates River, shooting RPGs as they approached. Their five boats were blown apart on the water. All of these attacks ended similarly. "It's not a fair fight," says Major Kevin Dunlop. "Trucks with machine guns against tanks and Bradleys can only have one outcome. We are slaughtering them."

On the other side of the Euphrates, east of Najaf, the 7th Cavalry ran into an even bigger fight. This time the main attack came during a swirling dust storm that made thermal night sights useless. Iraqi irregulars swarmed around the U.S. forces. The Americans were ordered to stay put and shoot at anything that moved. By midnight it was over. Two U.S. tanks were lost, blasted from behind—their most vulnerable spot— by antiaircraft guns mounted on pickups. Because of the M1's unique armor, no one on either tank was injured. And one of the tanks is recoverable.

The next rush-hour attack came right after dark the next day, but by this time the 2nd Brigade had set up "tollbooths"—heavy armor—on the roads leading from Najaf. "They attacked like morons," says Perkins. "But they kept coming." In one area guarded by two Bradleys, several hundred Iraqis were killed, according to the local battalion headquarters.

Civilians, meanwhile, continually wandered out of town to encourage and even beg the U.S. soldiers to take Najaf. They said *Fedayeen* irregulars were forcing local members of the al-Quads militia to fight by gathering their families and threatening to shoot them if they did not oppose the Americans. At one point, locals came out to thank the Americans for killing the area's Baath party leader, who they said had been executing civilians. The Baath leader, they said, had been killed in an air strike on a *Fedayeen* stronghold.

By the next morning, Perkins estimates, his unit had killed more than 1,200 attackers and taken the fight out of the rest. At first light, an Iraqi colonel walked up to an American position and surrendered. "He was a POW in the last Gulf War, so he had practice in surrendering when things are going bad," says Captain Cary Adams. The Iraqi colonel said he had only 200 of his 1,200 men left and claimed that originally there had been two other brigades in the town. One moved out during the night toward Baghdad, he said, while the other was hunkered down in government buildings around the city.

As the Iraqi attacks died down, the 101st Airborne Division began arriving to release the armored units for other missions. Brigadier General Benjamin Freakley, assistant division commander of the 101st, briefed the leaders of the companies that would be encircling Najaf. Everyone expected the remaining *Fedayeen* to attempt a break toward Baghdad even if it meant running the 101st's gauntlet. But if the *Fedayeen* stayed and conscripted the locals at gunpoint again, Freakley faced a moral conundrum: "Imagine someone walking into your home and saying either you fight or we will kill your wife and daughters. They are doing what any man would do to protect his family." It won't be easy killing men who are doing that.

* * * *

The 2-70 Armor Command Post was set up along Highway 8 in a stretch of desert where the sand resembled a fine talcum powder. Jeffery Ingram's staff personnel looked like a group of bad chefs in a hopeless bakery. When I stepped out of my hummer, the dust pooled in tufts of clouds, surrounded my boots and quickly climbed the length of my legs. Jim looked at me and laughed and said, "Now I'm sure we've landed on Mars." The closer I got to the command post the more I began to resemble the dust-covered soldiers working there. The executive officer was in the command post. He quickly apologized for the dust—as though he had any control over it. Despite the harsh conditions, the command post was exceptionally well organized and clean. I was impressed to discover that the resources available to an armor battalion far exceeded ours. There were floor mats, computer covers and hot coffee, none of which we had sufficient transport to take along with us.

As the executive officer ran us through the battalion's disposition, Lieutenant Colonel Ingram walked in. A tall and lanky man, he bent over to enter the tent and reached out his hand in welcome. Without missing a beat, he finished his executive officer's brief. When he finished, he contacted his forward company outside Najaf and told them to watch for my command group approaching from their rear. Ingram assured me I would learn more about Najaf from his Alpha Company commander, who was situated on the city's outskirts then with the staff and a two dimensional map in his command post. He was right.

As we neared Najaf, Kadhim came alive with excitement. After hours of rambling on about the possibility of seeing the Mosque of Ali, Kadhim was on the verge of realizing his dream. I must admit, up to this point, his promises to bless my children's children for a hundred years if I allowed him to see the mosque had seemed a bit pretentious and overenthusiastic. However, I was not prepared for what would happen next.

After clearing the last fold in the ground at the edge of the desert, it appeared out of nowhere—the glistening golden dome of the Mosque of Ali and the white façade of the city of An Najaf. The sudden mosaic of color, the golden mosque, the huge green palm trees, the deep pools of blue water lining the road, and the fields of bright yellow flowers was awe-inspiring against the dull backdrop of the open desert.

Even more overwhelming was Kadhim's reaction in the passenger seat of my hummer. First, he said a quick prayer and then fidgeted in childlike anticipation—scrambling inside our vehicle trying to get a better look at the Mosque. When the vehicle stopped, he burst from the vehicle and ran in front to pray. I was happy for him and I was proud that I'd helped make his dream possible.

Leaving Kadhim to his God, I walked forward to get a better view of the city. I could finally appreciate the elevation of the city and how it overlooked and dominated desert floor below. The now observable 300-foot sand and rubble escarpment at the base of this ancient city was beautiful to the tourist in me but horrifying to the commander. It was literally a cliff built by multiple ancient layers of older settlements, with a three thousand-year-old sand dune filling in the face of the chasm.

Ancient cities in the Middle East have level built upon level, as debris from old buildings is leveled off to accommodate new construction. This creates man-made hills, called "Tels" by archaeologists, which have noticeable escarpments, or slopes, of ancient debris. The oldest parts of the modern cities of Baghdad, Najaf, Erbil (in the Kurdish north of Iraq, where Alexander the Great fought the Battle of Arbala), Damascus, Syria and other cities all feature a Tel and sloping escarpment (or talus) at the oldest part of the city.

Our problem was atop the escarpment in the Tel of ancient Najaf. That makes them tough nuts to crack in the military sense, if the defender is determined. I was determined to break the defenders' will to resist *No Slack*'s dominance.

Around us, as far as I could see, there were rice dikes and paddies full of water lined by small yellow flowers. In front of us were Lieutenant Colonel Ingram's tanks. The first enemy artillery rounds landed nearby as I raised my binoculars to see what his tanks were firing at. The enemy artillery was close, very close to our position.

I had not yet seen incoming artillery, which served as a blunt reminder for me to stay focused, get what I needed quickly and get the hell out of there. As I gathered the information I needed, I heard a muffled plop to my rear in the road—it was Kadhim. My first instinct was to get down and wait to hear the gunshot, but no shots were fired. I yelled at Kadhim twice before I noticed he was just prostrating himself at the very sight of the Mosque of Ali. I slowly walked over to him lying face down in middle of the road and asked him if he was OK.

He arose and with tears in his eyes said, "Oh yes, I'm closer to my God and you have made this possible. We must free Najaf." As I helped him up, I realized that Kadhim's faith and the power of this mosque, the Shi'a equivalent of the Vatican, might in many ways be stronger than the combined firepower of my battalion and the Coalition moving toward Baghdad. We would need to tread lightly in Najaf and keep the religious significance of this city to the Shi'a in the forefront of our planning, even as I worked to find ways to leverage this Achilles' heel of Saddam's Regime.

THE RELIEF IN PLACE

That afternoon, Captain Tony New's Bravo Company moved forward to relieve Ingram's forward tank platoon immediately outside of

Najaf. Almost instantly, Bravo Company came under enemy artillery and mortar fire. As the day progressed, Bravo Company dug fighting positions along the rice dikes west of Najaf and began capturing prisoners along the road leading into the city. A quick assessment of these prisoners gave us our first hard evidence that the *Fedayeen* were forcing civilians to come out of the city to fight us.

The prisoners told us that the *Fedayeen* were holding their families at gunpoint and ordering the men to "go out and meet the Americans" or their families would be killed. This was a completely different situation than we expected, and we passed this new intelligence to brigade as quickly as possible. This claim by our prisoners was eventually confirmed and became one of the main reasons for the 101st Airborne Division's attack into Najaf, rather than just to surround and isolate it. We would attack to destroy the *Fedayeen* and free the citizens of Najaf from their tyranny.

While Bravo Company was digging in, we got word that the battalion would need to reposition to cover a third road entering Najaf from the south. Bravo Company would detach to our sister battalion while I took the rest of my battalion and moved south. Even though there were no reports of enemy activity from that avenue into Najaf, Colonel Hodges felt it necessary to check the route and ensure it didn't provide an unopposed enemy attack route into convoys moving north along Highway 8 to support the 3d ID.

I was furious about the order and went to brigade headquarters to talk to Colonel Hodges personally. *No Slack* had made contact with the enemy and was in an excellent position to attack; why in the hell would someone want me to give up the tactical advantage?

When I threw open the flap to the tent in the brigade command post, everyone knew why I was there. Recognizing my frustration on the radio, Major Frank met me and told me Colonel Hodges was not in the headquarters but he would do his best to answer my questions.

"Why would we give up this position when we know where the enemy is and have an opportunity to kill him?" I asked.

"I know sir," said Pat. "The sector we've been given is huge and we don't have the forces to cover every avenue in and out of Najaf. The colonel wants *No Slack* to check the southern route as soon as possible."

"Christ, Pat, how am I going to get down there? I will need all those trucks released back to division. It will take hours to reload them, drive back to Highway 8, negotiate the traffic jams south. And oh, by the way, all traffic going north has the right-of-way!" Continuing, I implored, "Then I have to cut cross-country along some damn goat trail to find a piss-ant road that is barely noticeable on the map."

Pat Frank was slow to reply so I almost yelled, "Christ, Pat, lets fight the fucking enemy right here in the palm of our hands, not some goddamn division staff officer's plan for where the enemy might be!" Pat knew I had been given a bad order and so did Colonel Hodges, but we all knew it was time to bite the bullet and support our commanders, even if they had not actually been on the ground yet to oversee the situation.

I realized Frank was doing the best he could when he modified the order and kept Bravo Company in contact with the enemy. This would buy us time to execute the order while keeping a hold on the enemy's throat to the west of Najaf. The key was to get to the southern road and quickly determine if the enemy was or could be using it against us. If not, we needed to get back to Tony New's Bravo Company quickly and continue the attack.

The lack of trucks in the battalion, and dwindling other resources necessary to move hundreds of infantrymen, forced me to order Charlie Company to walk south through the rice paddies while I moved the rest of the battalion by vehicle west to Highway 8, then south ten miles, and then to the south of Najaf. There were no north-south roads from our current location, so we essentially had to back-track over 50 miles of goat trails, dirt roads and desert. The move south was extremely difficult and took nearly eight hours, ending well after dark.

My forward command post sat on this unusually wet and squishy field and the damp soaked into my boots as I tracked Charlie Company's movement south through the rice paddies. I had ordered Charlie Company to move cross-country to our new position to see what was between the two major roads in the brigade's sector, and to determine if the enemy was establishing hide positions out of reach of our armor.

Up to this point, the armored forces had only patrolled and fought along the roads because of the water and restricted terrain. This move gave us a chance to see what lay between the roads. Luckily, the enemy was even less willing to brave this terrain than we were. Charlie Company spent the night crossing a series of rice paddies, all the while making comparisons to the jungles of Vietnam and Panama. As I struggled to stay awake, staring at the glare of the radio lights, I swatted mosquitoes and marveled that we were still technically in a desert.

Charlie Company (Cougar) emerged from the swamps of western Najaf as the sun came up. As Captain Matt Konz, a huge and ominous figure of a man from a small Iowa farming town, rendered his report, his Kuwaiti linguist kept trying to interrupt us and tell me how much the mission I had sent him on sucked. I was forced to ask Matt to wait while I addressed the grievances of his linguist. He told me he had no idea how difficult this "whole war thing" would be and promptly quit on the spot. I laughed and said, "You quit? You can't quit! Look around you. This is a war and we are 200 miles inside of Iraq."

"I don't care," he said. "I quit, and you don't own me!" I looked at Matt in surprise, hoping that he had heard what I thought I had heard. Matt grinned. I straightened up and looked the man in the eyes and said, "Fine, I accept your resignation."

He started to complain again, but I didn't have time for any more of his whining, so Matt and I walked away as he continued his report. The staff took care of getting rid of him.

I never saw him again.

Kadhim was made of sterner stuff and was more than happy to be right in the thick of things. After Matt finished his report, a small crowd of citizens started to form along the road next to our command post. I leaned inside my vehicle, grabbed my bullhorn and handed it to Kadhim, telling him to go earn his pay by talking to the people along the road. I wanted him to make my intentions known. Hearing my instructions to Kadhim, I could see Stewart Ramsey's ears perk up—a story! I told him to grab his cameras and go with Kadhim. "He's going to find out what's going on in Najaf."

After an hour of addressing an ever-growing crowd of Iraqis, Kadhim and the Sky News team were making quite an impression with the locals. The farmers in these small villages were cheering Kadhim, chanting religious slogans and singing at the news of our invasion of Iraq. Two of the local leaders and one sheik came out to talk to Kadhim, and they assured him that the *Fedayeen* had not come this far south and that they were not welcome in this part of Najaf. It was a good piece of human intelligence and would give us a good point of reference to confirm reports from our patrols moving toward Najaf.

Later that evening, I would get a chance to see the report that Stewart filed live to the Sky News desk in London, England. What surprised me was that while Kadhim walked among the cheering crowd, Stewart was saying on TV, "The Iraqis are truly happy to see the Americans. The Americans didn't stage this; it happened spontaneously when the American commander sent this former Iraqi citizen into the villages to tell the people they were here to destroy Saddam's regime."

I looked up from Stewart's five-inch TV screen, realizing that even though they had been with us for almost a month, the reporters still harbored stereotypes about the American military. How could I have ever staged such an event? I am sure what he was saying did not matter to the conspiracy crowd, but why did Stewart have to qualify the cheering crowds to his viewers, unless, of course, he believed his viewers wouldn't buy the footage unless he personally confirmed it was not staged?

I realized I had to push Stewart down to the men in the battalion and away from the command team and me. We were the institution and our actions and interviews would always be suspicious to Stewart's viewers. How could I convince his Arab viewers that our intentions were honorable, especially in Najaf, if all they heard and saw was what they believed was the "Bush" party line being parroted through me?

I needed to get cameras to the soldier level, where the men of *No Slack* could tell the story through their actions better than I could. Giving Stewart this level of access would finalize our trust in each other and help him show the world our honest and true intentions. These intentions would serve us well in Najaf. Words would fall short when most of those I wanted to communicate with spoke a different language; yet our actions in the village that day began to set a tone with the people of Najaf and, as we would later learn, the city's most important resident, the Grand Ayatollah Sayyid Ali al-Sistani of the Mosque of Ali, took notice.[8]

Delta Company, my most lethal and mobile company, equipped with twenty combat hummers with heavy machine guns, automatic grenade launchers and anti-tank missiles, completed their sweep of the road to the edge of Najaf and found no enemy positions or signs of *Fedayeen* along the route.

This confirmed the reports we had received from the local leaders speaking to Kadhim. They did, however, find hundreds of grateful Iraqi citizens. Apparently they were happy to see us and in need of our protection from the *Fedayeen* hiding in Najaf. While Captain Tom Ehrhart, my Delta Company commander, was talking to the village leaders near Najaf, Kadhim was wrapping up his meetings near our command post.

As Kadhim was returning to the command post, he suddenly found himself being heralded as a returning Iraqi hero, and the crowds grew as he walked along the single lane dirt road toward Najaf. They may have been simple farmers but they served as our first vital indication that the Shi'a might welcome the Coalition in Najaf.

Colonel Hodges decided to come to my sector to assess the road situation personally. I recommended that we meet where the road met the desert floor, so he wouldn't get blocked in by the large crowds forming along the route. It took me over an hour to move to the linkup point because of the crowds choking the narrow road to Highway 8. Once I cleared the road, I found a spot along a canal that gave Colonel Hodges an excellent view of the narrow road, two farm villages, and the hundreds of rice paddies between our position and Najaf.

I was hoping he would declare the route secure and let me take the battalion back to western Najaf. When he arrived, Colonel Hodges offered to "buy me lunch" as he dug into a box of Meals Ready to Eat (MREs) in the back of his hummer. I requested the meatloaf but settled for ravioli . . . I always seemed to settle for ravioli.

We climbed up the canal dike and sat facing Najaf and the narrow road. As we ate, a blue Kingfisher dove into the canal after minnows, unfazed that war had entered his domain. We discussed options in an almost surreal setting that made the war seem far off. The calm seemed to help the boss make his decision. I knew he had heard about my outburst with Pat Frank in his command post and I was embarrassed that I had let my emotions get the best of me; but I was not prepared to be overly pleasant or apologize just yet. I knew we needed to get back to our old position up north and I needed to convince Hodges it was the right thing to do.

As I contemplated how to do this with the least amount of fervor, Hodges suddenly said, "We're here to fight the enemy, Chris, not the stupid plan. There's no good reason to waste *No Slack* along this route. Take your men and go back to where you were and kill the enemy." Surprised and ecstatic, I stood up and saluted—"Yes, sir." Then I ran to my hummer, grabbed the radio and ordered the battalion back north.

After another grueling eight-hour move, *No Slack* was back on the western outskirts of Najaf. As Bravo Company prepared to close with and kill the enemy who were holding the citizens of Najaf hostage, Pete Rooks and the rest of Alpha Company arrived outside Najaf. The battalion was together for the first time since we had been forced to split up in Kuwait.

That evening I held a brainstorming session with my commanders and staff to develop a number of simple plans in an effort to prepare for multiple contingencies in and around Najaf. We were ready to move in and were only waiting for the brigade orders to do so. We finished around midnight and released the commanders to get some sleep. While the commanders were talking to the staff, I heard Colonel Hodges on the radio talking to the other battalion commanders. I gave the radio operator a stern look for not alerting me that Hodges was on the radio. It took me a moment to remember that I had ordered the radios turned down so it would not disrupt our planning session. The order had prevented me from hearing the boss talking to the rest of the brigade about upcoming operations in Najaf.

I took the radio mike, patted the young radio operator on the shoulder, and sat down just in time to hear Colonel Hodges ask Lieutenant Colonel Ed Palekas, from 3d Battalion, 327th Infantry Regiment, "What time are you going to attack?"

Once Ed finished discussing it with him, he asked Lieutenant Colonel Marcus De Oliveira the same question; then he asked me. I

looked at Majors Jim Crider and Pete Rooks, who by now were leaning over the radio to catch up on the conversation.

They shrugged in disbelief. "How could we have missed Colonel
Hodges' attack orders during our meeting?"

I asked Hodges if the intent was to conduct a coordinated brigade
attack or separate battalion attacks. He told me separate battalion
attacks. Again, I looked at Pete and Jim and smiled. Without hesitat-
ing I responded, "We will attack at 1500." Hodges approved.
"Roger," I said as the Colonel signed off.

Pete, Jim and the commanders looked at me. Surprise at my
response was evident on their faces. I quickly turned to the pad of
blank butcher chart next to the radios and began to draw an attack
picture on the paper.

"Why 1500?" Pete whispered into my ear.

"Because it gives us time to prepare and the sun will be at our
backs." I continued to draw on the butcher paper and outline my ideas
to Jim Crider on how we would attack. It was Crider's job to take my
ideas and turn them into an operations order for the company commanders to execute. Tomorrow would begin our battle for An Najaf.

OBJECTIVE FOX

Our mission was to seize a piece of terrain west of the city nicknamed
Objective Fox by the brigade staff, but we were not to enter the city.
After conducting our first leaders' reconnaissance, it was obvious that
the cost of seizing Objective Fox, which was directly below a 300-foot
escarpment, would be too high in terms of men and equipment. I
could not see any tangible value of holding such an exposed position.

Years earlier, during a major training exercise on the notional battlefields of Fort Polk, Louisiana, the 2d Armored Cavalry regimental
commander, Colonel Terry Wolff, told me, "I will never impale your
infantrymen on a city or obstacle without pounding it with every asset
I have at my disposal first." Wolff's words stood clear in my mind as
I looked at Objective Fox in disbelief. It was just such an obstacle,
4,000 years of blowing sand piled up 300 feet against a natural tectonic plate where the desert met the plateau of Najaf, overwatched by
a façade of three- to six-story hotels and apartment buildings.

Wolff's warning and promise to me rang loudly in my ears. It seemed that I was being told to impale my infantry on the heights of Najaf without first being allowed to pound the area with everything in the arsenal. "Well, not today and not with my soldiers; I will turn that tectonic plate into the western plains of Kansas before I attack."

The next morning, on the radio, I discussed my options and concerns about Objective Fox with Colonel Hodges. He approved my recommendation to conduct an armored reconnaissance to see how the *Fedayeen* would react when *No Slack* entered Objective Fox with tanks. I intended to send the tanks forward and draw fire. I had been told by Colonel Perkins two days earlier that his tanks had survived hits from everything the Iraqis had thrown at them. He did not think the Iraqis had anything that could destroy an M1 tank head-on. I hoped he was right as I was going to send the few tanks attached to me straight at the objective in order to draw fire. Once the enemy had shown his positions by firing, I would be able to destroy him at my leisure. With our weapons' stand-off ranges, I could inflict maximum casualties without exposing my infantry to direct fire from the 300-foot escarpment. It also allowed me to personally control the artillery, attack helicopters and close air support during our first battle.

My immediate tactical dilemma was attacking within sight of the Grand Mosque of Ali without damaging it. The Shi'a believed the Prophet Mohammad's son-in-law Ali was buried in the mosque, as well as Adam from the Garden of Eden and the great prophet Moses who led the Hebrews out of Egypt. It was imperative that we do everything possible to ensure that the mosque was not damaged during the fighting.

I had never worked with or even met the attached tank platoon's leader or his platoon sergeant before they received their orders. My instructions were simple as I pointed at the map on the hood of my hummer, "Your tanks will advance forward to the base of the escarpment, on the far side of the palm trees, and drive in a race track formation. I want you to become a 'shit magnet' for anyone on that hill with a gun. We will use the anti-tank systems, artillery, attack helicopters and Air Force to cover you."

My staff and commanders all turned to look at the young lieutenant. He acknowledged the order with little emotion. Standing behind him, the platoon sergeant smiled, looked down at the ground and shook his head in disbelief. If it hadn't been so deadly serious, it would have been funny. I felt sorry for the lieutenant who had to go back and tell his men that their job was to sit out in an open field and draw enemy fire so the rest of the battalion could kill the enemy—not a standard order for the young armor officer or his men.

By attacking at three p.m. we had the advantage of having the sun to our backs, coupled with the reflective effect of the water in the rice paddies, making it difficult for the enemy to pinpoint our positions or deduce our intentions. My mission was to find the enemy, determine his strength, and sting him hard. I wanted the enemy to know that *No Slack* was there to win and would stop at nothing short of complete victory.

Up to this point in the war, I didn't feel the Iraqis believed we were ready to enter their cities and fight them toe-to-toe. I wanted to dispel the perception that we were avoiding risk and unwilling to take casualties in a close city fight. I also had an opportunity to validate some long-held assumptions about the effectiveness and lethality of our anti-tank missile systems and to prove to the *Fedayeen* on the escarpment that *No Slack* was prepared to take the city with relentless and unconditional force. This armed reconnaissance would provide a dramatic display of our firepower and our ability to use it. It would also begin the process of separating the diehards from those Iraqis who might capitulate.

The only solid intelligence I had prior to the attack was from a few prisoners and from what Lieutenant Colonel Ingram had provided during our relief in place, which meant I knew precious little about the current disposition of the enemy in Najaf. However, Kadhim and the Iraqi villagers from the south had given me enough information that I was comfortable seizing the initiative and allowing *No Slack* to attack at the time and place of my choosing.

Though specific information about the enemy from higher intelligence sources was lacking, we did have a new source of information that proved crucial over the following days and weeks. It was a Special Forces A-Team from 5th Special Forces Group. The A-Team had operated in and around Najaf for weeks before our arrival and was able to give us a good idea of how the enemy defenses were arrayed. We had a general idea of what buildings along the cliff façade they occupied and what kinds of weapons they possessed. The A-Team's on-the-ground human intelligence provided my main rationale for using the tanks to draw fire from the enemy in Najaf.

As the brigade's attack into Najaf began, 1st Battalion met stiff resistance in southern Najaf at what the departing 3d ID had named checkpoint Charlie. We listened to their battle over the radio to glean lessons on enemy tactics and for any potential spillage of their battle into our sector. If this happened, we would have to rethink our attack and better coordinate it with 1st Battalion. Fortunately, their battle stayed within their sector and, to the best of our knowledge, pinned down a substantial number of defenders, keeping them from reinforcing the Iraqi defenses to our front.

Around noon, the battalion started to slowly assemble behind Bravo Company's defensive positions along the road. The tanks hid in an abandoned brick factory, Delta Company behind rock walls and rice dikes near an oasis, and my forward command post hid with the tanks in the brick factory. I didn't want to tip our hand and I hoped the timing of our attack would catch them off guard—no one attacks at three in the afternoon!

The plan was simple and would begin with an artillery barrage on what the A-Team identified as a *Fedayeen* command post along the Najaf facade. The enemy command post was in the most conspicuous building along the escarpment—a six-story white building that looked like a hotel. It wasn't on our maps, so it was less than four years old. As I was preparing to attack the building with artillery fire, the A-Team commander walked up and asked to speak to me. I held off on firing and listened as the team commander told me he couldn't guarantee that the *Fedayeen* were using the building. He was concerned that I was using his intelligence to bring devastating fires on a building that he only speculated was housing an enemy command post. He was right; I didn't have enough information to strike the building without provocation. I would need to get the enemy's attention another way. I had the field artillery targeting officer and my fire support NCO, Sergeant First Class Potts, recalculate the fires and spread them across the ridge of the escarpment to cover the tank platoon's advance into Objective Fox.

It only took the artillery minutes to recalculate and lay in the fires on the escarpment. I gave Crider the signal to initiate the attack and yelled back to the artillery team not to hit the mosque. The sound of the artillery passing overhead keyed the movement of Delta Company's lead platoon. The platoon rushed to the road intersection in front of us and began to scan the city for enemy targets with their long-range optics. One of my most aggressive and dedicated platoon leaders, First Lieutenant Eric Schnabel, commanded the lead platoon. Eric and I had spent many hours back at Fort Campbell and in Kuwait discussing the lethality and accuracy of his missile systems. Once this young officer and his men engaged the enemy along the façade of Najaf, they would make history by using anti-tank missiles to kill enemy infantry forces over a mile away hiding in buildings, houses and bunkers.

Delta Company's anti-tank missiles would give new meaning to the term "precision weapons." Never intended for this use, the anti-tank missiles would give me the ability to kill enemy infantry in homes, apartment buildings and office buildings without killing everyone in the building—something a 2,000-pound bomb from an Air Force jet or cruise missile could not do. The word "precision," to me, meant only killing those who needed killing, and not harming innocent people who might be hiding or being held in the same building. I saw no reason to level a building when I had the weapons to take out individual rooms or opponents. Winning the hearts and minds of Najaf's citizens would be a hell of a lot easier if I refrained from killing and maiming substantial numbers of civilians. Using anti-tank missiles in a precision firing role against fixed targets was a tactic I had wanted to validate since I had been an anti-tank company commander over a dozen years earlier.

In addition to the anti-tank missiles and their incredible ability to destroy enemy positions at long range, we had incorporated a number of sniper systems within the brigade to include the M-14 rifle. Not a new system to the Army, but an effective rifle that we managed to acquire before the invasion and train with our best marksmen. The 7.62 round of the M-14 has a much longer range than the standard 5.56 round of the M-16/M-4, offering a superior "one round knockdown power" to the battalion. This one weapon would prove its worth in the days and weeks to come, since not only did it make good its one shot/one kill reputation, but it also proved most valuable when fighting within the cities as its rounds penetrated cinder block, cars and tile. The value of the 7.62 round when fighting in built-up areas was undeniable.[9]

The artillery barrage snapped with a thunderclap as it landed across the ridge of the escarpment. In a flash, thousands of years of collected dust and sand filled the sky as the golden dome and most of the façade of Najaf disappeared in the barrage. Angered beyond belief, I threw my radio hand-mike in the front seat of my hummer and looked back at the artillery hummer and yelled, "What part of 'don't hit the fucking mosque' didn't you understand?" I looked back toward Najaf for what seemed an eternity, praying for the dust to settle and reveal that the mosque was still intact. It was, but I didn't apologize to the artillery team. They had gotten much too close and they knew it. I could see them feverishly recalculating their fire missions. Sergeant Potts, my fire support sergeant, looked at me trying to gauge my anger. I gave him a cold half-smile. "That was close, Potts—do it again and you're fired!"

The tanks rumbled past my position as our Air Force Tactical Control Party (TACP) sergeant yelled at me that he had aircraft stacked up at 2,000, 5,000, 8,000 and 10,000 feet above our position. He was preparing to bring in jet fighters armed with 500-, 1,000-, and 2,000-pound bombs. All we needed was someone stupid enough to shoot at us. Take the bait, damn it! I said to myself. Suddenly, with a pop and wiz, Schnabel's platoon began to fire their missiles at Najaf.

At first, I couldn't see the enemy, so I listened to the reports on the radio and followed the missiles to their targets with my binoculars. The windows across the façade of Najaf were full of men with heavy machine guns, rocket propelled grenades and rifle launched grenades firing wildly at Delta Company and the tank platoon. Even though the volume of fire was heavy, it was ineffective, falling well short of our positions. But now we knew where they were and the gunners of Delta Company were on them with accurate and deadly fires. As the battle across the escarpment developed, the oasis to Delta Company's front came alive with enemy mortar and small arm fires. I yelled at the Air Force Sergeant and asked him who and what he had on station first.

He replied, "F-16s with five 500-pounders, sir."

"Good. Put them in the palm trees to the front of Delta Company and shut down those enemy mortars."

The decision to drop the 500-pounders in front of the tanks forced me to slow their advance. If the Air Force failed to kill the enemy in the palm groves to his front, I hoped the tank platoon leader would use the additional time to consider how he was going to fight dismounted enemy infantry as he was sitting on Objective Fox. In the meantime, Delta Company continued to fire at will. Anti-tank missiles were screaming up the escarpment and flying directly into their intended targets—rooms and bunkers miles away. I turned and said to the men around me, "Precision. Now that's fucking precision. Not that 2,000 pounder killing everyone in the building—Air Force shit!"

The first two 500-pound bombs erupted in the palm grove and threw hundred-foot palm trees through the air like toothpicks. I was suddenly worried about my forward troops. I called Tom Ehrhart, who was forward with Schnabel, and asked if they were OK. He said, "It's getting hot down here, but not too bad." The next three bombs were more accurate and devastating. They hit the enemy mortar positions, setting off their rounds and propellant. The huge fireball and secondary explosions confirmed their destruction. The tanks were now free to advance into Fox.

Passing behind Schnabel's position with the tank platoon, Captain Tony New reported seeing enemy positions and receiving fire from the escarpment. Tony was my methodical warrior commander, small in stature yet huge in heart and passion. A Korean orphan adopted by American parents, he had beaten the odds and excelled in academics and had eventually been awarded an appointment to the US Military Academy at West Point. His troops loved his hands-on leadership style and keen sense of humor—something he would need on his first mission in harm's way.

Tony and Captain Matt Konz were moving forward with the tanks in an armored personnel carrier to see the terrain they would fight across the following day with their infantry companies. When they came under fire, I started to second guess my decision to send them both forward with the tanks. Risking two company commanders in this first preliminary battle now suddenly seemed like a bad idea.

However, if they were successful, they would have expert knowledge of the ground, which would help them accomplish their missions the next morning with minimal casualties. The risk was acceptable and I held my breath as they came under fire. Having them forward with a radio did pay one big dividend. I had two experienced company commanders feeding me valuable information about the battle beyond my observation and the enemy's ability to continue the fight, while the young tank platoon leader was able to fight his four tanks without worrying about sending me reports on his progress.

The tanks were on the far side of the palm grove now and under intense enemy fire from the city. They started systematically destroying the remnants of the enemy mortar positions and dismounted enemy infantry running through the palm grove. Although they were under a tremendous volume of fire from above, they were safely doing exactly what I had hoped—forcing the Iraqis to expose themselves to our artillery, attack helicopters, anti-tank missiles and snipers. With Delta Company sending missiles into windows almost two miles away, the artillery suppressing the escarpment and buildings, the Air Force delivering thousands of pounds of bombs on multiple buildings around the Mosque of Ali, and the division's OH-58 Armed Reconnaissance and Light Attack Helicopters rolling in on the enemy's artillery, mortar and infantry positions, I felt we had the enemy by the throat. We had the power to deliver fatal blows if they were stupid enough to continue the fight. They remained stuck on stupid for almost four hours as we pulverized them.

During those four hours, *No Slack* fought the most intense combined arms fight the 101st Airborne Division had seen since Vietnam. And just as I was about to decide whether or not to bring the infantry forward, Kadhim came over to me and quietly tugged on my sleeve. I didn't notice him at first and then he yelled, "Colonel, it's almost prayer time." I didn't know him well enough yet to pay him much attention and shrugged him off. He then pulled at my arm a second time and made eye contact, "Colonel, it's almost prayer time. The people want to go to the Mosque."

My first instinct was to pull my sidearm out and tell him to step back. Then I noticed the pain in his eyes. This was the mosque that had made this American from St. Louis, MO throw himself in the dirt and bless my family for ten generations. He was right. The Mosque was the key to taking Najaf, and Kadhim's insights were the next weapon I needed to employ against the enemy along the escarpment.

I quickly ordered the tanks, which were now clearing a minefield at the entrance to Najaf, to disengage and return to the brick factory. Delta Company would cover their withdrawal and the artillery would shift from high explosive rounds to smoke rounds to mask the movement. I withdrew the attack helicopters and staged them to our rear. I did not want to completely release them in case the plan didn't work.

"We are going to let the people go to the mosque and hopefully generate a lot of goodwill and make our peaceful intentions known through action, not bullets," I explained. I had Crider summon the speaker trucks forward and ordered Kadhim to get in the trucks and move to Delta Company's forward positions to announce to the people of Najaf that out of respect for Ali and Islam we would not fight the enemy during prayer time. I gave him the following message to read to the people over the speakers:

"We are the 101st Airborne Division and our mission is to destroy Saddam Hussein and his brutal regime. We respect your religion, the Mosque of Ali, and we do not wish to hurt the people of Najaf. You are free to go to prayers. May Allah be praised."

Kadhim continued the announcement as our tanks withdrew and as the enemy guns went silent. Moments later, without warning, the escarpment became covered with makeshift white flags. The families and children of Najaf were carrying them as they walked across the escarpment to the Mosque of Ali for prayers.

That evening I walked to the edge of one of the canals next to my command post and looked across the dark battlefield between Najaf and me—no men lost. We had accomplished our first mission and sustained zero casualties. Everything we learned had worked. We had used every resource available—Air Force jets, attack helicopters, artillery, tanks, anti-tank missiles, snipers, psychological operations, infantry and religion! I could feel my enemy's pain and anguish in the dark; we had punished, embarrassed and confused him, and his control over his force was waning. I had the advantage and I wouldn't give him an inch in the morning. I was sure we had broken his back; now I needed to either kill him or steal his final will to resist.

3

THE MOSQUE OF ALI

"It looks like the Liberation of Paris!"

ESTABLISHING THE FOOTHOLD

The next morning we were in position to resume the previous day's attack, but this time the infantry companies would have to move farther forward in order to seize a foothold in the city. Because of the terrain I was unable to alter the plan much due to the single road and flooded rice fields, but today I was confident we could break any resistance on the ridge and firmly establish ourselves in the city before noon. But I was unprepared for what was about to unfold once we commenced our attack—no resistance and welcoming crowds of restrained yet obviously happy Iraqi civilians. Our precision fires, personal restraint, compassion and cultural awareness were beginning to work . . . but how long would it last?

As Charlie Company passed the command team, I looked at Jim Crider and said, "Well, you may never see this again in your lifetime; hundreds of dismounted infantrymen moving in column to attack a city." Then I turned my attention back to the escarpment, leaned back in my vehicle and told my forward artillery observer to fire only smoke rounds in the first barrage. As I heard the rounds pass overhead, I ordered the tank platoon and engineer platoon forward to the minefield.

Captain Tom Ehrhart's heavy weapon platoons were set in their attack positions as the tanks passed behind them on the bend in the road. Tom's gunners were scanning the hotels, apartments and houses along the escarpment, but they reported negative enemy activity as the tanks neared the minefield at the edge of the city. Once the tanks were in position to provide covering fire for the engineers, First Lieutenant Evangelist and Sergeant First Class Kumm ordered their combat engineers out of their hummers and rushed forward to systematically destroy the mines along the road and dirt berms straddling the road.

Battlefield mine clearance technology hasn't changed much since my grandfather's days with the American Expeditionary Force in France in 1918. It remains as simple as it was then and just as dangerous. Two men provide cover for a third man who then moves into the minefield with a 100-foot strand of engineer tape with a pre-tied 20-inch loop at the end. Once he approaches a mine, he first checks for visible booby traps. If he finds none, he drops the tape loop over the mine and then works his way back to the hide position where the other two men are waiting. He gives a quick jerk of the line to move the mine three to four feet to see if it explodes. If it doesn't, he moves forward, picks up the mine and moves it to the side of the road. Once this is done, he begins the process all over again.

Methodically clearing the route into the city in this manner was taking time, and I was getting antsy. I was driving the tank platoon leader crazy with my constant request for reports. I had a thousand infantrymen bottled up on a single-lane road surrounded by water in every direction. I was feeling vulnerable and began pushing for a breakthrough.

Just then, Sergeant First Class Kumm reported that an elderly Iraqi man was walking toward them through the surface-laid minefield. The man, who appeared to be in his seventies, seemed to know exactly where to walk. We had suspected the locals knew a route through the minefield because dozens of them had been using the road over the past week. This man calmly came forward and signaled his intention to help the engineers. I ordered the counter-intelligence team to determine if the man was really going to help us breach the minefield.

This team included Specialist Kim Carr, a 20-something female Arabic linguist and former high school Spanish teacher who had joined the Army after 9/11. Kim was an extraordinary soldier who gained my respect from the moment I met her. She was bold, completely unafraid of risk, and intelligent. Yet she looked every bit the small-town high school teacher with a uniform that didn't quit fit and an oversized helmet on her head—but when she spoke, she knocked the Arab males off balance with her mastery of the Arabic language and her unwavering presence. Next to Kadhim, Specialist Carr was one of the greatest weapons I had in my inventory. When Carr arrived at the minefield, the man was in the process of showing the engineers where the mines were by pointing, smiling and drawing in the sand. In the days ahead, these universal communication techniques would often become our principal means of communicating until I could find or hire more linguists.

With the elderly man's help, the engineer platoon made quick work of the minefield. Kim Carr listened to the old man tell the story of the minefield and the plight of the citizens of Najaf. He had lost his 14-year-old son Armer in this minefield a month earlier when the *Fedayeen* emplaced it in response to the looming US invasion. Armer was his last son and was on his way to buy tomatoes at the market when he was killed in the newly laid minefield west of the city, which he knew nothing about until he stumbled upon it. Tears flowed from the old man's eyes as the mines were detected, disarmed and safely removed. The man's willingness to help us in plain view of the city, combined with the continued absence of enemy fire, and the growing crowds along the escarpment led me to believe we could enter the city standing straight up and without any more fighting.

Charlie and Bravo Companies quickly climbed up the road, taking cover west of the minefield, then quickly pushing to its far side as the engineers signaled the route was clear. They reached the top of the escarpment and positioned their heavy machine guns to cover their advance into the first three blocks of Najaf. Charlie Company was first, then Bravo Company, rapidly moving north within sight of the Golden Mosque of Ali, then setting up fighting positions at the main intersection leading into the heart of the city.

I had no intention of going house to house to spread the word of our arrival; I wanted to move through the streets and overtly let the citizens know we were there to kill or capture the *Fedayeen*, not to hurt or embarrass them by entering their homes and violating their religious and cultural norms. This became the main reason I wanted to avoid night operations within Najaf—I was determined to avoid contact, physical or visual, with local women.

Respect and understanding of the Arabs' cultural norms were paramount in taking control of Najaf. Any violation of these closely held beliefs would only fuel the resistance, and I felt I needed to stop the violence as quickly as possible in order to control the city and support 3d ID's march to Baghdad. This was going to be next to impossible if we used traditional US urban fighting techniques. To do it by the book meant we would have to push into each home, detain everyone in the house, search the house, and move to the next. These people were not the enemy and this method would only alienate them, bringing us down to the level of the *Fedayeen* in their eyes.

At this point, we hadn't received any hostile fire and conditions seemed ripe for restraint, so we restrained our actions. This was a risk I was prepared to accept.

I was struck at how the people of Najaf reacted when I smiled at them—it seemed to ease their fear. As the infantry companies pushed into the city, the tank platoon moved through the minefield and took up positions at the first intersection. I kept the mortar platoon, Delta Company and the battalion's logistic forces (called field trains) outside Najaf until I could determine how deep into the city we could push.

I set up my command team at the breach in the minefield while the companies moved into the center of the city. Delta Company was still at the road intersection scanning the façade of Najaf in order to cover the advance of Charlie and Bravo. They were reporting no enemy movement or visual contact at the previous day's enemy positions. The Special Forces A-Team and our psychological and counter-intelligence teams began to wade in and talk to the growing crowds.

After five days of little to no intelligence on Najaf from our higher intelligence sources, the volume and detail of the human intelligence we were receiving from the locals on the street was overwhelming. The crowds were telling us that we had destroyed the *Fedayeen* and Iraqi army positions across the escarpment the previous day. Any survivors had fled Najaf after prayers and had headed north to Hillah, a city farther up the Euphrates, south of Baghdad. After holding many of the families at gunpoint in the local high school, the *Fedayeen* had finally released them and fled during the night. However, the townspeople couldn't tell us if that meant that the *Fedayeen* had left the city or just melted into the population.

As I pondered all of the issues associated with fighting *Fedayeen* in civilian clothes, Kadhim interrupted me. He introduced me to the old man who had helped us clear the minefield. This man took me by the shoulders and forcefully kissed me on both cheeks, his unshaven face almost drawing blood from mine, and his breath thick from too many cups of tea and cigarettes, with tears in his eyes thanked me for freeing Najaf and begged me not to leave them this time. Still locked in the Iraqi's embrace, I looked at Kadhim and said, "Leave them this time? What's he talking about?"

Kadhim replied, "Yeah, like in 1991 when we [America] let the Shi'a be slaughtered by Saddam after we promised to help them if they rose up to overthrow Saddam. Do you remember that worthless promise, Colonel?"

I felt embarrassed for my country, and then forcefully returned the man's embrace and told him, "We won't let you down this time—I promise!"

* * * *

NOTE FROM JIM LACEY: The day before this event I had walked by an Iraqi household where the family was out cheering the arrival of the American forces. I spotted a picture of Saddam hanging on a wall inside the home. When an older gentleman saw what I was looking at he walked into the house and took the picture down. He then walked outside and let us watch him spit on the picture. When he was done, he walked back inside, carefully wiped the spit off the picture and hung it back up. An Iraqi interpreter, standing nearby, told me, "That picture will stay up until he is sure the Americans are staying and Saddam is not coming back."

* * * *

Major Pete Rooks called from the top of the escarpment to let me know he had found a walled compound at the entrance of the city. "It's a good place to establish the command post," he said. It was around the time I reached the top of the escarpment and my first instinct was to look back and confirm a suspicion I had. Turns out I was right; they could not see us on the desert floor. The sun was in their eyes and the water from the flooded oasis worsened the glare of the sun in the afternoon. Despite the technological innovations of war, sunrise and sunset remain constant factors in combat that may never change. This time it worked to our advantage.

SURVIVING IN THE SLUMS

Once I reached the compound, I quickly noticed something was seriously wrong. As I approached my hummer, I could see a swarm of flies on the windshield. In addition, through the windshield, I could see a very upset and uncomfortable look on my driver's face as he spoke on the radio. He thumped the windshield as he swatted the flies and yelled a muffled, "It's a flecking shouter haze!"

"What?" I yelled back.

Disgusted, he leaned out of the doorless vehicle, told the guy on the other end of the radio to standby, and yelled, "We're sitting in the middle of a FUCKING SLAUGHTERHOUSE, SIR!" In the blistering heat, I walked closer to the hummer and, admiring how well my chemical suit was pooling my sweat, thought, how bad could the flies really be? Then I looked into the hummer.

My God, they're everywhere.

"Yeah, they really seem to like your Gatorade, sir!" That's when I looked at my seat in the back of the hummer and noticed the mess of powdered Gatorade and Pringles caked with water from my overturned canteen. If that wasn't bad enough, there were thousands of flies, which were carrying every disease known to man, buzzing and sticking to my hummer seat—my only home for the foreseeable future.

Specialist Ray Bowers' candor was the primary reason I picked him as my driver. He was a combat veteran from Desert Shield/Desert Storm who had left the Army in the mid-90s, only to return in search of the lifestyle he had grown to love. The hiatus made him much older than the average specialist. In fact, he was only a couple of years younger than I. It was nice to have a peer around to break up the monotony of much younger soldiers. I enjoyed his company. We had a lot in common and he was very proactive when it came to making my life less complicated by keeping my command vehicle in top running order at all times. When I asked him why he decided to come back into the Army, he told me "[that] civilians are disorganized, they don't give a damn about their employees, and integrity is only a word in the dictionary to them. . . . I hated it out there."

Ray was a good partner in the command vehicle, and despite our difference in rank, we often argued like an old married couple. As the battalion commander's driver, he heard everything that the senior leaders of the battalion discussed. This knowledge made him a potential source of information and gossip for the rest of the battalion, but he never gave in to the temptations to spread rumors or take advantage of his position.

Besides the flies, the slaughterhouse was surrounded by packs of roving wild dogs who fed off the discarded animal carcasses, which were often just flung over the side of the escarpment. It was clearly not a good place for my command post and we needed to find another location quickly. We were not going to sleep in the streets of Najaf, nor were we going to occupy private homes. We needed to find a compound with defendable walls, enough height to give us clear fields of fire, and protected sleeping areas. This was not a new concept, but the reality of the squalor of western Najaf, the oldest part of the city (over 4,000 years old), instantly reminded me of the hideous conditions I had endured in Port au Prince, Haiti in 1994. The smell of the slaughterhouse and the biting flies were not limited to just this compound; it was the entire area. We were in the slums of Najaf, which was something you cannot determine by simply looking at a map.

In Haiti, I learned that compounds were essentially the "good ground" in urban warfare. They gave a unit the ability to defend, reinforce and resupply under secure conditions. An exceptional compound would have multiple story buildings inside, which would provide an observational advantage over any would-be attackers. But more importantly, closed compounds provided temporary quarters for soldiers where they could conduct personal hygiene, get some uninterrupted sleep, and develop a controlled field sanitation environment without being exposed to enemy fire. Haiti taught me that when soldiers concentrate in urban areas, so do flies, fleas, mites and rats. The tenacity of the enemy is always uncertain, but illness, incapacitation and disease are a certainty if you don't deliberately fight the elements of nature. We thought we were prepared for the wrath of nature in Iraq, but nature always seems to have a trick or two up her sleeve.

While in Iraq, the subject of field hygiene is matter that takes up a considerable portion of every chain of command's time. Once the troops return home, though, everyone quickly forgets about what is often the most sordid detail of war. First Sergeant Gregg (who appears elsewhere in this narrative) has captured the full complexity of the problem in this essay he sent me after the war. Finally, a very dark corner of war is illuminated.

* * * *

SCHITZSQUIE
By 1st Sergeant Ron Gregg

War is Hell, in more ways than most people can imagine. An issue that reporters and historians usually fail to capture, but is ever present in all soldier deployments is the latrine. Let's face it: this is not the most comfortable issue to talk about. It is in the planning phase of major operations that it should be discussed. Why? Well, imagine 720 dudes using four toilets for three weeks. Let's see . . . if each guy only used the toilet once a day . . . hmm, that gives him eight minutes. Imagine if your 8-minute window didn't open until 2:25 a.m.? Fortunately, we were a little more organized than that, and we did indeed have the foresight to plan for it. Actually there is a formula (believe it or not) for how many port-a-johns must be present to accommodate X number of soldiers for Y number of hours. What isn't cool is the fact that this is often impossible to support logistically, and which leads me to the meat of this article.

When the going gets tough, the tough plug their nose and drive on . . . or something like that. Necessity is indeed the mother of invention; I guess that makes logistics a mother *&$. This is not to say the logisticians are failing—not at all. It's just that a unit only gets so much cubic shipping space to go to war with, and bullets, food and other stuff sometimes rate higher on the priority list.

This issue first became apparent at a staging camp in Kuwait. Our latrine system was calculated almost perfectly.

Upon arrival, we had just enough port-a-johns to accommodate the needs of our soldiers. It was when the contract for the #%@*! Sucker Truck ran out, that we had issues. It is amazing how quickly these things fill up. Our contract was for them to be sucked out once a day. On two occasions he missed a day. Those were not good days.

The road to war is littered with crap. When out in the elements soldiers use the "cat-hole" method of waste disposal. This involves using one's entrenching tool (a small folding shovel) to dig a small hole, and bury the waste when the biological function is complete. Cat-holes are the best system for small units that are well dispersed; however, they are not ideal for large concentrations of soldiers. When soldiers are concentrated in say, company (120–150 troops) or battalion (700–900 troops) size elements, a more elaborate method must be used. Most often this is the "Slit Trench" or "Straddle Trench," which is simply a hole in the ground approximately six feet long, one foot wide and three feet deep. It looks like a shallow grave for a skinny guy. I would like to say that we had picture perfect slit trenches in every company assembly area in theater, but that would be a lie.

For the bulk of our travels, the ground was either so rocky it was like digging a hole in a sidewalk, or was so loose that the holes were so wide and shallow that they defeated the purpose. A slit trench that is too wide has great comedic potential but is otherwise useless. The concept of this method is that each soldier, after use, simply kicks a little dirt over his deposit before he leaves, much like the actions of a dog after he has made a similar deposit.

Cat-holes and slit trenches worked fine in the open, deserted terrain of Iraq. It was the urban areas that really challenged us. It was here that we spent most of our time and had to develop some more imaginative methods of waste disposal. What most people don't realize is that this is a very high priority in combat. When a large military unit stops for any more than an hour, this issue must be addressed with a sense of urgency.

The Night Deposit

Our first big challenge was in an abandoned military compound in An Najaf. To this day, I don't know what this place was, but it was new and beautiful. There were ten decent-sized rooms per building and about ten buildings. Our entire battalion parked in this compound for about three days. It stands to reason that Iraqi soldiers probably have the same human requirements that American soldiers do, thus there should have been toilets to accommodate the battalion. Yes, indeed. The Iraqi toilets are an issue themselves and are best avoided unless the water supply is unlimited. There were lots of Iraqi toilets but no water, so . . . back to the slit trench.

The limited areas that weren't covered in concrete were so sandy that the slit trenches looked more like elliptical dips in the sand. It was what we were stuck with, but led to the discovery of the "night deposit." This was the first non-doctrinal solution to the age-old problem. This involved using sewer access manholes as the place to do business. Because it made one look as if he was pooping on the sidewalk, it was best to go out during the hours of darkness to avoid any rude interruptions from fiery NCOs. In this manner one could make his contribution directly to the sewer system while squatting on nice flat concrete. It was a nice change, and almost felt luxurious. Just don't forget to put the lid back . . . the consequences are even more severe than at home.

The Chair

In Al Hillah, our first residence was a huge warehouse lot. There were probably fifteen gigantic warehouses on a lot about a mile square. A trench was already provided due to a sewer line repair that our attack interrupted. So there was this trench about four feet deep, with broken pipes and such at the bottom. The inspiration to use it hit me just as it was getting dark one night. I lit a cigar and set out on my adventure. A courteous young soldier pointed out the location to me and I walked up to the site. It was a sight alright.

Apparently the soldiers had gotten tired of squatting and

decided to improve the trench. There were now three chairs neatly arranged over it. When I say chairs, I'm referring to steel chairs with the seats removed. This apparatus provides the user with a large square frame on which to rest whatever part of his anatomy that he decides will support his weight during the operation. By itself, the chair was not a bad addition to the concept; the problem lay in the fact that the chairs were precariously balanced on some I-beams that somebody had scrounged and positioned across the trench. One had to walk out to the center of the trench on one beam, face about, then put the other foot on the other beam and hope that all four legs of the chair decided to behave during the whole process. On the night I used it, a squadron of hungry mosquitoes decided to take advantage of me, thus adding to the entertainment value of the experience. Swatting mosquitoes while balancing on a chair balanced on some I-beams, with your pants down around your ankles really should qualify somebody as a circus performance.

The Blackboard

Our next home was a school. Iraqi schools came complete with walls and locking gates. They also came with broken toilets and no water. Here we took the night deposit and the chair to the next level. My soldiers discovered a freestanding chalkboard in one of the classrooms. It was complete with sides, like a portable three-walled room, so they attached a toilet paper dispenser. Now they even had a place for graffiti, but no one indulged. They were too busy keeping their balance on the chair.

The Throne

We moved around a lot in Hillah. One of the attractions I got to see was one of Saddam's palaces. It had been ransacked by the local population a few days before I got there, but I did get to see his bathroom. It was complete with American-style toilets. Now, I'm not one to pilfer, loot or steal, but when I saw that the toilet seat was the only surviving part of Saddam's master bathroom, I took it, gold screws and all. I installed it that day on an ammo crate positioned over an open manhole, behind the former strip-joint we were living in. Needless to say, the soldiers were very happy with my contribution. That seat got lost somewhere along our journey, but it was good while it lasted.

The Volcano

The place we call Q-West, Quayyarah Airfield, was our next stop. The Iraqis had built a very impressive Air Force Base there; at least the structures we'd left standing were impressive. Once again, we needed to employ the manhole system. This time one of my sergeants made the contribution; this guy goes by the name of Monster. Well Sgt. Monster got his hands on our gasoline-powered cut-anything saw and wandered around looking for something to use it on. It wasn't long before he found what he was looking for and began making some real noise. Before long he came to get me so he could show me his creation. I must say that Sergeant Monster outdid himself. He had procured a tapered or cone-shaped piece of ductwork from one of the hangars and mounted a toilet seat on top of it. The result was this volcano-shaped affair secured over the top of an open manhole. There was only one problem with Monster's design: he built it to match his six- foot frame. It was truly a work of art, but the rest of us felt like Edith Anne in her big rocking chair . . . and that's the truth—raspberry!

The Schitzsquie

Monster's creation was such a raving success that it soon became necessary to build another. Soldiers from other companies were coming over to use our facility, and there was only the one. I had about 140 guys, so we had maximized the finite capacity of the Volcano. Thanks to our engineers, a large and very deep trench suddenly appeared somewhat near the Volcano. I immediately liked the idea of a new facility; the volcano had begun to erupt with flies, which was very disconcerting since it usually happened in response to a deposit. The problem with the large trench was spanning it. One of my guys procured an item I can best describe as a large steel hurdle. It had a wide base and a crossbar of steel tubing about five inches in diameter. The concept was to rest the back of one's knees on it and let the rest hang over the pit. I shied away from this design for two reasons. One, the pit was nearly six feet deep and if a soldier was to somehow lose balance, he might find himself dangling by his knees for a brief moment before he fell head-first into the pit. Yuck! The other reason was heat. The steel crossbar was painted dark olive drab. The summer sun even in northern Iraq can heat metal to egg-frying temperatures, and I for one did not want my eggs fried . . . if you know what I mean.

So what to do? I managed to find some odd-shaped I-beams lying about the area. I have no idea what their true purpose was but they were about three inches across at one end then gently tapered out to about six inches wide just past the center, and then they tapered back to about four inches. From the top, they looked like very long, angular, iron snowshoes. I took a couple pair of these and spanned the gap of the pit. I positioned them like skis. Hence the name: Schitzsquie. The idea was to create a secure platform over the center of the pit, where one could safely squat and do one's business. I preferred this open-air facility to the volcano. I got a couple guys to help me erect a camouflage net over it for privacy, and we were done.

The Inferno

Well, before long, the engineers got caught up with all of their bomb diffusing and minefield clearing and decided to get to work on the important things: outhouses. The first ones were a little rough around the edges, literally, but eventually they got the right-sized hole in the proper location and began producing them by the dozen. This style some folks will remember from the Vietnam era. The outhouse had a trapdoor in the back into which half of a 55-gallon drum could be placed and replaced. Unfortunately, somebody had to do the burning. Once or twice a day the barrels were pulled out and a mixture of gasoline and diesel were added to the already noxious contents. At this point, it would be ignited and some unfortunate soul would have to tend to it with a paddle. Eventually the contents would be up in smoke and the barrel placed back in the outhouse.

Full Circle
By the time I was leaving Q-West, nice new port-a-johns arrived. They were luxurious! The contractor was timely and there were plenty of them everywhere. With any luck, the rest of the soldiers won't be there so long that they end up having indoor plumbing.

After months of using such facilities, sitting on a porcelain toilet was one of my highest priorities upon returning home to the good ole US of A!

* * * *

Pete and I both agreed that we needed to get out of the slaughterhouse compound quickly. I told him, "We can't stay here, we will all get sick. We need to attack to seize compounds, strongpoints . . . places we can defend from and dig latrines." As usual, Pete was already focused on these details and was issuing orders to move the headquarters.

Pete grabbed Sergeant First Class Pernell Wilson, our master gunner who rode with me everywhere, and formed a quick patrol to find a new command post. That's how it's done in a unit with a good XO. He is responsible for the details of running the battalion, such as tracking logistics, setting up the command post, and ensuring someone is constantly sweating the small stuff so the commander can focus on fighting the battle. Pete had a meticulous eye for detail. He liked to sweat the small stuff and that's what made us such a good team. I hated details, deadlines, long meetings, logistics and setting up command posts. Pete took care of it for me so I could stay on the move; so I could command.

One of the details we had stressed before we deployed was buying all the components we would need to fight disease. We had spent over

$50,000 on lime, rat poison, traps, sulfur and fly swatters, and trained over 150 of our soldiers as field sanitation experts. It was time to put it all into practice to prevent the conditions from damaging our combat effectiveness.

As I walked out of the slaughterhouse compound, Pete yelled to me that the division commander was coming up the hill, but I had a lot on my mind and there was much to do. He then launched a patrol to find a new command post, while also sending orders to the companies to start identifying compounds in their zones where they could safely bed down as the sun began to set. Back at the main intersection entering western Najaf, our M1 tank platoon had taken up positions covering the three main roads that converged at the edge of Najaf. I didn't know it then, but *No Slack* was the 31st foreign army in the last 4,000 years to find itself at this intersection on the verge of taking control of the ancient city of An Najaf.

As I walked toward the rear of Charlie Company, I could feel the anxiety bubble in my stomach starting to ease. The infantry companies had managed to maneuver toward the Ali Mosque without taking enemy fire, and the streets were starting to fill with dozens of curious and friendly Iraqis. The road was jammed with infantrymen, cargo hummers and armed hummers with automatic grenade launchers, anti-tank missiles and heavy .50 caliber machine guns, all cautiously moving through the enemy minefield and into the city. Alpha Company was now moving into the city on foot and proceeding to a compound that Sergeant First Class Wilson had found in a schoolyard across the street from the slaughterhouse.

On the main street leading to the Mosque of Ali, I could see the Special Forces A-Team mingling with the tank platoon and the rear elements of Charlie Company. I moved up to their position in hopes of having a quick discussion with the A-team commander before we went into the planning process that evening. His team had been instrumental to the battalion's success thus far, and his recommendations for subsequent actions in Najaf would prove crucial to my planning.

The Special Forces team and their counterparts, a curious group of men called "OGA," which I later learned was an acronym for Other Governmental Agencies, had covertly operated in and around Najaf for over two months prior to our arrival, and were convinced that we should seek an audience with the senior Shiite cleric in Najaf, Ayatollah Sistani. They believed that Sistani's cooperation with the Coalition would be decisive not only in Najaf but in winning over public opinion within the entire Shi'a community, which would essentially stop the fighting in southern Iraq.

Because Sistani was the Grand Ayatollah, he was legally capable within the Islamic community to issue a formal *fatwa*, a form of religious proclamation similar to a Papal Bull or Encyclical. To the Shi'a, it would be a legal order as well as a religious injunction. It was hoped that such a proclamation could convince the Shiites to support the Coalition and assist in the overthrow of Saddam. Initial reports from the OGA's informants and emissaries were hopeful, but Ba'ath loyalists were still holding Sistani under house arrest, making our plans to seek his support even more difficult and dangerous as we neared the Mosque.

As I continued to walk toward my lead elements, I noticed an odd group of vehicles that didn't belong to the battalion. That's when I remembered that the commander of the 101st Airborne Division, Major General David H. Petraeus, was in the area. I hadn't seen General Petraeus since we crossed the berm and was anxious for news about the progress of the war. As I walked to his vehicle, I noticed the now ever-present embedded reporters, including Rick Atkinson from *The Washington Post*, whom I had met in Kuwait after the grenade attack.

As I neared the group I also noticed Colonel Hodges, who appeared to be giving General Petraeus a situation report. Once he saw me, he quickly motioned me over to provide an update on my progress and my plans for occupying the western sector of the city. This was the first time I discussed my plan to seek an audience with Sistani with anyone other than the Special Forces and OGA teams. General Petraeus acknowledged my plans and told me to "seek the advice" of the Ayatollah and ask him how we should occupy the city without causing significant collateral damage to the people and their holy places. I was relieved that this didn't offend Colonel Hodges, as I had not had an opportunity to discuss it with him first. As the days passed, I would appreciate Colonel Hodges' trust and confidence in the battalion and me. For him, it wasn't about looking good or getting credit; it was all about winning and doing the right thing.

As I walked away from the meeting, Rick Atkinson pulled me aside. Rick asked for my thoughts on the war thus far and I jokingly told him we had fought "the stupid, the weak and the brave." The phrase just sort of rolled off my tongue, but it had been milling around in my head since our first battle in Objective Fox. Rick nodded and began to write enthusiastically in his little green notebook. However, he didn't understand "the weak and the stupid" part. I told him the stupid were those who kept returning to the same windows that we engaged with anti-tank missiles only to die like those who had fought there moments earlier. The weak were those who ran to Hillah and were trapped by 2d Brigade of the 101st Airborne Division and subsequently destroyed by Air Force A-10 *Warthog* aircraft along Highway 8. My biggest concern was the brave. Where are the Iraqi regular soldiers we had fought the day before? There had been dozens of Iraqi regulars in Najaf, as evidenced by the large number of Iraqi uniforms and dead strewn along the road to the city, in their former battle positions and command posts. It appeared that many regulars had taken off their uniforms and faded into the population. I could feel them everywhere, watching us and trying to determine our next move. At the time, I could not imagine that regular soldiers would just take off their uniforms and go home.

* * * *

JIM LACEY: My memories of *No Slack*'s assault into Najaf are found in this article I wrote at the time. It was a pity that soon after this Chris and his battalion were sent to Al Hillah, while I remained with the 1st Brigade in Najaf.

SQUEEZING AN NAJAF
The 101st edges closer towards a battle to secure the town

By JIM LACEY

At dusk the 2-327 Infantry Battalion moved up to their assault positions for the next day. They found the enemy waiting for them.

Atop a hundred-foot ridge, paramilitary infantry and medium artillery had occupied a series of apartment complexes, from where they directed heavy fire on the advancing infantry. The U.S. troops immediately went to ground and called for help.

Earlier in the day, the battalion had made an armed reconnaissance into the area and came under sporadic fire, which they suppressed with some micro-scale shock and awe. It was assumed at the time that Iraqi forces would return when the reconnaissance units departed.

They did.

Alerted by the reconnaissance as to where the next U.S. thrust would come, they came out in force to stop it. For a few minutes, it seemed that every window along the ridge was spitting out machinegun bullets. Hoping to keep collateral damage to a minimum, battalion commander Lieutenant Colonel Chris Hughes called on his TOWs to silence the enemy guns. The TOW is a wire-guided anti-tank missile with a powerful blast, and those available to Lieutenant Colonel Hughes' forces are fitted with the new ITAS sights that allow the user to see an enemy's trigger finger 3,000 meters away in the dark.

Over the next few hours the battalion fired over 45 missiles into the apartment complex, almost all of them going directly through a window. By 9:00pm, it was a brave Iraqi who was willing to draw the attention of the deadly accurate TOWs, and enemy fire had almost completely ceased. Then one of the unit's artillery observers directed Lieutenant Colonel Hughes' attention to an artillery piece being rolled into position on the top of the ridge.

No sooner had Hughes trained his binoculars on the area than it exploded under the impact of a TOW missile. But Kiowa helicopters had spotted two others behind the ridge, and reported other enemy in the area. Hughes ordered the Kiowas to attack with their rockets and now called in his own artillery and some close air support from the Air Force. In blinding flashes of artillery and rocket impacts, the Iraqi artillery and their crews were destroyed.

For a brief lull there was no fire from either side, and the infantry began to slowly inch forward again. Almost immediately, they came under a fusillade of fire from a large white building on the far edge of the apartment complex. There was a brief moment of chatter on the radio: "We are taking heavy fire from our left." Close air support was already rolling in and an air liaison officer on the ground was designating the new target.

Hughes spoke into the microphone: "What building?"

"I say again," came the reply, "the white building."

In a blast of fire and smoke the building vanished as two 500-lb bombs smashed through its center.

Having met more resistance then he expected, Hughes continued to pound the ridgeline with mortars, artillery and over a dozen more air strikes.

Next morning, the commander ordered his five tanks up the road towards An Najaf. The anti-mine blade on the lead tank detonated three mines as it advanced, and engineers later cleared 66 more. Before the infantry started to advance, Hughes had the artillery fire a smoke screen in front of the suspected enemy positions. This was the last straw for a dozen of them, who promptly started waving white flags and walking towards American lines. A few minutes later the infantry began a cautious advance. There was no enemy fire and Hughes said, "We broke their back last night."

By early morning the battalion had secured a strong lodgment just inside the city, and its biggest problem became keeping the crowds of civilians away from U.S. positions. By the hundreds they came by to give the thumbs up sign, wave and smile. Special Forces soldiers asked the locals for help in spotting paramilitaries. Very few volunteered. A Special Forces soldier, who wished not to be identified, said, "It is amazing the hold Saddam has on these people. They are scared to death of him. Even with hundreds of soldiers in the area they are afraid he will return."

One man, ignoring the pleas of his friends, stepped forward and said he could help. He was taken to a map where he pointed to a position and said, "They are there now, twenty of them and vehicles." A helicopter was sent to investigate and reported military vehicles camouflaged in a yard. Within minutes, artillery and rocket fire rained in on the position, and for hours afterwards ammunition from a cache in the area continued to explode. The man returned to his friends who were now all smiles.

As the day dragged on, there were no further signs of enemy resistance in the area or in the areas of either of the other two battalions on the southern side of the city. An engineer sergeant said, "If this town were a woman you could stop buying her drinks now."

When the Division commander, Major General Petraeus, came by late in the afternoon he seemed to have come to much the same conclusion. "It is time to stop dipping around the edges," he said, "and jump into the pool. Tomorrow the 2-327 Battalion and its sister units will push deeper into the city and possibly determine once and for all who owns it."

* * * *

As I walked back to where I last saw Pete Rooks, Sergeant First Class Wilson intercepted me. Wilson was the battalion master gunner whose job was to constantly find ways to improve the effects of our weapons. Sergeant Wilson was not about to go through the war in the relatively academic position of master gunner; he was a ranger and needed to actively contribute to the fight. So whether I wanted it or not, he was my self-appointed bodyguard or, as he insisted on being called, "personal protection detail," a luxury normally afforded only the most senior of officers in the Army. Despite my complaining about his constant nagging and concern for my welfare, I was secretly grateful for his vigilant protection and concern for my safety. His watchful eye afforded me freedom of maneuver and enhanced my effectiveness on the battlefield.

Approaching the intersection, I could see he was excited; they had found three abandoned schools with plenty of space for the battalion. Twelve-foot walls surrounded the compounds, and iron gates protected the entrances. Additionally, these compounds seemed to house some of the tallest buildings in the city, affording us excellent observation and security.

"Perfect," I said, as Wilson walked me to the first compound. As we walked, he informed me that if I wandered off again he would shoot me himself.

An urban battlefield is a dynamic place. To say that the presence of soldiers is an interruption to the lives of those who live there is an obvious understatement. Yet, that fact did not really hit me until I entered our new command post at the "West Najaf Middle School for Girls." As I entered the schoolmarm's office, I found my map board, canteen and rucksack sitting next to an old gray metal desk with a red cushioned chair, green padded desktop cover, number two pencils in a coffee cup, an Arabic travel calendar, a box full of girls' scarves, a six-drawer filing cabinet, three couches, and a large black and white portrait of Saddam Hussein staring down on the room. All that was missing was the actual schoolmarm, who had been tasked to do much with so little.

As I settled into the office, I took a mental note of each item and its proper place; I would return them when we left. We would leave this school looking better than when we arrived. It wasn't their fault we were here. My heart went out to them as I surveyed the sparse conditions of their lives. It was also not their fault that we discovered that the *Fedayeen* had used the school as their command post prior to our arrival.

* * * *

JIM LACEY: The plight of innocent Iraqi civilians also struck me during the assault on Najaf. The following article presents my thoughts at the time.

LETTER FROM AN NAJAF: WAR AND POVERTY
As U.S. troops' storm through the town and surge towards Baghdad, they leave behind Iraqis who are fighting to survive amidst the rubble

By JIM LACEY

An Najaf, one of the holiest cities in Islam, is a crumbling slum. Poverty is not a condition found on the fringe areas of the city; it is endemic to the entire society. War has only made the dire situation more acute. Lives have been overturned. Lack of water and electricity add new miseries to an already arduous existence. The U.S. would like to think that its presence as "liberators" will give them hope for better life here. For now, however, the power vacuum created by the elimination of the Ba'ath Party makes the effort futile—and it may even threaten the long-term chances of pulling this village from poverty.

There are some images of war that stick with you forever—even ones that have nothing to do with combat. For the first four days in and around An Najaf, I was constantly following the action, as firefights and pitched battles sprung up in different parts of town. Now, as the 1st Brigade awaits orders to move further north, there is time to stop following the warriors and think about the people of An Najaf.

At dawn, a woman in a black shawl with six little ones in tow sheepishly approached a small American outpost. She held out a ration form. It was her day to come to pick up rice and flour to feed her family. Controlling the distribution of food staples had been one of the ways the Ba'ath Party had kept the population in check. With the party gone, she didn't know where to turn.

Army commanders here had already noted that Baath headquarters and the homes of party leaders were liberally stocked with 100-pound bags of rice and flour. Hoping to relieve the pressing food shortage they relaxed the no-looting rules and opened these locations for a local free for all. What ensued was dozens of miniature reenactments of the storming of the Bastille. Hundreds of people rushed into the buildings, emptying them of foodstuffs, furniture, farm tools and even lighting fixtures. This largess improved the lives of the fast, the young and the strong. It did nothing to help the woman with six hungry children to feed.

For the moment, soldiers found her enough food to hold

her over for a week or so. But what happens when the soldiers are gone?

Later in the morning the Brigade displaced its headquarters to the sight of some of the fiercest fighting on the first day. In one of the abandoned residences, now occupied by American soldiers, there are hundreds of photographs scattered about the floor. They show weddings, children playing, family gatherings and all of the happy moments that a family has shared. In the corner, there are children's toys piled in with most of the family wardrobe. From the room next door, soldiers carried out automatic weapons and mortars left by the paramilitary forces who had tossed out the family.

But the photographs stay in mind—photos of an innocent family that didn't deserve the upheaval and loss that comes with war.

In the doorway of what could charitably be described as a hovel stood an adorable five-year-old girl. With giant black eyes she looked out shyly from behind a half-open door to see what the soldiers were doing outside. A photographer noticed her and walked over to get a close-up, but the girl darted indoors. He asked through an interpreter if the girl would come out for a picture, which she eventually did. He offered to show her the picture, but she shook her head. "What do you want?" the photographer asked through the interpreter. The girl immediately brought her hand to her mouth and mimicked eating. "When did you last eat?" the photographer asked. The girl paused and then held up three fingers. The photographer went to talk to some soldiers and in violation of policy they brought over a case of MREs and gave it to the girl's mother, who rushed inside with it.

Moments later the translator pointed at two Iraqi men walking into the household and said they were going to take the food away. As the men left the house with the food, three heavily armed infantrymen walked over to politely convince them to give the food back. But what happens to the girl when the soldiers aren't here to intervene on her behalf?

In war, the burdens fall hardest on those least able to cope.

In this war, the burdens fall squarely on this town. The people here struggle day-to-day to survive—that's always been the case. But the brutal war might be justified if people here emerge with better lives. For that to happen, it will take a sustained American political presence and steady economic support until oil money and the miracle of capitalism begins to improve the general well-being. It will also take the will to maintain a strong military force in Iraq—at least until a stable democratic government has formed and taken root at the institutional level.

There is no other way to keep strong men from stealing food out of the mouths of five-year-old girls.

* * * *

The moment of reflection passed when Pete Rooks announced he had collected the battalion command group and was about to force the staff into a "What's next?" session. I looked at Pete, handed him a framed picture of Saddam and said, "Get rid of this fucking thing." He smiled and ushered in the staff. The staff provided an operational update from the three couches in the schoolmarm's office. Their attempts to be professional, while sitting on some of the lumpiest couches I have ever seen in my life, almost brought on tears of laughter. These warriors, with streams of sweat and dirt rolling down their faces, overburdened with combat equipment, were sitting in the principal's office briefing me on the progress of the war.

I began to laugh because I was sure most of them had been in this same position before when they were in school. As luck would have it, I found a ruler in the top drawer of the desk and used it to become the principal, systematically destroying Pete's meeting. Laughter was more important than a meeting at this point in the evening. It released the stress of the day and helped sustain each of them through yet another day on the battlefield. When the commanders walked out of the command post, I shook each one's hand and patted each shoulder. They needed to see and feel my confidence, and I needed each of them to know how proud I was of them. Tomorrow would bring us one step closer to destroying the Butcher of Baghdad.

HOW DO YOU MEET WITH AN AYATOLLAH?

That evening, as we brought the battalion into the security of the cantonment areas, the Special Forces team arrived to discuss the results of their meeting with three Iraqi emissaries and their recommendations on how to meet with Ayatollah Sistani. I was happy to see the A-Team captain and his two OGA members I had met earlier in the day. One of the OGA members was much older than I and he didn't wait for me to ask. He introduced himself and told me he was OGA.

"OGA," I said, "That's a new one on me." He told me it stood for Other Governmental Agencies. "Oh, the Agency," I mused. He and his partner looked at each other and smiled; they were CIA . . . I think. This particular operator, Bob, stood out because he was clearly in his mid-60s with a head full of gray hair, a gray beard, and steely blue eyes. It was an odd cover for the region, but what did I know? The soldiers in the battalion had already begun to call him "Santa Claus the Spook." Spook was a common term for a CIA operative. Bob was an odd sight in a sea of Arabs, with an M-4 rifle strapped across his chest, a whisper communications system around his neck, LL Bean shirt and trousers, Speedo sunglasses and fingerless driving gloves. When Bob and I spoke, we called each other sir; me out of respect for his age and he out of respect for my rank. It was fascinating seeing a man of his age in the thick of things. Soldiering is considered a young man's sport. Bob was not a young man, but we knew he was one of the best amongst us.

Bob's boss, Todd, was the leader of the OGA team. Little more than half Bob's age, I got the impression Todd was the professional operative, while the other gentlemen were former military with special skills needed to accomplish their mission. A fluent Arabic speaker, Todd obviously had an agenda and needed my battalion to complete his mission. This was a new situation for me. The Special Forces team had essentially walked out of the desert and attached themselves to my battalion, and now this OGA team appeared out of the shadows and alleys of Najaf. Both teams seemed to know each other and apparently had coordinated together prior to our arrival. But who was in charge? What was the grand strategy for Najaf?

My training had prepared me for this moment. During exercises at the Army's Joint Readiness Training Center (JRTC), Army units and their leaders are taught to coordinate with SF and other US Agencies on the battlefield during combat. Because of operational security, conventional commanders rarely knew the existence and locations of these autonomous units until higher-level commanders deemed such knowledge necessary. Like all conventional Army commanders, I was taught to seek out these small units in order to gain their assistance and support. However, what JRTC doesn't teach is: Who's in charge?

So in an odd moment during our discussions I asked, "Who's in charge here? Forgive me for not knowing, but I don't know."

"You are," both the SF Commander and OGA officer replied. This was news to me, but I nodded and accepted the responsibility and immediately began to treat their input as guidance instead of directives.

At the end of this first meeting, which became a planning session for the next day's activities, we agreed to meet in my compound and launch a patrol into the heart of Najaf to facilitate a meeting between our emissaries and the Ayatollah. I had already decided that this mission required an overt display of military might—tanks, infantry, heavy weapons, and the critical OH-58D Armed Reconnaissance and Light Attack Helicopters that had so effectively helped us fight our way into Najaf. However, our secret weapon was a man named Abdul Majorid al-Khoei. Khoei was the son of Sistani's predecessor, and as an Iraqi dissident, he had left the country and lived in the United Kingdom since 1991. I didn't know much about Khoei, but the OGA team offered to get him into Najaf and have him available to act as our intermediary with Sistani. They were confident that Khoei could get an audience. Once again I found myself in an odd position. The OGA guys were asking for my approval to implement an obviously well-coordinated and thought out agenda—but whose?

"How are you going to get him here before morning?"

"We can fly him in tonight," said Rick.

"From where?"

"Well, he's in Iran . . . or England . . . I think."

"Iran? Oh hell, forget I asked. Just get him here in the morning, I don't want to know anymore."

Bravo Company, under the command of Captain Tony New, would be the main effort for the battalion as we pushed to the mosque to get the emissaries to see Ayatollah Sistani and kill any enemy guards that might still be in his residence. Tony would have the tank platoon attached to protect his front and flanks in the event of trouble. With the four tanks, the SF team, an anti-tank platoon, the OGA team, and his 120 infantrymen, I felt the size of the force was too large for Tony to maneuver alone. If Tony got in a close fight, he would have his hands full fighting the infantry and tanks. I decided to go with him to assist with the attack helicopters, artillery and anti-tank systems if needed in order to free him to fight his infantry company.

The patrol was a large force. Essentially, it was a small task force with over 200 men. Tony acknowledged the orders and did not seem to mind me accompanying his operation. I tried hard not to over-supervise my officers, and deliberately maintained a good separation of command and control to allow them maximum initiative and freedom to maneuver. I did not want to get into the habit of micromanaging my company commanders before we reached Baghdad. Najaf was giving us an excellent opportunity to fine-tune our urban fighting skills and to prepare the men for what I believed was the greatest battle yet to come, on the streets of Baghdad. There I would not be able to micromanage them, so it was best not to try it now.

As the meeting broke up, I walked out of the schoolteacher's office and into the compound. It was well after dark. I eventually found my hummer by the breezeway and hesitantly walked to my seat to find some food. When I opened the door I found my seat wet but clean, a Meal Ready to Eat, a bottle of water, and a fresh can of Pringles. Even though it may seem minor now, at the time the discovery filled me simultaneously with relief and guilt. My Gatorade mess was gone but I hadn't cleaned it myself. Specialist Bowers was asleep on the hood of the hummer in his poncho liner (his preferred resting place because he could listen to the radio and jump into the vehicle quickly if we needed to move). He had taken the time to clean up my mess and prepare my dinner before going to sleep. I paused and silently thanked God for him. I also took time to reflect how my command burdens were eased by the skills, initiative and drive of each one of my men. For the thousandth time, I remembered my promise to their wives, children and parents that I would bring them all home safe. I intended to do just that.

Looking for some news and some company, I decided to track down the embedded reporters to see if they had found a safe place to sleep and to ensure they were prepared to participate in the morning's mission. In actuality, I was seeking some company my own age. Aside from Specialist Bowers, the embedded journalists were the only other men my age that I was in contact with on a regular basis. I spent about an hour with the press guys laughing about the slaughterhouse flies, the Gatorade disaster, and how much we missed indoor plumbing. They were men I could relax with outside my chain of command. After I was sure they were squared away, I withdrew.

Although there was a decent place to sleep in the schoolteacher's office, I wanted to sleep in the back of my hummer to stay close to the radios and be prepared to roll out on a moment's notice. I fell asleep as soon as my head hit my improvised bedroll, only to be awakened at 2 a.m. by a large explosion that rattled my vehicle.

"What the hell was that?" Specialist Bowers was standing on the hood of the hummer trying to see. I had fallen asleep with the radio mike on my chest, and after my normal tossing and turning had managed to get myself tangled up in the radio cord. Now I was trying to free myself as I fumbled in the dark to get a report. For the first two to five minutes, I only received negative replies from the units in and around Najaf, but it was becoming obvious the explosion came from the desert floor to the west of Najaf.

The headquarters' company commander, Captain Albert Garnica, my most experienced commander, reported that the explosion came from the vicinity of the mortar platoon to his east and that he was sending a mounted patrol to determine their status. The mortar platoon was located near the brick factory I had used as my command post during our assault into Najaf the day prior, and they were not responding to our radio calls. Suddenly the platoon leader, 1st Lieutenant Nick Grill, a wiry officer who grew up as an adrenaline junky, snowboarding and living life to the fullest, came on the command radio and reported that a missile had landed near his position, missing his platoon by only a couple hundred meters. Nick and some of his men were moving toward the impact to determine if it contained chemicals. I told Nick to cease, desist, return to his platoon and prepare to move.

Moments later, a second missile, clearly visible to everyone now awake, flew over Najaf and exploded in the desert, again near Nick's platoon. I felt like I had been teleported to England during the Battle of Britain, watching German V-2 rockets flying over our positions during World War II; but this was Iraq and the scene was not an old movie but in full color. Clearly the Iraqis were using old intelligence and firing at our last positions prior to sunset. If they had fired twelve hours earlier, the effects of these systems could have been catastrophic to the battalion, but for now I surmised there was no one watching and reporting on us. I ordered the mortar platoon to change locations as a precaution, but fortunately there were no more missile attacks. The enemy stayed quiet the rest of the night, though it was clear that they still had plenty of fight left in them.

The next morning, as we prepared to depart the compound, I went to the roof of the school to talk to the scout platoon leader and see his sniper positions. 1st Lieutenant Dave Gunther, an athletic natural leader who managed to win every competition and challenge I threw his way for two years, and his scouts had worked hard to build a team of snipers that would give the battalion more flexibility by providing precision fire in support of my infantry—screening the flanks of the battalion while on the move and killing key enemy leaders or destroying equipment from long ranges. The position on top of the school provided both our compounds with early warning and security at the hands of only a few snipers and spotters.

Dave's men were some of the best in the battalion, and they acted like it. Their pride, professionalism and enthusiasm were contagious; and Gunther was the source of their pride. While on the roof, I got my first view of the city, our exposed flank with 1st Battalion to our south, and my infantry positions throughout the old city. There were gaps in our defense and I needed to fix them before the enemy found them. When I reached the bottom of the stairs, I ran into Command Sergeant Major Montcalm. I told him about the gaps and he told me he would fix it as he scurried off. His sense of urgency allowed me to file the problem under the "taken care of" category in my mind and move on to today's primary mission: Ayatollah Sistani.

The A-Team and OGA were very excited about the emissaries and the possibility of getting an audience with Sistani through his former mentor's son, Ayatollah Khoei. Ground intelligence had confirmed that the Ba'ath guards at his house were no longer visible from the street. We hoped this indicated that they had retreated to the north with the rest of the Iraqi army. Unfortunately, hope is never a reliable tool in combat. So we approached the inner city as if it were well-defended. Movement through this ancient city was very restrictive and uncomfortable. I had two 70-ton tanks to our front, two to our rear, 180 equipment-laden infantrymen, four heavy weapons hummers and three Special Forces vehicles moving on the ground, while two troops of attack helicopters flew overhead. But the real force of the patrol was two loudspeaker trucks and two individuals with specialized skills: our Arab linguist Specialist Kim Carr and Mr. "Sergeant" Kadhim Al-Waeli.

As I walked between the infantry and the hummers, Kadhim stayed within arm's reach. We were discussing the protocol for passing information to Sistani and an agenda if we managed to gain an audience. As we talked, I kept placing my right hand over my heart, nodding at the elder men and saying *marhabba,* or hello. I was doing everything I could to read their reaction to our presence. As I continued to work the crowds along the street, I noticed that many of them looked like they just woke up. It was early, but they just didn't look like morning people. Kadhim laughed at my observation.

"When you don't have electricity, jobs or much of a future, there's really nothing to get up early for." His response surprised me, but made complete sense.

We walked to the next vehicle in the column, and by chance, it was the speaker truck. I stuck my head in the window and asked the team how they were doing. The two sergeants were enjoying the crowds and had noticed the same thing Kadhim and I had; these people were just waking up.

Then the team sergeant said, "Hey sir, how about some good old fashioned wake-up music?" I looked to Kadhim for his opinion. He smiled.

"Let it rip!"

When the music began, it startled me and Bravo Company, but not the Iraqis. The positive effect of the music was almost immediate as the Iraqis began to smile, cheer and sing. I stuck my head back in the truck and asked what the selected song was about. The psychosocial team told me it was about Ali's rightful ascension to the status of Caliph of all Islam. I turned to see a huge smile on Kadhim's face as he danced in the street with his Najaf brothers. Unfortunately, our first two attempts to negotiate with Sistani were met with confusion, false emissaries and covert *Fedayeen* resistance. But we were convinced the mission was worth the risk.

RIOT AT THE GOLDEN MOSQUE OF ALI

For the third straight day, we found ourselves seeking an audience with Grand Ayatollah Sistani. We were ever closer to the middle of Najaf and the famed Imam Ali Mosque—named for the founder and prophet of Shi'a Islam.

As we moved yet again downtown, the crowds grew, the waving increased and the worrisome smiles of the elders began to lose their dull look. *No Slack* stayed focused while scanning each window, gate, alley and roof as we moved closer to the Mosque. Constant scanning in a city quickly overwhelms a soldier's senses, adding to his stress and overall fatigue. This same stress and the spikes in adrenaline increase the body's core temperature, radically increasing a soldier's need for water and food. The deeper we probed into the city, the more and more I noticed the *No Slack* sergeants prodding their men to drink water and eat small foods like crackers, candy and peanut butter from their MREs.

As we cleared the streets, I nodded, smiled and spoke to as many soldiers as I could at each halt. As we spoke, I would press my memory for the name of a wife, child or parent. When time permitted, I would try to use a family name or ask a personal question to ease the incredible burden on each man's mind. It worked most of the time.

It was tough for me to imagine or anticipate the horrific situations I may place them in, and tried to not to dwell on it. No matter, it was always in the back of my mind. They were my men, my sons and younger brothers, and it was up to me to use them as instruments of American policy and power. I was to accomplish the mission at all costs, yet protect and care for my men. That is the greatest irony of command—a paradox that truly takes a good fifteen to twenty years to get used to. How to fight and win a battle while simultaneously conserving your primary resource: America's youth? The modern Army has tried to use clever phrases and slogans to minimize this "mission versus death" contradiction, but most attempts to do so are insulting to those who are willing to risk their lives for their country. The one phrase that bothered me the most was "soldiers first, mission always." It only existed to appease peacetime political correctness. The mission was always first, but it was still my job to find ways to win with minimal casualties. I was determined that no one in *No Slack* was going to die because I failed to be innovative and think. Only lazy and unimaginative commanders take needless casualties.

As I worked my way toward the front of the column, I passed a young stud who looked up at me and said, "Hey sir, when ya gonna let us kill someone?"

I shot back with, "If you shoot your rifle, I've failed. Let's give everyone else a chance to shoot these bastards before we have to."

He looked confused. I was ok with that. He would soon learn that war was not a game. Killing humans, even your enemy, was nothing I wished on anyone with good conscience. I would shoot all the artillery, drop all the Air Force's bombs and strafe the enemy with the division's attack helicopters before I would see one of my young soldiers in a street fight with the enemy at close quarters. I had to think, innovate—can I win without a fight? Should I even try? Yes, it was my sacred responsibility as their commander to try.

We had reached the main intersection south of the Mosque of Ali; this was the closest we had gotten in the last three days. The Golden Dome was just down the road. The road was lined with multi-storied buildings, cinderblock houses and a cobble stone road. It was a bullet shooting gallery waiting to happen. I walked the line of troops so I could gauge their physical condition while also trying to get a feel for the route to the mosque. I also never stopped working the crowd to the best of my ability. I returned to my small John Deere tractor, called a Gator, and sat down in the front seat to wait for a platoon of Bravo Company that was searching an empty school on our flank. The school would provide me an excellent position for the snipers to cover our advance to the Ayatollah's residence. Once the Bravo platoon was in the school, I decided to go in and get a look at the city from the roof and to study the route we would have to negotiate if Sistani decided to meet with Khoei.

When I returned to my "Gator," I decided to take my own advice and eat something.

* * * *

As with Mr. Jim Lacey, Mr. Wes Allison of the *St. Petersburg Times* was one of our embedded reporters. Wes was directly assigned to *No Slack* and spent every day with the battalion from Kuwait to Hillah. The articles attributed to Mr. Allison were written in harm's way and in some of the worst conditions the battalion faced in the early days of the war. Eventually I would learn that his daily dispatches were used by my wife and our family readiness group at Fort Campbell to track the battalion's daily operations . . . something I was unable to do. I will forever be in Wes' debt for providing our families the stories and letters we could not.

DISPATCH FROM THE 101ST

By WES ALLISON, *Times Staff Writer*

© St. Petersburg Times, published April 3, 2003

The relationships between senior officers and the noncommissioned officers who work closely with them are often complicated. The officer may be in charge, but a good non-com is no sycophant. They spend a lot of time together, in difficult situations, often under stress.

And rank or no rank, men are men.

It was getting hot Thursday morning and Lt. Col. Chris Hughes, commander of the 2nd Battalion of the 327th Infantry, was waiting in the middle of a wide avenue in Najaf, hoping for a meeting with a cleric who never showed.

He and the man assigned to protect him in combat, Sgt.

1st Class Pernell Wilson, were snacking on field rations when a disagreement arose about whether Wilson had correctly given headquarters their position.

Wilson, 33, of Philadelphia is a master gunner with a shaved head and dark shades and big arms. He may work for the colonel, but he's no yes man.

Hughes, joking, called him his "map b__."

"Is this the way you talk to someone who's going to take a bullet for you, sir?" Wilson said. "You wouldn't take a bullet for me," Hughes countered. "You'd be throwing me down and shooting over my head. I know you. You're not taking a bullet for me."

"Well it sounded good." Wilson paused. "Would you take a bullet for me?"

Hughes took a bite of a MRE cookie. "Sure."

Wilson: "And you don't think I'd take a bullet for you?"

"You'd take a bullet for me just to spite me."

Wilson: "I'm going to be a pain in your a_ for the rest of this deployment."

"Well, then, nothing's going to change."

* * * *

As I picked through my MRE, First Sergeant Ron Gregg, the top sergeant in Bravo Company, told me that Ayatollah Khoei had arrived and that the SF team wanted me to move to the front of the column to meet with him.

He then winked at me and said, "The Special Forces captain wants you to come forward nonchalantly so the media guys don't follow you. Khoei wants to keep a low profile until he's had a chance to talk to Sistani." Gregg and I quietly laughed as we walked as "nonchalantly" as possible through hundreds of men, guns and tanks on our way to the front of the column. First Sergeant Gregg was one of the best men in the battalion; I wouldn't truly appreciate how good he was until the sun set on this particular day.

Khoei was in the back of one of the SF vehicles with his face covered; he simply nodded when we were introduced. I understood his desire to remain anonymous while outside the mosque. He was taking a tremendous risk being here and I needed to ensure his safety. After meeting him, I was summoned over to the hood of another vehicle to discuss strategy. The OGA team was waiting for one of their primary emissaries who was meeting with Sistani. They were optimistic as we discussed how to get Khoei through the crowd and up to Sistani's residence. Sistani's house was 150 yards up the road and we needed to try and keep the move low key while providing Khoei adequate security. The plan was for the SF team to take him in as *No Slack* secured the route and provided a quick reaction force in case the SF team and OGA got into trouble.

It seemed simple enough until the emissary returned and started to tell us Sistani's demands. First, he wanted US protection since he was concerned for his safety after his Iraqi guards had left in the middle of the night, leaving him and his students unprotected. Second, he wanted to meet with Khoei and the American commander who had allowed his people to go to prayers during the fighting.

"He wants to meet with me?" I asked in surprise.

"Yes, he was impressed with your actions this week and your words—he wants to meet you," said the elder emissary.

I was stunned. Bob from the OGA began to laugh, and Todd looked at me and said, "This is a tremendous opportunity; we can't pass this up!" Never for one minute did I think Sistani would ever allow an audience with an "infidel." But Todd was right; this was an opportunity to stop the fighting in the south and possibly gain the support of the Shi'a in Iraq and the Middle East. I sent word back to Pete Rooks to contact brigade and let them know that I was going to negotiate an audience with the Ayatollah.

How does one meet with an Ayatollah? The question was on the table and two captains, a 60-year-old OGA warrior, a young CIA operative, an Iraqi dissident, Kadhim, and I were trying to figure out the answer. As I looked at the men of Bravo Company, the crowd and the ever-present reporters, including Al Jazeera, I knew this was quickly becoming an international strategic event. I had a chance to make a huge difference and there was no time for hesitation. I accepted Sistani's terms but offered one demand of my own. I wanted to send my speaker trucks forward so he could come out of his residence and tell the world he was inviting my battalion to protect him and asking me into his residence to talk. The man had been under house arrest for over fifteen years and the last thing I wanted to do was make it look like I was arresting him—live on Al Jezeera and CNN.

Later I would learn that Sistani had a number of secrets that prevented him from addressing the crowd in Najaf that day, including the fact that he received most of his religious training in Iran and spoke with a heavy Iranian accent. This is a little known fact that to this day has left him isolated and hesitant to vocally counter the radical rantings of Muqtada al-Sadr, a mere layman with no Islamic credentials and who has no reservations acknowledging his relationships with the Persians of Iran while pretending to speak for the Iraqi Shia.

The emissary understood my concerns, and after conferring with Khoei he returned to Sistani's residence to pass on my request. After his departure, I received word that the embedded reporters from brigade were on their way and that General Petraeus was preparing to come to our location as well. I was frustrated at the sudden attention and didn't want this first meeting to grow any larger. Just then, two hummers full of reporters from the brigade headquarters came barreling down the road in front of Sistani's house. They stopped in front of me with huge smiles on their faces: Jim Lacey from *Time* magazine, Mark Strassman from CBS and a boat-load of others.

"Hey Colonel Hughes, what's happening?" they yelled. Their behavior was anything but nonchalant.

"Get that goddamn hummer out of here, I will explain later," I shouted. I motioned to my rear and looked behind me to see Khoei stepping out of his vehicle. He had removed his scarf and looked upset. I called First Sergeant Gregg over and told him to get control of the reporters and keep them away from Khoei and the OGA guys. He gave me the thumbs up and I walked back to the front of the Special Forces SUV.

Suddenly I heard a familiar voice yelling from in front of the SUV near Khoei. "Hey, are you the fucking linguist? Tell these people to get the fuck back before I bust some heads!" I stopped dead in my tracks and looked around the back of the SF vehicle to see 1st Lieutenant Eric Schnabel telling Ayatollah Khoei to "get off his ass and tell these people to get the fuck back!"

"Eric, shut up and get over here," I said. Eric stepped away from the Ayatollah and hustled to the back of the vehicle. "Eric," I said, "he's not a linguist. He's . . . aw shit, I'll tell you later."

"But sir, how do I get these people to get back?"

I barked, "Use the international sign for get the fuck back," and pointing at Khoei told Eric, "Stay away from him!" I then quickly demonstrated by waving my hands reverently in a back to front motion. Confused and frustrated, Eric walked back toward the crowd and tried to use the hand signal I had shown him. He had no idea he had just insulted one of the top Ayatollahs in the Shi'a world, not to mention our best chance to get an audience with Sistani. I reluctantly walked over to Khoei and apologized for Eric's behavior.

Khoei looked at me and said, "He's young."

"That he is sir . . . thanks for understanding," I said, relieved that Eric hadn't dissolved our international relations with Khoei.

As I walked back to the vehicle, I told myself to remember this run-in between Khoei and Schnabel. Though frustrating now, I knew it would be hilarious later. Laughing to myself, I looked up and noticed the emissary returning from Sistani's quarters. The emissary and Todd motioned me over. Sistani agreed that the crowd needed to know he was inviting us to his compound, but he was too afraid to move out of his compound and use the speaker trucks. Sistani had recommended a compromise. He would have his students file out into the streets and let the crowd know he wanted us to come to his compound and meet. Todd and I agreed that it was a fair compromise and, concerned that Sistani's patience was wearing thin, we quickly agreed. We didn't want to stress the meeting protocols to a point where we unnecessarily placed his life at risk. Moments later, the emissary returned with a huge grin on his face, "His eminence has agreed and his students are moving into the crowd to announce your invitation."

I waited long enough to see these "students" of Sistani's; they were not what I expected. They were older men with white and black turbans, long robes and neatly groomed beards. They swiftly moved into the crowds on the road to the mosque, outside Sistani's compound and around my battalion. The sudden and euphoric actions of the crowd reminded me of Pope John Paul's first appearance in Vatican Square in 1978. The people of Najaf hadn't publicly seen their Ayatollah for years, and the possibility of him making an appearance spread like wildfire through the streets of Najaf. Window shutters were banging open, and people were running toward us from every alleyway, street and rooftop. The intensity of the situation was reaching a fever pitch and we needed to take action before we lost control. The overwhelming force of *No Slack* was growing relatively weaker by the moment.

The senior cleric from Sistani's office approached our emissary and told him we were clear to move to Sistani's compound. The Ayatollah's wishes were clear to the crowd and the students would act as escorts.

"Good, we need to move. Captain New, get your men up. Let's go!"

And with that order, the entire patrol picked up and started to slowly proceed down the Golden Road to the Mosque of Ali. I started to make my way back to my Gator when suddenly there was a huge crash to my left rear. As I turned to see where the sound came from, something hit me in the left corner of my sunglasses. As I staggered back, something else hit me in the back of the helmet.

What the hell was that?

Someone behind me yelled, "They're throwing rocks!"

"Rocks? No, he invited us. Where the hell are those fucking students?"

I looked back to the front of the column in time to see a large vegetable cart being pushed into the street and turned on its side by a large and angry mob.

Now I was pissed. I put my head down and started to briskly walk to the front of the column. This is a mistake, I thought. These people don't understand we were invited! Closer to the quickly growing riot, I took my M-4 rifle off safe and prepared to shoot a couple of rounds into the air to get their attention. OK, so you get their attention, then what—what do you say? How long will the pause last—will it be a pause or will it be an excuse for someone in the crowd to shoot back? I put my M-4 back on safe as I neared the front of the column. The SF A-team and my lead platoon were already intermixed with the crowd and beginning to push and shove. This was about to erupt out of control. Someone was either going to accidentally shoot their weapon, or feel threatened and shoot into this crowd. I knew someone was causing this riot and I had to stop it—NOW.

I had to do something visually that couldn't be mistaken for a hostile act by the crowd, the bad guys, the media or my men. Reasoning with the crowd was futile—I could barely hear myself think over the growing riot. Trying to speak would only pull me into the chaos. So I turned my M-4 rifle upside down and yelled, "Take a knee! Everyone take a knee!" It was all I could come up with. I needed the men to stop entering this mob and "taking a knee" is what infantrymen do when they stop. It lowers a soldier's profile, stops them from making noise, and lets them rest. The moment the column of *No Slack* soldiers stopped and took a knee, the mood of the crowd softened, almost as if it became confused and curious. I had learned in Haiti that crowds have personalities. This crowd paused, a safer and surer pause then one that would have come if I had chosen to fire warning shots.

"*No Slack*, point your weapons toward the ground—show no hostile intent," I shouted. The crowd paused again and people in the front began to smile and sit down with my soldiers. "OK," I'm thinking, "so most of these people don't know what the hell's going on, someone is pushing and agitating them from behind."

Taking advantage of the lull in the crowd's mood, I quickly walked over to the speaker truck, stuck my head in the driver's side window, and told the sergeant inside to get a linguist and tell these people we were invited. He pointed outside the passenger side of the hummer at the Iraqi colonel that the SF team had brought with them. He was a defector, and before I could get his attention he began to speak to the crowd on the loudspeaker. The moment he began to speak, the crowd erupted back into an angry mob. I don't know what he said, but they quickly pinned him against the side of the hummer in protest. I told the sergeant to unplug his ass and lock their doors. Screw him!

Realizing that the crowd was going in the wrong direction, I walked back to the front of the column and, pacing behind the wall of *No Slack* soldiers, told them to smile.

"Smile men, they have to know we were invited—SMILE!" Slowly but surely the men began to smile. They were short, awkward and forced smiles, as would be expected from young men facing down an out-of-control mob. Running out of options, I turned my rifle upside down and tried to work the crowd. Shaking hands and smiling my ass off, but it was too late for that. The Iraqi colonel had ruined it for us, and it was obvious that there were agitators in the crowd that wanted us to fire on them. We had managed the situation well, but I needed to break this off. It didn't make any sense to muscle through this crowd to meet with Ayatollah Sistani. To do so would feed right into the hands of the *Fedayeen* and Ba'ath party officials in the crowd. They wanted me to screw this up, not just for the people of Najaf, but for the world. Thanks to the press, the world was watching. *No Slack* would maintain the moral high ground today; I walked back to the speaker truck.

"*No Slack*," I shouted into the microphone, "We're going to pull back and let them sort this out themselves. Everyone pull back." And with that, the men stood up and began to walk backward. When I saw the men walking backward, it bothered me . . . it looked like we were defeated and withdrawing. There was no way the world or the *Fedayeen* were going to get a picture of *No Slack* retreating.

"Just turn around and move—just turn around, men, and walk away," I yelled across the column and the street. It was a risk, but so was each unexpected action we had taken up to that point. It was another curveball to throw at the instigators of this now obviously staged riot—something else to make them think twice. I wanted them to know that *No Slack* was not the least bit afraid of them. So the men turned and walked away for the whole world to see. This move allowed me to speak to the Arab world with actions that could not be twisted or manipulated. We were leaving as men and were not the least bit afraid. T.E. Lawrence had learned 85 years earlier that Arabs respect a man who turns his back on an aggressor without fear. I needed a way for the world to see we were not afraid. If we had continued to back off facing the crowd as we had been trained, the Arab press and those who wished us to fail could have used this visual against us as we neared Baghdad, with headlines like "The Americans retreated from an unarmed crowd, they are afraid to fight." It was a chance I could not take.

As we cleared the crowd and started to get some distance between us, I remembered something Kadhim had taught me. He had told me to place my right hand over my heart and slightly bow to show respect. The gesture meant, "Allah be praised" or "God bless your heart," and had worked well for me up to this point in the city. So, as *No Slack* turned the corner toward our compound, I turned back to the stunned crowd, stopped, placed my right hand over my heart and slowly bowed, turned around, looked at my radio operator and said, "Have a nice day."

Later that evening, when we were waiting for the emissary to return to the headquarters, we got word from our informants that Ayatollah Sistani had issued a formal *fatwa* to the people of Najaf.

"Do not interfere with the American forces entering Iraq, Praise be to Allah, Grand Ayatollah Sistani of the Mosque of Ali."

The fighting ended the next day as *No Slack*, and our sister battalions 1-327th, *"Above the Rest,"* 3-327th, *"Battle Force,"* and the *Bastogne* Brigade Combat Team reported An Najaf secure.

* * * *

...IN ONE CITY, AMERICAN SOLDIERS ENCOUNTERED A CROWD OF IRAQI CITIZENS WHO THOUGHT OUR TROOPS WERE ABOUT TO STORM A NEARBY MOSQUE. JUST THEN, LT. COLONEL CHRIS HUGHES ORDERED HIS MEN TO GET DOWN ON ONE KNEE AND POINT THEIR WEAPONS TO THE GROUND. THIS GESTURE OF RESPECT HELPED DEFUSE A DANGER-OUS SITUATION AND MADE OUR PEACEFUL INTEN-TIONS CLEAR.

—PRESIDENT BUSH
April 12th, 2003, radio address on war's progress

* * * *

JIM LACEY: I still have very strong memories of this event. Chris' actions that day are still the most remarkable example of quick thinking I have ever seen in a combat situation. The following article was written later that evening.

ARMED WITH THEIR TEETH

By JIM LACEY

It may have been the most unusual directive of Gulf War II. "Soldiers of 2nd Battalion," ordered Lt. Colonel Chris Hughes. "Smile!" With that, infantrymen of the 101st Airborne Division, armed to the teeth, began flashing their choppers at a crowd that had grown restless as the soldiers approached the mosque at the Tomb of Ali in Najaf, one of Shiite Islam's holiest sites. The tactic helped win over a crowd that had more questions than answers. Were the soldiers going to storm the mosque, as some agitators were shouting? Were they liberators? Or conquerors? Were they really going to kill Saddam Hussein this time?

Najaf's civilians watched with hope and concern last week as the 101st made repeated incursions into the city, rooting out the remnants of regular and irregular Iraqi forces. After four days of cautiously advancing—sometimes fighting house to house, sometimes guided by civilians who pointed out the positions of Saddam's men—the Division's 1st Brigade gained control of the area on Wednesday. The following day Najaf had the feel of a liberated city. Smiling citizens crowded every street around the American positions. There was a constant stream of people willing to give information and loudly condemn Saddam. American soldiers who a day before had been in close combat were now basking in the cheers and applause, their arms tired from returning friendly waves.

There were women and children in the crowds, but only the men did any talking. They would say the word Saddam and spit. Or run up to U.S. soldiers and shout "George Bush good." Said Sergeant Reuben Rivera: "The American people, particularly the movie stars against us being here, need to see this. These people need us. Look how happy they are." The locals at last seemed convinced that Saddam could not reach back and hurt them, as had happened after Gulf War I. "All they ask is, When will the Americans kill Saddam?" said a Kuwaiti translator traveling with the 101st. "They say it over and over, as if I did not hear them. I tell them that the Americans will kill him and not to worry."

But the euphoria was almost lost over the mosque incident. It began when the local imam, who had spent twenty years under house arrest until the city fell and his captors fled, asked American soldiers to protect him and the mosque. He neglected to explain this, however, to the crowds outside. As the soldiers of Bravo Company of the 2nd Battalion, who had formed a tight perimeter on the street, began heading toward the mosque, citizens started shouting and moving forward. With rabble rousers (later identified by Iraqis as Ba'ath Party members) shouting, "The Americans are storming the mosque," the crowd began to chant and shake their fists. That's when Hughes made his move. Grabbing a microphone he calmly announced over a loudspeaker, "*No Slack* soldiers, take a knee and point your weapons at the ground." Seconds later every one of the men was on a knee, and not a single weapon was pointing at the crowd. Then he gave the smile order.

It worked. Hughes kept his men like that for about five minutes and then returned to the microphone. "Soldiers of *No Slack*, we are going to stand up and then walk slowly back to base. You will not point any guns at the crowd, and you will smile at everyone." A minute later, the Smilin' Second was walking away from the mosque, and the Iraqis began intermingling with them, patting them on the back and giving them thumbs-up signs again.

* * * *

After receiving the fatwa from Ayatollah Sistani, the city of Najaf fell silent and started to return to normal, or whatever normal is in Najaf. We unexpectedly found ourselves moving about the city with relative ease, and in some neighborhoods we were greeted like heroes and liberators. The fighting was over in Najaf, but combat still continued to our north.

Just when I thought the war was going to pass *No Slack* by, Colonel Hodges ordered the battalion to the northern outskirts of Najaf to prepare for possible orders to move toward Baghdad.

Our recon teams managed to find an abandoned military compound that appeared brand new and never used before our arrival. It was nice to be out of the slums of Najaf, and not having to live with the stench of rotting sewage and the constant nagging of homicidal flies was worth the move, but this compound was no Taj Mahal.

It consisted of stark, single-floor cinderblock buildings with concrete floors, unfinished windows and doorways, zero vegetation or shade, all encircled by a foreboding 10-foot wall. It was perfect for force protection, but it would yet again compel us to dig latrines in close proximity to where we slept, ate and lived.

As the days passed waiting for orders, time within this military compound started to drag, and the men were getting antsy for news on the progress of the war and where we could be committed to help the offensive. Similar to our wait in Kuwait, my hummer and the Blue Force Tracker system became our only link to the outside world. Specialist Bowers, now promoted to Sergeant, began to pass updates to the men from our hummer as he watched the computer and read the ever-present messages on the e-mail board. The blue force tracker once again was transformed from a combat system to *No Slack*'s version of a Saturday night drive-in movie theater as the men anxiously watched the blue icons maneuvering south of Karbala pass. Why were they stopped . . . were they in a big fight? How much longer would we be in Najaf?

The morning was cold and I found myself, the oldest guy in the Task Force, having to get up earlier than most to use the latrine. CSM Montcalm had found the only possible location for our new latrines in the northwest corner of the compound—the only problem was that the whole camp could see you doing your business, so in a vain attempt at some privacy, I went early. It was early enough to pass the morning security detail coming off the wall. They were tired, yet anxious for news of rejoining the war. I gave them what I knew and hurried them off to get some sleep before the heat became too unbearable.

As I returned to my duties, I felt a cold stab at my heart when I heard machine gun rounds cook off somewhere from within a building to my rear. It was most likely an accidental discharge—inside the compound!

The cold, crisp sound of automatic machine gun fire was unmistakable and nauseating. People were being shot and there was nothing I could do about it. My mind raced as I went through my commander's mental checklist. I could run to the incident, scream commands and get in the middle of the mayhem, or I could calmly walk to the scene and let the sergeants and junior officers do their jobs. It was an accidental discharge, I was sure of it now, and someone would need to keep a cool head.

If there were dead *No Slack* soldiers in that room, I had to be the calm, stoic one—there would be hard decisions to make. So with my commander's mask firmly affixed, I moved to the scene and prepared for the worst.

As I neared the incident building, I could see the junior leaders of *No Slack* securing the scene, treating the wounded, and passing commands and coordinates for the Medical Evacuation helicopter. Major Pete Rooks walked toward me slowly as he organized his thoughts in order to render his report.

As Pete approached, I prepared myself for five dead and six wounded—seemed about right considering it was a machine gun, firing around 20–30 rounds in an enclosed cinder block room full of sleeping men. I was prepared for the worst report of my life.

Pete stopped in front of me with his ever-present notebook open and looked up with tears in his eyes. "Sir, we have three wounded; one in the ankle, one in the foot and one in the groin. All are stable and MEDEVAC is in-bound." He then closed his notebook and looked at me with a long face. Almost in shock I blurted out, "Only three?"

"Yes Sir, we were very lucky, the men were wearing their body armor while they were sleeping. We were damn lucky."

"Holy shit, Pete, that's the understatement of the year . . . thank God!"

I pushed past Pete almost in disbelief, thinking "only three." How could it only be three when that machine gun should have killed half the men in that room? I quickly found the first wounded soldier and bent down to talk to him.

It was the Mortar Platoon leader, Lieutenant Nick Grill. "How are you Nick?" Despite his obvious pain, Nick was surprisingly upbeat and in good spirits. He told me he was fine as he tried to sit up and make his report.

After giving me a quick rundown of what had happened and the condition of his two wounded soldiers, he did something I will never forget and always respect. He told me he was worried about the young private who had shot up his platoon. "Sir, we will be fine, but I need you to look after my soldier, you know, the kid who shot us. He is devastated—it wasn't his fault, it was an accident."

The other two wounded soldiers were just as upbeat considering their predicament and were just as concerned about the young soldier who had shot them and what I might do to him.

I eased their concerns and marveled at their principles. Here were three wounded men more concerned about the fate of their comrade than their own personal welfare. Where do we find men like this?

After getting a chance to talk to each man and the battalion surgeon, I was confident and relieved that they would all recover from their wounds, but I wasn't so sure about the young private who had shot them.

As the wounded began to depart, I turned my attention to the most critically wounded soldier that morning—the private who had accidentally shot his friends and brothers.

Rightfully, the platoon sergeant who had been saved by his Bible in the top left pocket of his shirt that morning, stopping a bullet within Genesis, had hidden the young private in the front seat of his hummer. He took me to the soldier and introduced us. He had just joined the battalion prior to our deployment so I didn't recognize him. "Let's take a walk, young man."

We left the hummer, walked to the middle of the compound, and stopped to watch the last wounded soldier being loaded on the MEDEVAC helicopter. Once the dust had settled, I asked him if he was OK. He was shaken, although more composed than I would have been given the situation. Nonetheless, when he spoke he immediately became apologetic and tried to calmly and rationally explain what had happened, ever cognizant that everyone in the battalion was watching our conversation in the middle of the open compound. "Sir, what will they do with me? Will I be court-martialed; will I go to prison; will they survive? I can't live with myself, I'm sorry . . . so, so sorry."

His passion, concern and fear were all I needed to perceive in order to know there was no punishment on earth worse than the punishment he would inflict on himself for the rest of his life. We had no time for punishment; he had done nothing wrong. It was an accident, and now we needed to get past the issue.

My heart went out to him, but I had to keep my commander's mask on. What should I do, what could I do to make this right?

"So what do you do in the mortar platoon?" "Sir?" "What do you do in the platoon?" I repeated. "I'm a loader and I carry the M-249 Squad Automatic Weapon." "OK, I need you to keep doing that if you're up to it. Are you up to it?"

"Sir, I just shot three of my teammates. I can't go back, they will hate me!" "Well, as you can see I'm a little shorthanded in the mortar platoon right now and really need you to go back and help the team. Will you do that for me?"

"Are you sure, Sir?" "Yes, you made a mistake, it was an accident. We all know it was an accident and we need you more now than ever before. You're not going to jail, getting court-martialed, or even an Article 15 (a form of non-judicial punishment), but I have to do something so everyone can see I punished you. You understand that everyone needs to think I punished you so they know the matter is resolved, right? So I'm going to cut off your stripes for all to see." I took out my knife. "You and I both know that if I don't file the paperwork the Army will still consider you a Private First Class, but for now we will call you 'Private.' I will give you your stripes back after we get rid of Saddam. It will be our little secret. Now act like I just chewed your ass while I cut off your stripes."

The platoon sergeant and I agreed to watch the new private and ensure he was brought back into the team quickly and given much to do. We needed to ensure he didn't focus on what had happened. He recovered quickly, and months later no one was happier to see the return of two of his teammates when they rejoined us in northern Iraq, completely recovered and prepared to fight another day.

In reflection, I was reminded of a statement once made by Dr. Martin Luther King, who said: "The ultimate measure of a man is not where he stands in moments of comfort and convenience, but where he stands in moments of challenge and controversy." This incident did much to boost my belief and trust in my sergeants and junior leaders. All reacted well and showed a calm that would be most necessary in the days and weeks that lay ahead.

* * * *

DISPATCH FROM THE 101ST
In machine gun accident, 3 wounded, 1 devastated

By WES ALLISON

(Published April 7, 2003)

NAJAF, Iraq—The burst lasted just three seconds, but it was long enough to catch the ear of every U.S. soldier on this captured Iraqi army post, sending some scrambling for their rifles and others scrambling for cover.

It was also long enough to fire 24 bullets, their hot brass casings clattering to the bloodied tile floor.

A young lieutenant hopped out of the barracks room on one foot, shouting for a medic. He lay down, and then directed the men who rushed to his aid to look inside.

A sergeant was down, blood filling his left boot. A specialist took a bullet in the thigh, precariously near his groin.

When the commotion cleared, a young private first class sat outside the doorway alone, hanging his head between his knees. He had joined a mortar platoon of the 2nd Battalion, 327th Infantry of the 101st Airborne Division only six weeks ago, a few days before the unit left Fort Campbell, KY, for war with Iraq. Before that, he was in basic training.

Accidental discharges, as the Army calls such shootings, are an inevitable part of war, when thousands of soldiers are carrying and cleaning loaded guns. It is precisely for this reason that most Army units weren't issued ammunition until after they had been in Kuwait for several weeks, right as the war started.

This battalion had its first accidental discharge last week, when a guard handed another guard a sniper rifle during their shift change. The safety was off, and one of them bumped the trigger. No one was injured.

"When you have 18-year-olds with guns and things that

blow up, they are going to make mistakes," Lt. Col. Chris Hughes, commander of the 2nd Battalion, called *No Slack*, told his staff Sunday as he reiterated a battalion rule: No loaded machine guns indoors.

Since last week, *No Slack* has been conducting search and destroy operations around Najaf, a city about 80 miles south of Baghdad. This weekend it moved into a compound of low, concrete barracks in an abandoned Iraqi army post on the desert's edge, north of town.

The private was cleaning his M-249 machine gun after guard duty when the shooting occurred. The M-249 is called a SAW, for squad automatic weapon, and it is a serious machine gun. It weighs about 14 pounds and fires 5.56-millimeter bullets at up to 725 rounds per minute.

It is primarily used to lay down a field of fire, forcing enemy soldiers to hug the ground or die.

According to the incident report, the private was breaking down his gun to clean it and had removed the butt stock and the trigger mechanism. The trigger mechanism not only allows the gun to fire, but also stops the gun from firing when the soldier isn't pulling the trigger.

On Sunday morning something was stuck, and the private was banging at the bolt. When it freed, the firing pin struck a bullet in the chamber. With no trigger mechanism to stop it, the ammunition belt just kept feeding into the gun, and lead kept coming out.

The private dropped the gun and briefly sought cover against the smooth concrete wall. The SAW chattered and danced around the floor clockwise, spraying bullets off the tile floor and the concrete walls as a half dozen soldiers vainly sought cover.

A Sony Walkman was blown to bits. There were rips—but not holes—in at least two protective vests. A ricochet smacked into a soldier's Bible, but the lead never got past Genesis.

The private dove onto his weapon and the belt broke. The gun was quiet.

The lieutenant, the private's platoon leader, was shot once

in the ankle. The bullet traveled up his calf and lodged behind his knee.

The specialist was hit in a hand, an elbow and his left upper thigh.

The sergeant was hit behind the left knee and in his left foot. The bullet bit off his third toe.

A Blackhawk medical evacuation helicopter landed in the dirt parking lot, and soldiers fed the three stretchers into its belly. As of late Sunday night, all three men were in good condition.

When Hughes, the *No Slack* commander, got around to the miserable looking young man outside the door, he didn't snap or snarl, berate or bawl. They took a little walk, and Hughes took the sharp knife from his vest and quietly snipped the black, private first-class symbols from the young man's lapels.

The investigation found the soldier had been adequately trained on the SAW and was responsible for the accident because he failed to unload the gun before cleaning it, the first step in any manual.

The report also noted he has been a good soldier with a positive attitude, motivated to learn. He may get his rank back when his battalion returns to Fort Campbell.

The dust from the Blackhawk settled, and the business of waging war returned to normal. *No Slack* received orders for its next mission and began the reconnaissance, searching for soldiers to shoot on purpose.

* * * *

4

AL HILLAH—
THE BATTLE FOR BABYLON

"It's your city, don't screw it up!"

THE FEINT ATTACK

On April 7, 2003, Colonel Hodges summoned me to his command tent outside of Najaf. He had received word that *No Slack* would be attached to 3d Brigade, effective immediately. He showed me the location of Colonel Mike Linnington's command post along Highway 8 to our north and told me that I needed to get there as quickly as possible. In the morning they were planning to attack the city of Al-Hillah, the site of ancient Babylon on the Euphrates River.

Word from Hodges' staff was that *No Slack* would conduct a feint attack into the south of Hillah to tie down defending Iraqi forces south of the town in order to facilitate 3d Brigade's main attack from the west. A feint is a distracting or deceptive maneuver, a mock attack. It was a term I had heard often in the Army, but now it struck me that I had no idea how to "fake" an attack. Colonel Hodges noticed the confusion in my face and smiled his familiar calm, yet sarcastic, grin: "Get up to 3d Brigade, get yourself some tanks, and feint the hell out of them-there Iraqis."

Then for the first time in the war, I saw concern in his eyes. He had already been forced to detach one of his battalions to the 3d Infantry Division, and now he was sending a second to 3d Brigade while he was being left behind in Najaf. There are few things more difficult for a commander than having to relinquish control of his troops during a fight. Hodges was being left behind and I understood his pain. I assured him I would see him soon in Babylon, the capital of the cradle of civilization.

After Colonel Hodges departed, I turned to my operations officer, Jim Crider, and issued an order to have Captain Tom Ehrhart and his Delta Company conduct a visual reconnaissance along the southern route to Hillah. They were to ensure that the bridges along the Euphrates were still intact and to check out possible enemy positions.

Within 30 minutes, Delta Company left the compound and I jumped in my hummer and moved north to Colonel Linnington's command post. Colonel Linnington had always struck me as a picture perfect officer: tall, chiseled features, and lean. He would look different when I found him that day. I needed to speak to him immediately in order to start planning and ensuring that his staff knew our disposition, strength and logistical status before they were too far along in their own planning. I also hoped to convince my new brigade commander that I would need a tank platoon for the operation if he wanted me to make the feint look convincing; especially since I planned to take southern Hillah if possible. To do that, I would need tanks.

It took over an hour to get to his command post. While I was en route, Captain Ehrhart radioed that he had reached the southern outskirts of Hillah and was conducting a visual reconnaissance from within Babylon University. He reported no enemy contact en route and the bridges were intact, but he could see enemy trenches and fighting positions straddling the roads and rice dikes along the main roads leading to the city. I told him to pull back, establish an assault position, and prepare to receive the battalion that evening.

The 3d Brigade was setting up along the main road heading into Hillah from the west. The Hillah road intersecting Highway 8 featured an odd display of tanks, fuel trucks, destroyed Iraqi trucks, burned out or mangled civilian vehicles and clouds of dust in every direction. Dozens of vehicles from just as many units were crisscrossing the intersection, on and off the road, busily going somewhere fast. Despite all the activity and planned chaos, 3d Brigade had managed to find the only grass covered field I had seen in months on which to set up their command post. It was a striking contrast of green grass, palm trees, dust, diesel fumes and the dirtiest soldiers I had seen since we had crossed the berm.

When I first saw Colonel Linnington, I hardly recognized him. The once tall, lean and striking commander was filthy, unshaven, hunched over and exhausted. I hadn't realized how inhospitable and horrible it had been for 3d Brigade stuck out in the barren western desert for the past three weeks. Despite the bad conditions and his personal appearance, he was suddenly energetic, poised and indisputably in command when he saw me. The 3d Brigade had been in the desert for more than twenty days and they looked the worse for it, but the ordeal had only made them more dangerous and ready to fight.

No Slack was honored to be on their right flank.

Colonel Linnington was happy to see me and was quick to take me to a map and show me his plan for taking Hillah. It was a simple and deadly plan, and he confirmed his intent to use *No Slack* in a feint attack to pin down Iraqi forces in southern Hillah. His quick and clear description enabled me to quickly grasp his intent and relay instructions to my staff. I provided him with some lessons we had gleaned from our fight in Najaf and then busily moved on to other matters.

I wanted to study the plan and develop my own battle concept using 3d Brigade's command post. As I read the details of the battle plan, I suddenly realized that Captain Ehrhart had already accomplished two-thirds of our tasks. By conducting the leader's recon to the south of Hillah, Ehrhart had essentially conducted the feint a day early. I quickly found Colonel Linnington and showed him where my soldiers were located. He simply looked at me and said, "No use paying for the same real estate twice." I then worked with his staff to modify our tasks to ensure the feint still supported the overall concept for the attack. The brigade operations order wouldn't be issued for hours, so I took advantage of the downtime to catch up on some personal hygiene and sleep, luxuries that would escape me in the days and weeks ahead.

After the best sleep I had had in over three weeks, Major Crider and I were able to develop a sound concept and pass most of the details to the battalion staff on the radio before the brigade's operations order came that evening. I needed to stay at the brigade command post to back brief Colonel Linnington on my plan and get his final approval before returning to my new CP south of Hillah. I was comfortable with my executive officer, Major Pete Rooks, and his abil-

ity to form the staff, reposition the battalion and develop sound orders
in my absence. He justified that confidence by moving the entire battalion to the secure staging area south of Hillah, positioning our
artillery battery, and resupplying the battalion before I linked up with
them after dark.

The brigade operations order and back briefs went quickly, since
by this point the battalion was very good at receiving and executing
verbal orders. So when I returned to our new position, the order was
well organized and ready to issue to the commanders. As usual, Major
Rooks had given the commanders enough information to issue orders
to their platoons prior to my arrival. Allowing junior leaders to issue
warning orders early is crucial for platoon, squad and team leaders
because these junior leaders need every moment of time possible to
organize, rehearse and prepare for combat. The *No Slack* noncommissioned officers were some of the best I had ever worked with in
over twenty years of service. They had their battle drills down to a science and they understood the importance of pre-combat checks. Most
importantly, they loved and cared for their soldiers. My goal was
always to give them as much time as I could to prepare and they never
failed their soldiers or me.

When I arrived at the new assembly area, I noticed a Bradley platoon within our perimeter. I had been promised a tank platoon, but
some confusion had led to a Bradley platoon receiving orders to assist
in our attack instead. The lightly skinned vehicles would cause some
minor changes in our plan, but they were still a welcome sight and
proved to be an exceptional force multiplier in the following days.

Unbeknownst to me, the 2d Brigade of the 101st Division had
launched a feint attack into southern Hillah two days prior to our
arrival. Weeks later I would learn that this brigade, supported by 2nd
Battalion, 70th Armored Regiment, commanded by Lieutenant
Colonel Jeff Ingram, and 3-101st Aviation Battalion, commanded by
Lieutenant Colonel Jim Richardson, had met stiff resistance from dug-
in Iraqi infantry along the southern road into Hillah. The Iraqis had
expertly used artillery and direct fires during the fight. Brigadier
General Freakley, the assistant division commander of the 101st, had
mentioned the use of planned artillery fires by the Iraqis, but I failed
to make the connection and ask the right questions at the operations

order briefing. We were hours from attacking up the same road that had cost the life of one US soldier already.

The brigade's plan was simple. *No Slack* would attack slowly from the south, with the Bradleys leading. Delta Company would be on their flanks providing long-range anti-tank support along with fires from heavy machine guns and automatic grenade launchers, if required. In order, B, C and A companies would follow in dismounted columns. With direct covering fires from our D Company and indirect fires from B Battery, 2-320th Field Artillery, the Bradleys would clear the route to Hillah and seize a series of battle positions leading to Objective Lynx, a major road intersection inside the city. The three dismounted infantry companies would seize and hold all terrain cleared by the heavy teams. We advanced one pre-determined phase line at a time, maintaining good fighting order, as we were cleared by the brigade commander to move north. The brigade was using *No Slack* to fix the Iraqis in the south so they couldn't reinforce the enemy defenses in the west, as 3rd Brigade executed the main attack into Hillah. Each time the brigade broke through an enemy defensive line, they would order us to move to the next phase line in order to increase pressure on the Iraqis until 3d Brigade could fully deploy and seize the city.

On April 8, the attack began with the Bradley platoon quickly seizing key objectives along the outskirts of Hillah. Sporadic small arms fire fell meaninglessly around the Bradleys as Delta Company engaged a series of compounds and trenches with TOW Missiles, .50 caliber machine guns, and MK-19 automatic grenade launchers. The sight of the Bradleys began to flush enemy vehicles out of alleys, garages, and from walled military compounds to our front. The Iraqis' most fearsome vehicle was a French Roland Air Defense system with SA-16 surface to air missiles in the erect-and-fire mode. Once our infantry had spotted the Roland, it became a two-hour chase to destroy this lethal system.

The cat-and-mouse game between the Bradley platoon and the Roland was finally concluded when two American F-16s screamed in and destroyed the Roland. The F-16s miraculously demolished the vehicle between the Hillah Hospital and a high school without damaging either building. Our Air Force Tactical Air Control Party, deployed from the Idaho Air National Guard, had proven, yet again, their value during a close fight.

The enemy's infantry presented only token resistance and quickly faded into the city to our north. As our infantry worked their way to the outskirts of the city, we seized a fuel depot, a major food-for-oil warehouse compound, a large weapons factory, two military training compounds and an Iraqi National Guard headquarters. We also discovered huge caches of ammunition, weapons, Iraqi equipment and uniforms. It was obvious that the Iraqis had decided to drop their uniforms and run north. Helmets, gas masks, atropine injectors for chemical warfare, military uniforms and military vehicles were strewn about the former Iraqi defenses. The discarded chemical gear was a stark reminder that we were nearing Karbala, the place the brigade chemical officer had identified as the perceived line in the sand that Saddam would use to employ chemical or nuclear weapons. The abandoned gear led me to believe that either the Iraqis didn't believe Saddam would use WMDs or that they were moving far enough north that the WMDs would have no effect on them. In either case, I started mentally planning the fight on a contaminated battlefield.

Questions clouded my mind. Could we really fight in a contaminated environment? Could we sustain the offensive in hot chemical protective equipment? How would we deal with the massive civilian casualties if Saddam used chemcial weapons? In any case, we would need to stay close to a water source; we would need to hug the Euphrates River to conduct hasty decontamination operations so we could stay in the fight. But where would that poisoned water go, and would it kill civilians if I used it to decontaminate the battalion? I didn't get much sleep in Hillah.

SERGEANT MAJOR GADGET

The discovery of the food-for-oil compound was a significant stroke of luck that would prove invaluable to the battalion and 82nd Airborne Division in the following weeks. The eight football field-sized warehouses were full of black tea from Vietnam, soap and shampoo from Jordon, sugar from Indonesia, Sri Lanka and Guam, rice from Cambodia and Thailand, and baby food and powdered formula from Europe. I knew that the people of Hillah were dependant on the program and would need help as soon as we could begin stability operations. I hoped this food would help us gain control and order in Hillah after the fighting subsided.

Upon entering the warehouse compound, I was brought up short by the sight of Command Sergeant Major Montcalm zipping around in a heavy forklift, moving bags of wheat and rice to reinforce the walls. I paused to laugh, remembering the unconventional predeployment training we had conducted with our NCOs and officers.

Light infantry is very vulnerable and sometimes hampered by the sheer amount of equipment they must carry. Over the years, I learned that it is important to think outside the box and lighten the burden whenever possible. I knew that we would probably find abandoned vehicles along our route and wanted to be able to commandeer them for our use. With that in mind, I took all of my squad leaders and above to a junkyard and had a "less then savory" character teach them seven different ways to hotwire a vehicle. My boss was not too pleased at my initiative and told me, in rather colorful terms, what would happen to me if any of my soldiers put their newfound knowledge to use during their leisure hours back home in Kentucky. No one had more fun during this training than my Command Sergeant Major.

Montcalm is known as "Sergeant Major Gadget" due to his love of inventing. His eyes gleamed when we found six huge tractor-trailer semis in the warehouse complex. These trucks appeared to be brand new and were in excellent working condition. He knew exactly what to do with them, and assured me that *No Slack* would no longer need to rely on division or corps transportation assets for the rest of the war. With the assistance of my maintenance sergeant and a blow torch, Montcalm turned the trucks into traveling foxholes by cutting firing ports along the sides. The trucks were so big that we could load more than 40 soldiers and all their gear onto them, or just use them to transport the soldiers' equipment so they wouldn't have to carry so much while dismounted. These trucks accompanied us during the rest of our stay in Iraq.

THE FINAL PUSH

April 8, 2003 passed in a flurry of sporadic contact, mass explosions by the engineer platoon destroying enemy caches, mounting civilian traffic and door-to-door searches before I decided to stop our advance in order to seize and clear buildings for the night. We had taken all of our objectives with only one casualty and I wanted to be in a good position to repel any potential counterattack when the sun went down. We were exhausted and anyone watching would know this as well.

Like in Najaf, we seized compounds with high walls, two to three-story buildings and accessible roads, which gave us interior lines to defend from, making it possible for resupply and to get some rest while only needing minimal force to secure ourselves. It also gave us a chance to conduct sound personal hygiene.

That night 3d Brigade prepared for their final push into the center of the city. They had met stiffer resistance than we had, but they had managed to get to their objectives before nightfall. At three a.m., their second attack began with a tremendous artillery barrage that struck the primary Ba'ath headquarters, three Iraqi military compounds and two *Fedayeen* training sites. *No Slack* was responsible for attacking a suspected terrorist training camp to the west of our current position. Intelligence led us to believe that a large number of foreign nationals were housed in this compound and that they regularly trained at the Iraqi military compound we had taken earlier in the day.

Our scouts and B Company had placed eyes on this target earlier in the day, and I wanted to see it for myself before attacking it with artillery and close air support. Unexpectedly, I saw a complex of three seven-story apartment buildings with children's toys on the grounds, a couple of swing sets, and laundry hanging out to dry on the balconies. I decided to intimidate the target with illumination artillery rounds until we could positively identify enemy forces in the apartment complex. Though difficult, I felt that this was the most rational decision. If I was wrong, we would have terrorists in our midst the entire time we were in Hillah; if I was right, we'd have avoided needlessly killing civilians. I decided to err on the side of caution.

I needed to prove to the people of Hillah, much like the citizens of Najaf, that we were there to help and not to steal their religion or to randomly murder Muslims. Killing a large number of civilians would immediately derail those efforts. I could not forget Sergeant Akbar's rational for launching a grenade attack on his fellow soldiers in Kuwait. If an American soldier could be convinced we were going to kill innocent Muslims, what would the people of Hillah think if I indiscriminately bombed apartment buildings? As we had learned in Najaf, Stability And Support Operations (SASO) must be executed in conjunction with combat operations. There is no sequential transition from combat to SASO; rather, they should be concurrent. The operational risk of killing innocent civilians far outweighed any potential threat from the possible terrorists hiding in that apartment complex. I knew that if any terrorists came out of the building, my soldiers would make sure they did not return to it.

* * * *

JIM LACEY: It was obvious to me that throughout the war every American unit did everything possible to minimize civilian casualties. That is why I was struck by many post-war articles claiming that Americans had killed thousands. One CNN story in particular told about hundreds of dead and wounded civilians taken to a hospital in Najaf. That reporter had taken the word of an Iraqi doctor and obviously failed to tour the hospital. I did visit the hospital and penned this story after viewing CNN as it tried to paint American troops as callous murderers.

NAJAF SISTERS
The truth about civilian casualties.

© 2003 by National Review Online, www.nationalreview.com.
Reprinted by permission.

By JIM LACEY

On the fifth floor of Najaf's Teaching Hospital lay two sisters injured by American forces during the liberation of the city. Esraa, a wide-eyed six-year-old, had just undergone surgery to amputate her leg below the knee; it had become infected after a shrapnel wound. In the bed beside her lay her 14-year-old sister, Nor. She had taken two shrapnel wounds to the leg, but was expected to make a complete recovery. Dr. Ali, who was accompanying me, said he knew the girls and that their house had been near some of the most severe fighting in Najaf.

Both girls were awake when I entered the room, but did not attempt to speak. When I tried, through Dr. Ali, to express some measure of the sorrow I felt for them, the only reply came from the family members: "It is as Allah wills." It may be the will of Allah, but it was done by the hand of man. War can exact a terrible price from the innocents caught up in it, and Esraa and Nor were paying that price in full.

Unbelievably, they were the only two children I found in the hospital.

At the end of almost four days of shelling, air attacks, and hard infantry fighting, I went to visit the hospital with a measure of trepidation. Having witnessed much of the battle and seen the destruction in the areas where paramilitary forces had put up a fight, I fully expected to encounter dozens—if not hundreds—of children like Nor and Esraa. Despite the sadness I felt for the damage done to the lives of both girls, I will be forever thankful I did not find what I expected.

If it had been in any city in America, Najaf's hospital would have been closed down. The building is in a severe state of disrepair and there is filth everywhere. Bloody gloves and medical equipment litter the hallways. Urine and blood samples lie around rooms collecting flies. The burn unit's door is locked to keep it sterile, despite there being a large window missing in the door. A doctor explained as I got on an elevator, "Sometimes it lets us out. Sometimes it does not." He smiled and added, "It is like Saddam."

Immediately upon my arrival, I was surrounded by doctors and staff eager to show me around and answer questions. I asked the only female doctor present how many patients they had treated who had been injured in the fighting, and how many of them were men. She replied that they had treated about 600 patients and that they were mostly men. Dr. Ali quickly corrected her and they began to argue in Arabic. He then announced that it had been about half men and half women.

Dr. Ali insisted on being my escort for the remainder of the visit. He explained that the hospital's fifth and sixth floors were reserved for civilians who had been injured in the war. Men were on the sixth floor, women and children on the floor below.

The first room off the elevator was filled with the men who had suffered the worst injuries. None of them spoke as the doctor showed me each of their many wounds.

I went from room to room without saying a word. It was hard to look at the broken bodies lying in such unsanitary conditions, but I also noticed something else. There was only one man who seemed to be over age 40 on the entire floor. Of the 46 patients I counted, 45 appeared to be in their early twenties.

When I visited the women's and children's floor, most of the rooms were empty. Besides Esraa and Nor, there was only one middle-aged woman, who had been wounded in the side by shrapnel. She also was expected to make a full recovery.

I asked Dr. Ali why, if these were all civilian casualties, there was not an even distribution of males and females and among age groups. Why did the overwhelming number of them appear to be men of military age? He offered no explanation, but continued to insist that the men were all civilians. He then added that many civilians had been killed, too, and that I should check the morgue and see.

When I did try to check the morgue, they would not allow me to see any of the wrapped bodies, but did let me go through the paperwork. At my request, a clerk pointed out where the name was supposed to be on each form. Most of the name blocks were blank. Pressed for an explanation he said, "They are not known here." It was only then that it struck me that most of the men lying in the hospital had no family around them—unlike Esraa and Nor, who were surrounded by family members. The clerk's statement probably meant that these men were fighters from Baghdad who had no relatives in Najaf.

Besides what I saw at the hospital, I do know of at least one three-year-old girl killed during the fighting. She had been living with her family in a block of homes that received heavy

Iraqi mortar fire the night before American troops moved into the area. Iraqi paramilitary forces reportedly would telephone to houses along the routes from which they were expecting the Americans to approach. If anyone answered the phone, they fired the mortars. The adults in the house knew not to answer the phone; the little girl did not.

As we were leaving, Dr. Ali explained that he was wearing mourning clothes for his brother, who had just died of cancer. He went on to explain that the disease had been caused by some weapon America had used in the first Gulf War, in which his brother had been a soldier. He added, "America is at fault for [my] brother and many others and [will] need to make it right in Iraq."

It is heartbreaking to witness suffering like Esraa's and Nor's. But the truth is that, considering the intensity of the fighting, the civilian casualties in this war were remarkably few. There are several reasons for this. While American weapons have become much more lethal, they have also become more discriminate, allowing commanders to hit the exact target they are aiming at and avoid collateral damage. The low level of casualties is also a testament to the skill and bravery of many of our young soldiers, who often accepted significant additional risks to themselves in order to ensure minimal civilian losses.

Wars always involve an element of brutality. The suffering of innocents is particularly hard to bear. Only the prospect of better lives for the overwhelming majority of the people of Iraq will ever begin to repay Esraa for the loss of her leg. It will require a sustained effort— by both the U.S. and the Iraqi people—to ensure that she can one day be a part of the celebrations that were going on in the streets around her hospital room as I left.

As for Dr. Ali, he surely had his own reasons for lying, and for trying to paint America in a bad light.

* * * *

On the morning of April 9, the city of Hillah suddenly came to life with Iraqi citizens in the streets, both in cars and on foot, carrying flags and signs and wearing enormous smiles on their faces. It became obvious that either whatever they had feared was gone or they were brilliantly tempting us to let our guard down. We had not expected an outpouring of support such as we experienced in Najaf, yet Hillah seemed anxious to get back to normal, and our presence was not going to keep them cooped up in their homes any longer.

As I stood across the street from an Iraqi compound watching B Company prepare to destroy a weapons cache, I suddenly heard the 3d Brigade Command Center issuing orders on the radio. The brigade operations officer was instructing the other battalions to prepare for a relief in place. I got on the radio and listened for my orders, but received none. After the group discussion on the radio, I contacted the operations officer separately and asked for my orders. He told me that I was not moving north with 3rd Brigade and he wasn't sure what my next mission was. While mulling over this information, my driver spotted a familiar icon on the blue force tracker computer in my hummer. Sergeant Bowers announced, with much flair and humor, "Sir, Eagle-Six approaching from our rear." It was Major General Petraeus. My driver had gotten quite good at recognizing the icons of my bosses and got great enjoyment out of announcing their approach to see my reaction.

As Major General Petraeus stepped out of his vehicle, I had the premonition that he was going to leave *No Slack* in Hillah just as 1-327th had been left in Najaf. After some simple pleasantries, he said, "Chris I'm leaving you in control of Hillah, I need you to relieve the battalions of 3rd Brigade of the 101st, known as the *Rakkassans,* as quickly as you can so we can move them north to Karbala. Once you've relieved 3d Brigade, you will go back under the control of Colonel Hodges and 1st Brigade. Good luck, we will see you in Baghdad." And with that, he was off. I wouldn't see him again until the commander's conference in Mosul some two months later.

As the 101st continued the attack north, I was out of communications with my higher headquarters for approximately 8–10 hours until we finally reestablished radio contact with Colonel Hodges. The 1st

Brigade was in the process of moving its command and logistical trains between Najaf and Hillah and would need to centrally position itself to control both 1st and 2d battalions. I asked about 3-327th, commanded by my good friend Lieutenant Colonel Ed Palekas, and learned they had been detached from 1st Brigade and were moving north to join the 3d ID for the fight into Baghdad. *No Slack* spent the rest of the day completing the relief in place and settling into our new positions throughout the city.

The staff was busy establishing contingency plans for any possibilities as we assumed control of the entire city of Hillah, home to over 300,000 Iraqi citizens, not all of whom were happy we were there. For me, I was not very happy that we would be left out of the final assault on Baghdad.

COUGAR'S FIGHT

On the morning of April 10, we started to send mounted and dismounted patrols into the city to determine the extent of the damage from the previous day's fighting and to conduct initial assessments of what we needed to return the city to a state of normalcy. My command post remained in an empty warehouse in the food-for-oil compound. I was sitting in a folding chair in the CP reading a newspaper when the first burst of automatic machine gun fire rang out to our north. The sounds echoed in the warehouses, which made it difficult to determine where they were coming from.

C Company reported contact with a white car filled with men brandishing AK-47 machine guns and they'd exchanged gunfire. Immediately afterward, another force made contact with a similar vehicle and a sentry reported armed men climbing over a wall near C Company. The intruders appeared to be raiding the former Iraqi military compound and weapons factory.

It was unclear if we had one or two contacts, but as the small arms and machine-gun fire increased, Majors Crider and Rooks looked at me with confused expressions on their faces and concern in their eyes as I did not react or even get up from my seat. Up until this point, I had personally controlled every battle and they expected me to do the same in this case. However, I was still very concerned about not micromanaging my commanders. I had been too controlling and was secretly hoping for a small contact so I could step back and let one of the company commanders handle it without getting directly involved. I needed to prepare my commanders for the decentralized fighting I anticipated if we did get the call to enter Baghdad. This seemed like the perfect time to let Captain Konz fight a battle on his own.

I called my staff over and explained my goal. I wanted Captain Konz to stay on the battalion command radio frequency so that I could monitor his fight and let him know that the battalion mortars and Apaches were at his call as needed. From the sound of it, he had most of his heavy machine guns in the fight and had begun to use his company mortars. I could feel the stares of the battle staff and command post personnel as I tried my best to continue to read the paper without emotion and keep my nose out of C Company's fight.

As the fight continued, I developed my personal engagement criteria and decided I would only get involved in the fight if the commander asked for my help, a second unit came in contact, or it looked like C Company would take a casualty. I instructed my mobile command team to pack up, deploy the vehicles into the middle of the compound, and get my vehicle radios up and operational. I also gathered my Air Force liaison team together and told them to go outside and get some air-on-station in case this escalating firefight grew into a full-fledged enemy counterattack. As I walked back into the command warehouse, the battalion 81mm mortars next to my building fired a volley of high explosive rounds for C Company—they had a full-fledged fight on their hands.

On the battalion radio, I could hear Captain Konz bringing in three Apache attack helicopters in on the enemy positions. The Apaches positioned directly over my compound and began to fire their 30mm machine guns and Hellfire missiles. The deafening sounds of mortars firing and 30mm chain-gun casings bouncing off the roof of the metal warehouse gave the impression that we were in the middle of the fight even though we were over a thousand meters away.

For Captain Konz, this fight was the culmination of years of training, exercises, live fires, military schooling, professional reading, blood, sweat, determination, guts and valor. Listening to him calmly and coolly orchestrate this battle was one of the high points of my life as a leader. Everything we had trained for was working and he knew exactly what to do. I was so very proud of him and his men.

My reverie was cut short as the Bradley platoon reported contact at a second location in Hillah. It was now time for me to engage. The Bradleys were north of C Company's position and were receiving small arms fire from several two- and three-story buildings near the hospital. The Bradley platoon leader and his platoon sergeant had already attacked and managed to stop the enemy's progress toward C Company's compound.

Now, with two units in contact, I was concerned this might be the start of an enemy counterattack to retake Hillah.

I moved to my mobile command team in the center of the compound and heard Lt. Colonel Jim Richardson, the Apache battalion commander, talking to Captain Konz on my command frequency. I picked up the radio and got an assessment from him. From the air, he reported that he couldn't see any additional enemy forces moving into our flanks or rear and confirmed Captain Konz's assessment that most of the enemy was either destroyed or pinned down in a three story military barracks north of C Company's position. From all the information available, it appeared that the attack consisted of approximately 20–40 enemy personnel and C Company had managed to corner them in a former Iraqi barracks in a compound adjacent to their own. The Bradleys had killed a second group of Iraqis attempting to reinforce the main enemy assault. My remaining companies reported negative contact and the rest of Hillah was silent.

As C Company tightened the noose around the enemy in the barracks, I was impressed with the enemy's ability to survive direct hits from our 60mm and 81mm mortars and multiple Hellfire missiles from our Apaches. The fight was now in its second hour and I was becoming worried that exhaustion would have a negative effect on my soldiers and their decision-making ability. It was time for me to end this firefight.

I turned to my Air Force JTAC team and asked them for immediate close air support. Within moments, two British Tornado pilots answered my air controller. The barracks housing the remaining Iraqi fighters were dangerously close to most of my battalion, the Hillah Hospital and an unnamed mosque. After the pilots made two passes to positively identify the target, they were confident they could hit the target, but they were carrying 1,000 lb bombs and needed a minimum safe distance of 700 meters to ensure no friendly casualties. Captain Konz had forces that were within 500 meters and any attempts to withdraw them would expose them to direct fire from the enemy barracks. I was not willing to take friendly casualties.

However, there was something different about this enemy. Their tactics were unorthodox and overly aggressive in light of the force they obviously faced and I couldn't let them escape. Captain Konz and I both felt that if we let up our pressure on the Iraqis and repositioned ourselves, they would take advantage of this lull and either escape or engage our repositioning forces. The urban environment made withdrawing, while maintaining pressure, next to impossible, so I asked Captain Konz if his guys could maintain contact with the enemy while finding cover within the 500 meter danger zone. He said he could and immediately placed his men under cover. As soon as I confirmed that he was set, I passed control of the Tornados to Lt. Colonel Richardson, who could see the target from his helicopter, as the Tornados released their deadly load. The impact of the two 1,000 lb bombs nearly knocked me off my feet, but they were dead solid perfect. As the dust settled, the building ceased to exist, as had the enemy fire. The buildings on the left and right appeared untouched by the attack.

As C Company cleared the compound, enemy casualties began to flow to my compound for aid and evacuation. The wounded were in various forms of uniforms and civilian clothes. They were dazed and beaten, but still defiant as we treated them and prepared them for medical evacuation. Kadhim came to the field aid station to see if he could glean any information from the enemy wounded. Suddenly, he lost his cool and started to yell wildly at the injured men. I pulled him aside and demanded an explanation; he looked at me with tears of rage in his eyes and said, "They are Jordanians and Palestinians." Then he pulled away and pointed at one of them on a litter and said with contempt, "and Syrians," before stomping away. I realized that the terrorists had found us and their deadly tactics suddenly made sense. They wanted jihad and we had helped them. These wounded men were defiant and angry only because they had failed to die.

ESTABLISHING A GOVERNMENT IN HILLAH

The responsibility for 300,000 people weighed heavily on my mind as I tried to maintain a balance between the immediacy of helping the citizens of Hillah, defending against possible enemy attacks, and posturing for the possibility of being called forward to fight in Baghdad. As we planned for all contingencies, we received no specific guidance on what to do next. I was pondering how I would convince these people we were not there to oppress them, steal their faith and make their lives any worse than they already were? I also had to be prepared to face the fact that my soldiers had killed their sons, husbands and brothers. Would they trust us? Could we trust them?

Army doctrine had always taught me that when a unit transitions from combat to peace enforcement it should be replaced by another force so it doesn't have to work and negotiate with the families and friends of the dead. That is the difference between theory and practice. The doctrine looked good on paper, but wasn't always possible on the ground. The Army didn't have the luxury of rotating us out with another battalion as the war raged to our north. I was left to find a way to make it work and in very short order.

As my staff and I pondered our next move, the companies were settling into different locations throughout the city. A Company maintained control of the food-for-oil compound and my headquarters. C Company was now in control of a former military compound and weapons factory, D Company moved into a gymnasium and adjoining compound, and B Company was in a school near the center of the city. The Bradley platoon was reassigned to brigade and we never saw them again.

In the plus-column, we picked up a new Special Forces Team (A-Team) commanded by Captain Jason Barnes. They moved into one of Saddam's elaborate palaces in the reconstructed city of Babylon on the north end of Hillah. Additionally, the Najaf OGA team appeared out of nowhere and joined *No Slack* for a second time, aggressively helping us to develop the best options for our next move.

The OGA team leader told me that he had coordinated with a group of prominent Iraqis who were prepared to take control of Hillah and act as an interim government. I agreed to meet with these local leaders to determine their intent and to decide whether or not to support them.

Colonel Hodges hadn't directed us to establish a local government, but it seemed like the next logical step in returning the city to normal, and I had learned in Najaf that my leaders were willing to give me great latitude to do what I felt was right and necessary. I contacted Colonel Hodges on the radio and told him my plan to meet with these Iraqis. I will never forget what he said: "Well, your gut has served us well so far. Be careful and keep me informed of the results."

I set down the radio hand-mike, looked at Major Rooks, and said, "We are going to win this war with guidance like that." That Colonel Hodges had such confidence in himself, his subordinate commanders and his soldiers impressed me then and, given the stakes involved, is even more impressive in hindsight. To me, that is the essence of leadership.

BABYLON

Then a mighty angel picked up a stone and threw it into the sea, saying: In this way, Babylon the great city will be thrown down violently and never be found again. [10]

"Astonished and humbled" best describes the feelings I had when I first saw the reconstructed city of Babylon. It was a scene straight from the pages of the Old Testament and I got a lump in my throat thinking of the men who had passed through these gates. The local workers, whose tribe had lived outside the gates of Babylon for thousands of years, told me that Saddam had rebuilt the city to defy the world and prove he was the reincarnation of King Nebuchadnezzar, the conqueror of Jerusalem.

The new city was only yards away from the original ruins along the Euphrates River—grandiose city gates, spectacular and ornate walls, stone paved roads, lush courtyards, shops, royal mistress quarters, lavish dining halls, lakes, gardens, an amphitheater, and of course, the Palace.

Saddam's goal was to build three palaces on 500-foot manufactured earthen berms overlooking the ruins in defiance of the Jewish

God's decree that Babylon would never be found again. It was a gross display of power and wealth designed to convince the people of Iraq that Saddam was an equal to the ancient king who had punished the Zionist infidels. I couldn't help but wonder if I was standing where a young teenager named Daniel once stood interpreting the dreams of King Nebuchadnezzar over 2,500 years earlier.

> Then the king Nebuchadnezzar fell upon his face, and worshipped Daniel, and commanded that they should offer an oblation and sweet odours unto him. The king answered unto Daniel, and said, of a truth it is, that your God is a God of gods, and a Lord of kings, and a revealer of secrets, seeing thou couldest reveal this secret. Then the king made Daniel a great man, and gave him many great gifts, and made him ruler over the whole province of Babylon and chief of the governors over all the wise men of Babylon.[11]

The palace was filled with brass and Italian marble inscriptions depicting reenactments of the siege and sacking of Jerusalem in 586 B.C. Other monuments and declarations of the perceived Iraqi victory over Iran during the Iran/Iraq War, and of course, Saddam's great national victory over the American Coalition in 1991 filled the walls. Kadhim translated one such inscription in the main ballroom at the bottom of a large brass battle scene, I asked him to stop so I could get my notebook to write it down. The inscription read:

> As for the nation or kingdom that does not serve Nebuchadnezzar king of Babylon and does not place its neck under the yoke of the king of Babylon, that nation I will punish by sword, famine, and plague

Later that night my chaplain, Captain Scott Brown, helped me find the passage in my green Army-issued King James Bible. However, as Captain Brown pointed out, Saddam had taken the quote out of context and omitted "until through him I have destroyed it."[12] The irony of the situation was sobering and intimidating and the pressure to do the right thing for the people of Hillah was more important now than ever before. If helping them meant the end of the shooting war for *No Slack*, then I would do whatever it took to maintain the peace.

BUILDING GOVERNMENT FROM THE "BOTTOM UP"

The OGA and A-Team members met me at the Mistress Quarters and gave me a quick tour of the compound before this august body of Iraqi businessmen and local leaders began to arrive. Kadhim and I discussed protocol and prepared to use all our senses to observe and assess these men. The OGA had brought some new faces with them, a combination of Egyptian, Jordanian and Iraqi linguists. One of the Iraqis was a former Iraqi army colonel who exuded a particular kind of confidence. I had met him before in Najaf when he—intentionally or unintentionally—stirred up a crowd in front of the Ali Mosque in Najaf. He had deserted from the Iraqi army prior to the invasion, and that made me willing to give him a second chance. However, I did not yet understand his agenda, and the fact that Kadhim did not trust him made me a bit skittish about accepting his advice.

As we continued to wait for the Iraqis, the team sergeant from the A-Team we had worked with in Najaf approached me and asked if I had heard that Ayatollah Khoei had been stabbed to death on the steps of the Ali Mosque. This was the first I had heard of it, and his death was a shock that struck me personally. Khoei had played a key role in helping the coalition to free Najaf and I prayed his death wouldn't set the Shi'a back in their goal to free Iraq. I walked out of the meeting hall and into the gardens along the Euphrates River, and for the next few minutes this Christian soldier from America prayed for the soul of a Muslim Ayatollah from Iraq in the ancient city of Babylon. No ideologies, no politics, just one comrade bidding another comrade farewell and Godspeed. Later I would learn that a few Iraqi Shiite leaders, including Ayatollahs Hassan Jawaheri, Amer al-Manshadawi and Saeed al-Saedi, had vowed to pursue Khoei's work of "peace and reconciliation" and "joint efforts to rebuild a new Iraq with the help of the liberating coalition." I could only pray that in time Khoei's dream would become a reality . . . a free Najaf.

Word came from the front gate that the Iraqis were arriving under the protection of additional members of the OGA. I had not met this group yet and was growing concerned that I didn't know how large an organization this OGA was. How many of them were in my sector? What they were up to? Where were they staying? Even, who was in charge? I pushed these concerns aside as a convoy of red, white and black Mercedes and BMWs pulled up in front of the meeting hall. I looked at Kadhim as these men, who seemed at home in plush surroundings, emerged from their cars and said, "I bet they've been here before." It was an ominous sight and my defenses went up as fast as my blood pressure.

Before their arrival, Kadhim had had a run-in with one of the Iraqi linguists working for the OGA, and the OGA team leader asked me to keep him out of the room during this initial meeting. I didn't understand why and was tempted to refuse to participate in the proceedings without Kadhim. The team leader promised to discuss the issue with me in detail later, which he never did, and said that if I left, we would lose our best chance to get the citizens of Hillah to help us. I knew he needed my uniform and rank, but I could not understand why Kadhim was suddenly a liability. It was hard asking Kadhim to stay outside, but he was still able to see each of the participants as they milled around before and after the meeting. Additionally, we convinced the Iraqis to let us take their pictures so we could make identification badges to help them gain safe passage in the coming days.

Eighteen men finally sat down in the chairs arranged in the great hall. Most were dressed in traditional black and gold sheik attire, but others sported tailored Western-style suits, and a few wore open collar shirts. The OGA team leader opened the meeting in Arabic with pleasantries and compliments, and then had each of the men introduce himself and identify whom they were representing within the province. Once this was complete, he turned the floor over to his linguist and me. I had rehearsed my speech with Kadhim, knowing that I had only one chance to strike the exactly right note and gain their support.

"*Salaam Alakham, Allah Akbar*. (Hello and Welcome, God be Praised.) My name is Lieutenant Colonel Chris Hughes from the 101st Airborne Division. It is my honor to represent my commanding general, Major General David H. Petraeus from the United States of America. It has been my dream for over twelve years to sit in this great hall and discuss the expectations and conduct of the citizens of Hillah in a free and sovereign Iraq. My forces in Hillah are not an occupation force; we are a liberation force designed to provide protection and humanitarian assistance until a free government can take control of Hillah and care for its citizens. As I learned in Najaf while working with His Holiness the Ayatollah Sistani, I will not assume I know what your people need or desire to return to a state of normalcy. I plan to use this august body of civic and business leaders to advise me initially until the Hillah government is established. I give you my word as an officer that I will support a government that strives to help the people, wishes to get beyond this war, and will openly renounce Saddam Hussein's regime. With this statement, I will now be silent as I seek your counsel and consider your advice. *Allahu Akbar* and thank you."

By the end of the meeting, the eighteen had selected a mayor of Hillah and a city council—although I got the impression the selections were made long before this meeting. After the men left, the OGA team, the A-Team Commander, the Iraqi colonel and a few others met to discuss strategy. The mayor and city council would come to the city and make their existence known to the people when they felt the conditions were right. The battalion was to provide security and legitimacy when they were ready. The OGA and A-Team would help them organize and begin to seek local support through their contacts. It all seemed in order; it all seemed feasible; it all seemed too easy. And I didn't trust it.

In essence, the OGA team had followed the top down approach to forming a government by taking a group of self-identified big shots at their word. I wanted more of a bottom up approach, working up from the grass roots.

After returning to headquarters, I put the staff to work investigating the new Iraqi council members. I wanted to know everything about them, especially what roles they had played in the previous regime. I also wanted to know whether they were Shi'a or Sunni, and what the local reaction would be when we showed their pictures around. We would need to work fast to gather as much information as possible to ensure we weren't putting remnants of Saddam's regime back into power. The key to solving this puzzle was Kadhim and the other Free Iraqi Forces (FIF) in the division. I trusted Kadhim, as he had proven himself time and time again. If he told me that these men were untrustworthy, then I knew he was probably right.

After reporting the particulars of the meeting to Colonel Hodges, luck once again played its hand. Major General Petraeus' interpreter, Lieutenant Joe, was from Hillah and wanted to visit his family whom he hadn't seen in over ten years. A returning hero had proven an effective tool in Najaf, and we now had the opportunity to do it again in Hillah. The next morning Colonel Hodges and Lieutenant Joe came to my headquarters and we escorted them to the center of Hillah.

The reunion was jubilant, emotional and overwhelming. The neighborhood's streets filled with people as Joe's family ran from house to house announcing his arrival. His mother and sisters fell to their knees and wailed and cried. Colonel Hodges looked at me and we quickly left the house. This was a private reunion and we needed to step back and let the family have some time together. Outside, hundreds of happy children and curious men immediately surrounded us. Specialist Carr was helping me to talk to the people and confirm their joy at Joe's return. As we worked the crowd, we found out that a school about 200 meters from Joe's residence was full of ammunition and the locals were concerned that the children might go into the school and accidentally cause an explosion.

I took a small patrol from Colonel Hodges' security detail to take a quick look at the school. We had plenty of help showing us where the weapons and ammunition were. The fact that they were willing to help us made us confident it wasn't a trap. What they showed us was criminal and completely against every rule of human decency. While there were no books or pencils, every classroom had mortar, artillery and RPG rounds stacked to the ceiling. The courtyard in the middle of the school was full of cased land mines, ammunition and three anti-aircraft guns. One spark and the entire neighborhood would cease to exist.

After reporting to Colonel Hodges, I contacted Major Rooks and instructed him to get the engineer platoon to the school immediately to secure the munitions. This became our primary mission for the day, not only for safety reasons but to demonstrate to the locals that we would address their needs with a sense of urgency. If I could get the same type of positive reaction for cleaning up this mess that we got when Joe's family announced his return, perhaps the news that we were truly here to help would spread.

The extraction of the munitions went on through the night. We removed over six truckloads of high explosives and weapons and took them to the southern outskirts of Hillah for disposal. During the process, Lieutenant Joe had a chance to look at the pictures of the Iraqis I had met during the Babylon Palace meeting. His reaction was quick and vehement: "This man is a murderer. This one kills children. This one is Ba'ath . . . this man hates Shi'a . . . he was sent here by Saddam before the war to ensure the *Fedayeen* fought us." It was my worst nightmare, and although I knew I had to take his comments with a grain of salt, it was the only human intelligence I had on the proposed council.

I gave Joe the picture collage we made of the Iraqis vying for power and asked him to confirm our suspicions and help me to assemble a true government for Hillah. Before I left Joe at the gate of his family's home, he agreed to help us and promised to come to my headquarters within the week. I decided to take a chance on the Free Iraqi Forces once again.

Two days later, two Iraqi men came to our front gate claiming to be representatives of a newly elected government of Hillah. I queried the guard to tell me how they were dressed and what kind of car did they own. He told me they were in open collared shirts and had arrived in a taxi. I looked at Major Rooks and stage whispered, "I guess Joe's been busy."

I had the XO receive the men at the compound gate and take them to an office near the front entrance. I told him to confirm their story and arrange a meeting. I learned in Najaf that I couldn't always make myself available to emissaries and representatives. In order to increase my power as a commander with the Iraqis, I had to limit my exposure to only their senior leaders. The men told Major Rooks they represented Lieutenant Joe and a council of men who had met in the Hillah mosque, and they had been democratically elected to represent Hillah. They wished to arrange a meeting with me and the council to determine our next move. I told my XO to congratulate the men and tell them I would meet with the entire council the next day in my headquarters.

That evening I contacted the A-Team commander and first sergeant to ask them what they thought would happen if I determined the local council was more credible than the OGA-proposed council. They had a relationship with the OGA and I hoped they could provide some insight on its organization and authority. Captain Barnes had no idea what the impact would be and said he would ask the OGA team leader that night.

The next morning Joe and his newly elected council arrived at our headquarters. Lieutenant Joe assured me that these men represented the people of Hillah. They were local leaders, businessmen and scholars from Babylon University. According to Joe, the election had taken place two days earlier in the Hillah mosque, and the local cleric Mohamed Lataf Abdulla had validated the results. Abdulla was prepared to make the official announcement to the city during evening prayers if I supported the council's legitimacy.

After meeting with the group for over an hour, I asked for a quick break and walked the compound to consider their proposal. I worried that the OGA council was part of a bigger plan that I was unaware of and that I was about to ruin it. I didn't have nearly enough information, but I didn't have the time or resources to gather more. Although they had been present in Najaf, the OGA had not questioned any of my decisions there. I was not willing to give in to them now. Their solution just did not feel right. As Colonel Hodges had told me earlier, my gut was usually right, so I would go with my gut. I had no other choice.

I returned to the meeting and shook hands with Eskendar Juad, the new mayor of Hillah, and declared my support for his council. I also agreed to assign A Company, under the command of Captain Steve Thomas, as the security unit for the mayor, his staff and the new mayor's office. The council had already identified a complex in the center of the city, and we would take over the facility the following morning. The council returned to the city, and the staff of *No Slack* settled in for a long night of planning and preparation. Foremost to our planning was getting word to the OGA that I had decided to support an alternate council and would not throw my support behind the one they had proposed. I never saw the OGA team or their council again.

* * * *

JIM LACEY: The "expert" OGA team had also selected the government for Najaf prior to leaving for Al-Hillah. Unfortunately there was no Chris Hughes to protect the people of Najaf from the OGA-selected government's depredations. Even at the time, it was obvious to anyone who took the time to look, that the OGA and their Special Forces buddies were screwing up. The Najaf Council was finally arrested en masse at the order of the CPA and Central Iraqi Government six months later. The following article gives you my observations at the time and will give the reader a small taste of what can happen if there is no one like Chris Hughes to apply common sense and adult supervision.

WE ARE MAKING OUR FIRST WRONG TURN IN IRAQ
What the country needs now is the rule of law. It isn't getting it.

By JIM LACEY

When U.S. Special Forces teams went into Afghanistan looking for allies they found a battle-tested, hardened army of veterans waiting for them. All the Northern Alliance needed was leadership, modern communications and the support of devastating American firepower. Within a couple of months, Special Ops troops led Northern Alliance fighters down from their mountain strongholds to sweep away the Taliban and enter Kabul, a success that has become the paradigm of how Special Forces and Air Power in concert can conquer a country. Now the Special Forces are making a similar attempt in Iraq. What they have created so far is a parody of the Northern Alliance—one that should trouble U.S. leaders, and one that could spell trouble for the future stability of Iraq.

In the months before the 3rd Infantry Division crossed the border from Kuwait, Special Forces teams entered Iraq. One of their primary missions was to establish the conditions and train fighters for a revolt in the Shia areas in the south of the country. But they failed to spark the anticipated revolt. In retrospect, it's easy to see why; the Shia have been burned before by what they thought were U.S. promises of support. A Shia rebellion against Saddam in the aftermath of the first Gulf War was brutally suppressed, and no one here, remembering the tens of thousands killed then, was willing to commit to support the U.S. until it was absolutely certain that Saddam was going to be permanently removed as a threat.

Of course, when you get to that point, you really don't need a popular revolt. A Shia uprising was supposed to wipe out the Baath Party and destroy any paramilitary cadres along the line of the Coalition advance. American forces accomplished both of these missions. Still, the Afghanistan model called for a popular revolt, and in An Najaf last week Special Ops soldiers set out to recruit one.

So it was that when American Combat Engineers got ready to blow up the statue of Saddam in the An Najaf city center, two-dozen fighters calling themselves "the Coalition for Iraqi National Unity" were on hand. They rode into the square on top of heavily armed Special Forces Honda trucks, full of smiles and waving to anyone with a camera. Throughout the day they were only too glad to pose for pictures in their newly issued equipment while brandishing AK-47s, often begging to be photographed. They all professed to want Saddam dead and shouted their willingness to fight his forces anywhere in An Najaf. Bold talk, considering the 101st Airborne had just completed sending Saddam's loyalist cadres to the great beyond. I asked one of the Special Forces soldiers how he knew these guys were not fighting for Saddam the day before.

"Some of them probably were," he replied. "But they have had a conversion."

The Coalition for Iraqi National Unity's spokesman, and second in charge, is a cleric who teaches at a local mosque. Even if you accept the power of the clerics in this region, is it really wise to place them in charge of a U.S.-sponsored military force? It seems too great a concentration of power, given the volatile mix of religion and politics in the area.

It didn't help when the cleric, Hassan Mussawi, began talking about his party. Asked about reports that his forces were looting the local people, he responded, "People who accuse us of looting are extremists who are against national unity." The best answer he can come up with when asked about the seven late-model Nissans and a very new looking Mercedes in the courtyard is, "This is what the people give us to fight Saddam." When asked if the U.S. supplies the vast quantities of food his men have on hand he says, "We are self financing; the people give us what we need."

These must be some remarkably generous people to turn over so much food when they have so little themselves, and to give up new cars when the average automobile here is 25 years old. The impoverished masses near the headquarters also turned over chairs, dishes, pots, blankets and a host of other items of everyday living.

Mussawi's army is made up mostly of upper middle-aged men and youngsters, several well under sixteen, in what looks like a father-and-son operation. The first thing one notices about all of the older "patriots" is that none of them have missed a meal in a long time. Given the lean look of the general population, it does not appear that the people taking part in this uprising suffered much under Saddam's regime. In fact, if their waistlines are a measure of success, then these are prosperous men.

Their claims to military prowess are limited to nocturnal raids with Special Forces soldiers to capture or kill Saddam loyalists still in An Najaf. "We try and arrest our enemies," Mussawi says, "but if they resist we have to kill them." To date, everyone appears to have resisted. One of the Special Forces soldiers on the way out to lead one of these nocturnal raids yelled out to a group of reporters, "You guys can make yourselves useful in the morning by washing the blood off our trucks."

When Special Forces soldiers are asked how they know the people being identified are Saddam loyalists, the general reply is, "We have to trust that they know who their enemies are."

Still, their enemies might not be the enemies of the United States or even the people of An Najaf. Almost a week after the city has been liberated, it is hard to comprehend that U.S. Special Forces would condone and maybe even assist in techniques of blind justice when even they admit they do not know much of the history of the people being targeted.

The people of Southern Iraq are overjoyed that America has rescued them from Saddam, but there is no open revolt here. What is here instead is a ragtag group of old men and boys on the U.S. payroll who are likely looting their own people and settling private scores.

With Saddam's power broken, the need for a revolt has passed. By extension there is no need to create a new paramilitary force of uncertain loyalty. It would be better to disarm and disband this little army before it grows, through American largess, into another force to oppress the population here. It is time to give democracy a chance to flourish. That will not happen if armed thugs are allowed to dominate a rebuilding civil society. Special Forces teams have done a lot to assist in the successful invasion of Iraq. However, their military mission in An Najaf is over now and it is time to bring them back under adult supervision. What An Najaf needs now is the rule of law, not continued rule of the gun.

* * * *

EASTER IN BABYLON

The longer we operated in Hillah, the more visitors from other U.S. units showed up for a tour of Babylon. The most frequent and persistent visitors to Hillah were the chaplains of all denominations from across our division. My own chaplain, Captain Scott Brown, was so enamored and awestruck at being this close to biblical Babylon that he found many innovative ways to visit the site as part of his daily rounds.

One day in mid-April, I found out that the brigade chaplains had pooled their resources and were preparing to ask me for permission to conduct Easter Sunrise Services at the Palace Mount overlooking the city of Babylon. Perhaps they sensed this was a proposal that I would find impossible to refuse.

Captain Brown, a Southern Baptist Minister and former Cobra pilot who fought in Desert Storm, was not your typical chaplain. He was older than most captains in the Army, closer to my age. His age, experience and contagiously optimistic and energetic personality made him like an older brother to the soldiers, a role model to the officers and my closest confident and friend. When Captain Brown had an idea, it was impossible to talk him out of it, especially when he was right. He knew our soldiers and their spiritual needs well. The men needed this service; many had killed and most had seen death up close for the first time in their lives. A service of this magnitude was necessary for the psychological health and welfare of the men.

The thought of a Christian Easter Service in Babylon both fascinated and scared the hell out of me, and I worried about taking an unnecessary risk. I worried about pulling it off without causing some sort of international incident, especially moving hundreds of soldiers to the palace without being attacked. The city had been peaceful since April 10 and there were no obvious signs of enemy activity. We were fully engaged with the new Hillah council and there was no apparent reason to believe that the relationship would change any time soon. As a result, I gave tentative approval for the service, but stressed to the staff that the service must be treated like a combat operation. I wanted an operations order, contingency plans for every possible threat, and a concept of operation designed to mitigate any threats that may arise. The planning began in earnest for the first Easter Sunrise Service in Babylon in at least 35 years.

The service brought all faiths in the battalion together on that Easter morning. I even spoke to three young men who didn't believe in any form of religion, but they came to the service because they felt it had historical significance and they wanted to participate. The sunrise was awe-inspiring as it cleared the walls of the ruins and climbed to the palace mount. Captain Brown rose to the occasion, and hundreds of soldiers attended the multiple services on either side of the palace. Men came from *No Slack*, the 2-230th Field Artillery and other units from the brigade who managed to make their way to

Hillah that clear and cool Sunday morning. The operation was flaw-less. I don't think the people of Hillah even noticed the six large grain trucks shuttling soldiers to and from the ruins of Babylon. In any event, the people of Hillah had a religious event of their own to occu-py their minds: the return of the Hajj and the pilgrimage to Karbala.

THE FIRST PILGRIMAGE[13]

The Hillah city council exceeded our greatest expectations. The city came to life over the following weeks with electricity restored, com-merce back on the streets and elaborate preparations for the Shiite pil-grimage, the *Zeyarah*. The Hajj is the Muslim pilgrimage to Mecca made by both Sunnis and Shi'a and is one of the five basic precepts of Islam. Its performance is one of the essentials, and its non-perfor-mance is a grave sin. Shi'a had the additional *Zeyarah* obligation around their annual Ashura, a day of mourning for the loss of Hussayn bin-Ali, the grandson of the Prophet, venerated by the Shi'a as the Third Imam.

Saddam had banned the Hajj Zeyarah during his reign and now tens of thousands of Shi'a were eager to make the pilgrimage to Najaf and Karbala. Intelligence had told us that the pilgrimage had actually started in late February and would run through the end of April, with an anticipated climax in Karbala on or about April 20.

Hillah stood directly in the path of the pilgrimage from Najaf, Diwaniya, Samawah and Kidhir. While the mayor of Hillah expressed great joy about the resumption of the feast, he was also gravely con-cerned. I thought he was concerned that the pilgrims would react badly to an American military presence, but he was much more wor-ried that the citizens of Hillah were not prepared to support the pil-grims themselves. The route needed to be secured and there needed to be ample rest stops in addition to plentiful food and water points for the pilgrims as they passed through. The rest stops throughout Hillah were free and designed to help the tired travelers to present themselves to Allah. If the mayor failed to provide for the pilgrims, he would offend his city and fail in the eyes of Allah.

The challenge now was to support local efforts to bear the resource strain of the pilgrimage while remaining unobtrusively in the background. As I had expected, the Division was not as optimistic about my non-violent assessment of the march and wanted to ensure that our presence in the two holiest cities of Shi'a Islam did not invoke negative and hostile actions by the pilgrims. We therefore took great measures to maintain as low a profile as possible, and only light infantry was allowed along the route—no tanks or Bradleys. Direct visible support to the pilgrims was also forbidden. It was essential that the Iraqis do the Hajj Zeyarah on their own to reestablish confidence in their own abilities and in their local leaders.

The pilgrimage in Hillah would help our new government to gain legitimacy not only within its own community, but with the surrounding communities as well. Our new city government did it alone, and the pilgrimage season came and went with no hostilities and no hitches.

The mayor of Hillah and his executive council were now the legitimate government of Hillah, the first free government in the recent history of Iraq. A small group of brave Iraqi patriots who were more concerned for their fellow Iraqis than their own personal safety conducted this 28-day experiment in freedom, democracy and peace, which continues in Hillah to this day. *No Slack* was justifiably proud of its first successful attempt to help establish a local government. The lessons and tools gained in Hillah would serve us well as we continued to move north.

On April 26, indeed, *No Slack* received orders to resume its march north. The 1st Marine Expeditionary Force (1MEF) was moving south from eastern Baghdad to take control of central Iraq, the Palace of Babylon, and the city of Hillah. The Palace of Babylon would become its headquarters. *No Slack* was relieved by 1st Battalion, 4th Marines, on April 28 and began a 300-mile air/ground movement to Quayyarah West Airfield, 40 miles south of Mosul, Iraq.

The Kurdish Autonomous Zone in northern Iraq, first established by the
United States in 1991.

5

NORTHERN IRAQ

"What do you mean you don't speak Kurdish?"

THE KURDS ARE TOO FAR SOUTH

The flight of helicopters taking us north began to pass over the western edge of Baghdad about twenty minutes into our flight. Sitting on the aluminum floor of the helicopter, I had to rise up on my knees to see the Tigris River out the left door and Highway 8 out the right. It was hard to believe it was over. According to the rumors and reports we were getting from the Iraqis and remaining American press in Hillah, the battle for Baghdad had ended on April 9, 2003. This allegedly occurred after a number of armored Thunder Runs by the 3d Infantry Division had penetrated the inner city, and Saddam's regime had suddenly stopped holding news conferences on TV. Reports confirmed that the same battalions we had relieved in Najaf from Col. David Perkins' 2d Brigade were now in control of the enemy's capital.

From the helicopter window, it did appear that life was returning to normal in Baghdad. The destroyed Iraqi military vehicles were pushed off the highways. The streets were full of people and the roads were clogged with traffic. As we cleared the city, I was shocked to see green palms, wheat and vegetable fields, rice paddies and dozens of roadside farmer markets selling fresh goods. The closeness of the Tigris and Euphrates river basins in this part of the desert gave origin to this famous and ancient city. As I peered off into the distance from the helicopter, the explosion of color below loomed in sharp contrast to the haze of colorless desert on the horizon. It served as a constant symbol of the harshness of this land that its people endured.

The pilots gave me the six-minute warning as we approached the landing zone. The battalion had rehearsed for a forced entry into the Quayyarah West (Q-West) Airfield, not knowing for sure if any retreating Iraqi forces had occupied the area or if it was still abandoned as we'd been told. A team of AH-64 Apache helicopters, which protected our flight north, escorted the lift of Blackhawks carrying my infantrymen. Before the six minute warning, the Apaches had gone forward to observe the landing zones and survey the airfield to ensure that there were no enemy forces that might interdict our air assault. As we braced for a potential fight, I got word over the headset that the airfield was clear and that Major Pat Frank from Brigade had already secured the airfield with a small force the day before. It was good news and we landed in a secure but guarded posture.

Pat met me at the landing zone and gave me a quick rundown of how he planned to lay out the Brigade on the airfield as it arrived by ground and air over the next three days. *No Slack*'s mission was to establish and provide security as the Brigade took over the airfield. First Brigade was to secure the airfield for the Division, which would give Major General Petraeus a significant force outside of Mosul. This force gave the Division the flexibility required for responding to threats along the Iranian and Syrian borders, while also dealing with the initial expansion and aggressiveness of the Kurds.

Unknown to me at the time, the Assistant Division Commander, Brigadier General Benjamin Freakley, was directing the withdrawal of the Kurds from the Mosul region. Apparently the Kurds had come south with the 10th Special Forces Group (SFG) to place pressure on the 5th Iraqi Corps that was defending northern Iraq at the beginning of the war. The Kurds had been instrumental in pinning the Iraqis down in the north and preventing them from turning south to reinforce the defenses of Baghdad—an accomplishment we were very thankful for. But their presence so far south was a violation of their agreement with the 10th SFG and the American government. By being this far south, they were infuriating the Turks, agitating the Iranians, and rekindling hundreds of years of hatred and distrust in this region of the Middle East. To prevent potential conflict and third country intervention, the 101st Airborne Division was given the mission of pushing the Kurds back north of an established zone of separation between the Iraqis and the Kurds called the "Green Line," located across the northeastern quarter of Iraq.

As the Kurdish situation festered, *No Slack* was eventually directed to air assault into an area northwest of Mosul to secure an oil pumping station, oil refinery and water production station, which were being threatened by looters and retreating Kurdish army units. We had unconfirmed reports that Kurdish army units had seized some of these facilities and had failed to withdraw after a formal request from the 101st Airborne Division. The Kurds were exploiting the facilities and were preparing to destroy them on their departure to prevent their use by the same Iraqis who had tormented, gassed and murdered them for the past 25 years. I didn't condone their actions, but I sure understood them.

I reflected again on my studies of Oriental philosophers, this time Tu Mu from the 9th century: "He who excels at resolving difficulties does so before they arise. He who excels in conquering his enemies triumphs before threats materialize." I would soon have an opportunity to test this theory in practice.

On one particular mission, we had Bravo Company air-assault near a water pumping station and oil refinery west of Mosul. Captain New and I landed at the water station and Sergeant First Class Maloney and his platoon landed inside the refinery about three miles to our east. The seizure of the water station was uneventful, but our first reports from the refinery indicated it was under the control of a Kurdish army unit. After surveying the water station, my ground command team arrived with our hummers and sufficient combat power to go to the refinery and see what Maloney's platoon had found. Once I got in my hummer, I could hear Maloney telling New that the refinery was crawling with Kurdish military and they were taking the Iraqi fuel trucks full of benzene and convoying them north.

I mounted up my command team and two heavy weapon vehicles from Delta Company and quickly moved to the refinery. While en route, I contacted the Apaches that had escorted us during the air assault and told them to move to the refinery in order to protect Maloney's platoon and give me a head count of the Kurds. I was especially interested in the possibility the Kurds had tanks or armored personnel carriers. I didn't want to pick a fight, but they weren't supposed to be this far south and my orders were clear: "All Kurdish units must move north of the green line without delay."

When I reached the refinery, it was immediately clear that a significant Kurdish force was guarding the refinery compound. Maloney's platoon was in an "over-watch" position on a berm within the refinery and was prepared to attack the Kurds if my discussions failed. The road to the refinery curved around the outside of a perimeter fence and ended at a two-lane blacktop road. This blacktop road was a main highway into Mosul and led north to the green line. Leading with the heavy weapons, we drove down the road to the front gate and positioned across the street from the main entrance of the refinery. When we pulled up, my Air Force sergeant confirmed that he had two F-16s with 1,000-pound bombs on board if we got in trouble. They would remain on station for 30 minutes.

As I got out of my hummer, a 5,000-gallon Iraqi gas truck pulled out of the facility and turned up the road to the north. We had caught them in the act . . . they were obviously stealing the fuel, along with the trucks and anything else they could take north. As I walked across the street, I turned to Major Jim Crider, "They look like a junior ROTC detachment, but with guns!"

The Kurdish soldier at the front gate had two belts of machine gun bullets wrapped around his torso, crossing at his chest like the Frito Bandito. The others around him were similarly dressed and armed with heavy machine guns, grenades hanging on them in John Wayne fashion, and wearing a mixture of military and civilian clothes. A second gas truck was at the main gate preparing to leave when I approached. I waved to the driver and guards and told them in English, "Stop the truck."

The Kurds were cautious, but they seemed to understand my order and stopped the truck inside the compound. Once they stopped short of the front gate, I motioned to the rank on my helmet and asked if I could speak to someone in charge. When there was no response from the exterior guards, I asked the Frito Bandito if I could speak to his commander. Without hesitation, he motioned for another man to go to the guard house. When he emerged, he had a short, gray-haired man in tow with no hat, weapons or military markings on his flat green uniform. The man grunted at me and waved for me to enter the compound. Feeling less than comfortable facing down this group with only my 9mm pistol, I waved for him to come out and talk to me.

"No, no," he said, waving again for me to come in. Reluctantly I entered the compound with Jim, Sergeant First Class Wilson and my new linguist. There were eight more Kurds inside the guardhouse and, after passing the gate, I could see another 15 or 20 by the trucks near the gas pumps.

"I count 30," said Jim discreetly.

"Yeah, me too," I whispered as we entered the shack. "Wilson, keep your eyes peeled."

"Roger sir."

Now that we were in the shack I decided to take the initiative. "My name is Lieutenant Colonel Hughes from the United States. I've been sent here by the commander of the 101st Airborne Division." After a slight pause to wait for my linguist to do his thing, I stopped. Realizing that my linguist was not translating, I turned around, "Well, tell him what I said!"

"I don't speak Kurdish, I'm an Arabic linguist," he said, shrugging his shoulders as if to say, "Duh, colonel!"

God, I missed Kadhim. He would have at least told me the Kurds didn't speak Arabic. I never thought to ask this guy if he spoke Kurdish. It never occurred to me that two ancient cultures within the same country would not know how to speak to each other.

"Someone must speak English or Arabic. Do any of you guys speak English?" I asked. The men in the shack gave me a deadpan look; I was really starting to believe that no one spoke Arabic or English except me and this stupid linguist who had suddenly become nothing more than a paperweight. These guards were a tough crowd and I was having a hard time even drawing a smile from them. I motioned for the gray-haired guy to use his phone in hopes he could call someone to speak with us. Luckily, he seemed to understand and made the call.

When he finished speaking, he pointed at his wristwatch to show me a time, which I assumed was the arrival time for the person he had called. I decided not to waste any more effort with this group and went back to my vehicle to see who or what would show up at the given time.

Meanwhile, my communications guy had set up our satellite radio to give a report to Division in hopes they could find us a Kurdish linguist. As we waited for the guys at Division to find a Kurdish liaison officer, we stood across the street and continued to count the number of Kurds in the refinery. Moments later, Maloney reported that a large group of armed Kurds was entering the western end of the refinery and heading our way. Suddenly 30 Kurds became 70, then 100; eventually over 120 Kurds were visible inside the compound. Moments later, a convoy of Mercedes sedans and Toyota pickup trucks sped into the refinery. I looked at Jim and said, "Well, they either have someone who can speak English or someone who can order them to attack. Get ready for both."

I walked toward the men exiting the sedans. The gray-haired man had his hat on now and saluted the newcomers as they exited their cars. He spoke to them briefly and then motioned to me standing in the middle of the road. The men gathered themselves and began to walk toward me.

The roles of the three men who approached me were obvious. The tall man in uniform was the senior Kurdish commander in the area. He wore the rank of a one-star general, but didn't speak. The second man, a skinny weasel of a guy, appeared to be the older man's son or advisor. I was hoping he spoke English. And the older man, dressed in a double breasted suit, was the Kurdish elder or elected leader. He was the only Kurd who smiled at me that day. He took my hand and shook it hard, and with his huge yellow teeth said "Hello" in English. His second sentence was in Kurdish.

For ten minutes the three of us tried to find a way to communicate. Hand gestures, drawing pictures in notebooks, pointing to the four winds, and even pretending to get in a car and driving north. My only message was for them to leave this place and go north of the Green Line. Their only message was that they didn't understand my message. So we decided to wait for a linguist on the radio with Division. As the wait dragged out, I got frustrated as the Kurds started to resume their thievery by trying to sneak refinery equipment out the back gate of the facility. Maloney spotted them and reported over the radio that they were filling three of the large tanker trucks with fuel from the front gate. I had to put an end to this, but it seemed impossible without the ability to communicate. The chances of sparking a firefight were increasing.

After meeting dozens of English speaking Iraqis on our trek north, I found it hard to believe that these obviously educated men didn't speak English, or at least Arabic, so I devised a plan to make them talk or act. I took the radio and told the Apache commander to land his three helicopters behind my position in the middle of a wheat field facing the refinery. Minutes later, the three birds began to land. It was an impressive and intimidating sight. Acting as if this kind of activity was an everyday occurrence, I ignored the Apaches and continued to talk on the radio. I was in contact with my good friend, the senior operations officer for the Division, Lieutenant Colonel Ricky Gibbs. Ricky was aware of my situation and was desperately trying to find a Kurdish linguist in the Division command post. They had one, but no one could find the guy to get him on the radio in order to tell these guys in Kurdish to leave the refinery. As we spoke, I watched the leader of the group and the Kurdish general discussing their options for dealing with the situation. The Kurds had more than 200 men in the refinery by now, and additional Kurds continued to arrive by pick-up truck and taxi as the situation dragged on.

It was time to get tough and let them know I'd had enough—it was time for them to leave and I had to show them I wasn't bluffing. I got on my radio and told the Apache commander to take off and hover his aircraft behind my hummer at about 200 feet. I needed to convince the Kurdish commander that I would kick his ass if he wanted to start a fight. I needed a display of power, so I enlisted the Apache commander's help.

"You guys watch my hands. When I motion right, you bank right; when I motion left, bank left; when I circle my arm over my head, take your aircraft and circle the Kurds and me. Let's give 'em a good scare." My final instruction would clear up the situation if things went wrong: "If I drop to the ground it means they shot me—kill every Kurd in the compound. You guys got that?"

"Roger that sir."

Jim flashed me his famous cautionary look, and without a word walked behind the hummer and prepared the men for a possible shoot-out with the Kurds. The two heavy weapon vehicles were ready to cover the front gate with their .50 caliber machine guns and automatic grenade launchers. Two F-16s were on station at 5,000 feet, and Maloney was in position to attack the Kurds from their rear and could block the Kurds from reinforcing the front gate. We were ready to call their bluff or force them to comply with our orders.

I walked across the road toward the three men and their body guards next to the three Mercedes. I stopped about 50 feet short of the Kurds and slowly lifted my left arm and pointed. The Apache abruptly lurched from the wheat field and banked hard to its left for about 100 yards and then leveled-off as it swiveled its Gatling gun back and forth at the group of Kurdish leaders. Without losing eye contact with the group, I repeated the signal with my right arm, and again the Apache banked hard and locked into position in strict compliance to my hand signals. I never looked back and kept my stare on the men. We obviously had their attention now and I could see the concern in their faces. The talking was over . . . it was time to comply or die, and I only had one last move up my sleeve short of fighting. I raised my arm and circled it over my head. The Apache slowly began to circle the Kurds with its gun fixed on the cars like a hawk preparing to strike.

"I've got three of these bastards and they do whatever I tell them to do . . . NOW what the FUCK do you got? I'm tired of fuckin' talking! Get your shit and get north of the green line before I really get pissed!"

The three of them had crouched behind their cars and now cautiously began to straighten up as the Apache slowly circled the front gate. At the sight of the Apache and my yelling, the weasely guy suddenly spoke up—in English!

"You want us to leave? I'm sorry, we didn't understand. We are friends . . . we will leave."

"You bet your ass I want you to leave. I want you to leave now! Leave the benzene behind and get north of the green line. NOW! Do you understand?"

"We understand."

And with that, the older man quickly gave instructions to the gray-haired man, and the three Kurdish leaders departed north in their convoy of sedans. There were no pleasantries, just an immediate compliance to my orders. The first group of Kurdish soldiers to follow them left in dozens of white Toyota pickup trucks and sedans. After that, the lower enlisted men came out of the refinery and walked to a bus stop about 500 yards from the front gate. Carrying their guns and ammo, they took the next public bus going north. The final group that exited the refinery flagged down taxis at the front gate and drove north as well. I had never seen anything like it, but in less than an hour they were gone.

Back at the vehicle, Sergeant Bowers told me General Freakley was flying to our location and would be here in less than two minutes with a Kurdish linguist. Jim and I looked at each other, paused, and then burst into laughter. "Those sons-of-bitches spoke English the whole time. I should have shot 'em," I said.

It was a sudden release of nervous emotion and anxiety. I sat down in my hummer and felt a rush of relief shiver up my spine. Just then, Sergeant First Class Wilson walked up to Jim and me, leaning against the hummer, and with a deep breath and sigh said, "Sir that's the scaredest I've ever been in my life. I thought we were all dead. Let's not do that again, please!"

Nearly a year later I would be asked in Washington, DC if there was one technology the US industrial base could invest in to make a difference in Iraq. In reply I stated: "I cannot fathom how Captain James T. Kirk of the Starship *Enterprise* can fly anywhere in the galaxy, meet an alien race and simply hit his lapel pen to hold an intelligent conversation, yet with all our technology I cannot intelligently communicate with a race of people we have known throughout our entire existence as a nation. Take all the money you're wasting on counter-IED gizmos and give me one good English-to-Arabic translation devise, and we can cut the violence by 80 percent. Most of the violence in Iraq is due to a lack of communication!"

OPERATION EINDHOVEN

A week after the incident with the Kurdish army, *No Slack* was ordered to conduct a battalion air assault into an area northwest of Q-West airfield nicknamed Eindhoven. Colonel Hodges named this key area south of Mosul Area of Operations (AO) Eindhoven in honor of the 101st's role in Operation Market Garden during WWII. Market Garden was the largest airborne invasion in history, intended to seize key bridges in Holland leading to the Ruhr, the German industrial heartland, in an attempt to end the war before Christmas in 1944.

In northern Iraq, AO Eindhoven and AO Veghel (named after another embattled Dutch town) dominated the key north/south roads along the Tigris River from Tikrit to Mosul and was a major thruway for the Iraqi army prior to our arrival. It was believed that Izzat Ibrahim Al-Duri was using the Tigris Valley and highway system in Eindhoven to hide in and coordinate Iraqi resistance against Coalition forces in Baghdad.

To our south, AO Veghel was key because it contained the only bridge across the Tigris between Tikrit and Mosul, in the town of Quayyarah. This key bridge facilitated trade and east-west movement across the Tigris between the Kurdish Green Zone near Irbil and Mosul. The combination of Eindhoven and Veghel gave 1st Brigade responsibility for over 25,000 square kilometers of terrain south of Mosul. Eindhoven, which was *No Slack*'s area of responsibility, covered over 11,000 square kilometers. It was also the home region of 60 percent of the Iraqi officers' corps; it was the heart of Sunni country. I soon learned that this district had a tradition of service to the Iraqi army and took great pride in its historical service to Iraq. Ninety percent of the town leaders, upon whom I would eventually come to rely and trust, were not only Sunnis but retired and former Iraqi officers.

The air assault into Eindhoven took over three hours, with Charlie Company attacking to seize the town of Ash Shurah, Bravo Company the village of Shuryrat, and Alpha Company the town of Al Hawil. The battalion scout platoon and snipers were sent to the outskirts of Sayyid Awyah, and Delta Company launched a ground assault across the Quayyarah bridge to secure the road network east of the Tigris River. The initial assault into Eindhoven met no resistance, but there was a guarded curiosity by the citizens of each of the three towns we now occupied. Once it became clear we would face no organized resistance, the brigade extracted the covering artillery battery. I ordered the commanders to attempt to make contact with local leaders and begin to conduct initial assessments of their towns to determine what type of humanitarian assistance was needed.

As the companies entered the towns, we no longer needed to maintain an airborne command aloft, so I landed and set up a forward battalion command post in the rolling wheat fields west of Ash Shurah. The ground command team linked up with us and we began to establish radio relay sites to ensure communications with brigade in the event we needed attack helicopters and artillery support. While establishing the command post, I received a report that an armed convoy of three vehicles—two white Toyota pickup trucks, with approximately fourteen armed Iraqis in the back, and a black Mercedes—was quickly approaching Ash h from the east.

Captain Konz had already established a blocking position east of Ash Shurah using a railroad overpass with a platoon of infantry and a heavy weapons platoon from Delta Company. I ordered two division Apache attack helicopters on station to drop to Konz's company radio frequency and work directly with him to stop the unknown group of vehicles from approaching his position. I then moved my mobile command post to the railroad overpass to collocate with Captain Konz.

As I arrived, the Apaches were targeting the convoy from behind a railroad berm and passing news of their progress to Matt Konz. Matt had established a strong position and would easily dispatch this group if they became hostile. We could not see them as they approached because of a hill to our front, so we relied on the Apache progress reports. Suddenly the three vehicles broke the horizon to our front about half a mile away. They suddenly veered to their left and crossed to our front along a small road, bypassing the road leading into Ash Shurah and moving south at high speed.

As this happened, Captain Konz sprang his trap. The Apaches appeared from behind the elevated railroad tracks and the heavy weapon vehicles moved out of their hide positions so the Mercedes could clearly see them. The three vehicles suddenly came to a quick stop in a cloud of dust and sand. An oddly calm moment passed, and then the rear door to the black Mercedes abruptly opened. A well dressed man calmly stepped out of the car, looked up at the helicopter, and motioned to his guards. Five of the armed guards jumped out of the first pickup and moved to the Mercedes. As we braced for what looked like a possible attack, the man adjusted his dark sunglasses, buttoned his suit jacket, and turned away from us as he walked up a small hill next to his car. That's when I first noticed that the hill was a cemetery.

Captain Konz ordered his men to hold their fire as we watched the man and his guards walk up the hill and then as he demonstratively displayed his respects to a grave near the top. He was only at the grave for a few minutes, but he openly prostrated himself and it was quite obvious he wanted people to see him. Just as suddenly, he returned to his car. Once he reached his car, he motioned for his guards to get back in the pickup and he moved slowly to the front of his vehicle and held up a piece of paper toward Captain Konz's men.

Konz ordered one of the heavy weapons vehicles to move forward and determine the Iraqi's intent. The platoon leader in the vehicle collected the paper, moved to his radio, and read the paper to Captain Konz and me. The note was a message from General Petraeus and the letter granted this man, Marsham Al Jubari, and his security detail unfettered movement within the 101st area of operation. The letter of introduction from my commanding general, on an official two star letterhead, seemed authentic enough, so I moved forward to meet Mr. Al Jubari and ask him his intent.

When I arrived, much to my surprise, Mr. Al Jubari walked up to me, shook my hand and welcomed me to the Ninawa Province of Iraq, all in fluent English. Mr. Al Jubari told me he had been in exile since 1993 and had just returned to Iraq prior to the 101st's arrival in Mosul. He told me Ash Shurah was his hometown and that he was paying respects to his mother's grave. He also told me he was on his way to meet with local sheiks and tribal leaders in East Ash Shurah. Without hesitation, he invited me to accompany him to a luncheon so he could introduce me to the community leaders.

Although this was not my first invitation to a luncheon with local Iraqi leaders, it was a very tenuous situation considering we hadn't secured East Ash Shurah. Furthermore, this man had fourteen armed guards in uniforms that were hidden away in cars, and we were in a Sunni Province.

I did not have confirmation of his legitimacy from brigade yet, but this was an exceptional opportunity that would get my foot in the door with the local leaders. Moreover, it would also help me establish a relationship with an opportunist from Mosul with international connections. Marsham was clearly a wealthy businessman who had returned home with an agenda, and I hoped to figure out what it was and leverage it to our advantage in the future.

My command team followed Mr. Al Jubari's convoy up the road to the small town called East Ash Shurah, where we were met by a few dozen family members in the street and led to the Al Jubari family meeting hall. While en route, I contacted Captain Konz on the radio and put him in charge of securing the area. He also needed to report the meeting and location to brigade to let Colonel Hodges know we had made contact with what appeared to be an influential group of tribal leaders. Matt and I quickly discussed a contingency plan if the meeting turned sour. It outlined a simple procedure: "You stay close enough to hear shots; if you hear shots, come get me and Major Crider out of there; or if we're not back in an hour, come in and get us."

As Major James Crider and I were preparing to leave my vehicle, we quickly discussed our nonverbal strategy: smile, don't appear afraid, don't expose the bottom of your feet, avoid discussing Saddam, eat whatever they put in front of you, and remove your combat gear. Jim and I were nervous about being in such close company with twenty unknown Iraqis, but realized we had to take the risk. Kadhim would have made this much easier, but he was needed at brigade.

Iraqi meeting halls are normally 20-foot by 60-foot tile floor rooms lined with rugs, sitting pillows, and adorned with pictures and maps of the tribe's former sheiks, martyrs, families' lands, and political contacts within the government or occupation force. This hall had numerous pictures of the family sheiks from the Al Jubari tribe with British commanders from the early 1900s, Iraqi leaders and princes from the mid-1930s, and the most recent picture of the sheik's father smiling and shaking hands with Saddam Hussein and his former vice president, Izzat Al-Duri, in a reception line. Marsham and an elderly gentleman awkwardly smiled at me when I stopped and looked at the picture, and then motioned for me to sit at the head of the room to Marsham's right. As I worked my way to the front of the room, Marsham was being hugged and kissed by his elders, cousins and brothers like a conquering hero.

When Jim and I were shown to our pillows, we slowly and confidently removed our combat gear. We had to act self-assured within the sanctuary of Al Jubari's hospitality by removing our body armor and helmets and leaning our rifles against the wall in the corner of the room. Even so, neither of us relinquished our side arms, but we forced a smile. We also constantly scanned the room and kept our backs against the wall. As Marsham started to talk to his family in Arabic, I mentally worked through at least four horrific scenarios on how to fight and escape if things got ugly. I know Jim was thinking through many more as I began to speak to the audience in an attempt to make our intent known.

FOG, FRICTION, AND LUCK

Another 9th-century Chinese philosopher, Chang Yu, came to mind at this juncture with his words: "Benevolence and righteousness may be used to govern a state but cannot be used to administer an army. Expediency and flexibility are used in administering an army, but cannot be used in governing a state."

The chance meeting with Marsham Al Jubari and his tribe had once again proven to the battalion that detailed planning was essential in combat, but luck was the great equalizer in war. The Al-Jubari tribe helped the battalion to establish credible contacts throughout Eindhoven and aided in the quick return of local Iraqi police forces, city shops and stores, public utilities, propane and food distribution, reopening of schools, markets and gas stations, and establishing conditions for the elections of local officials.

Even though Ash Shurah was our center of gravity within Eindhoven, Hammam Al Alil, in our northern sector, was our largest and most hostile city. As reports started to come in that the Agricultural University in Hammam Al Alil was being looted, I had to dispatch Charlie Company north quicker than planned, which forced us to adjust the relationships within our sector to control Hammam Al Alil. This meant that Captain Matt Konz would have to leave Ash Shurah and Captain Anthony New, the Bravo Company commander, would now have to begin to build relationships and trust in Ash Shurah as well as the other cities he was already responsible for. This transition would cost us time, both operationally and personally, because I would have to get more involved in the day-to-day activities of Ash

Shurah to help Captain New gain credibility with Sheik Ahmed Al Jubari.

Experience had taught me to avoid changes in relationships during stability and support operations if possible. Relationship changes can cause a loss in momentum and set an operation back weeks as trust and confidence is reestablished. But this particular change was mission critical in order to support the 101st Division's role in Mosul. While Hammam was not our center of gravity, it was a burr under General Petraeus' saddle because some of the most influential leaders in Mosul were from Hammam. Notable Hammam leaders came from the local academic community and were using the Agricultural University looting as a rallying point for complaints about the reconstruction of Mosul. My boss didn't need this distraction while working to stabilize Mosul, so I took the risk of changing relationships by sending Captain Konz to take control of Hammam Al Alil and the Agricultural University while expanding Captain New's area of operation to include Ash Shurah.

THE WILD, WILD WEST—HAMMUM AL ALIL

Hammam Al Alil straddled the Tigris River and was a major hub of trade and commerce for Mosul. Human intelligence sources told us that a large majority of young men from the 5th Iraqi Corps, who initially fought and then disbanded to the north of Mosul, lived in Hammam Al Alil. Though they had left their pride on the battlefield, they returned home with their weapons.

As Charlie Company approached the Agricultural University on the outskirts of Hammam, the Apaches reported hundreds of looters tearing the campus apart. Reacting to the report, Captain Konz quickly dismounted his troops from trucks and maneuvered his force. The looters were quickly surrounded and pinned against a perimeter wall around the campus. In very short order, using helicopters, infantry, heavy weapons hummers and a loudspeaker team, Konz managed to quell the trapped mob without a shot and took dozens of detainees.

As I entered the University Campus, it was obvious that the looting had gone on for several days before our arrival. Scarcely anything was left except the buildings. Even the windows and doorframes were gone. As Major Crider and I turned down one street, we saw two men dragging an entire street light pole across a small field. The two men were not afraid and stopped to look at us like two deer spotting their first car. I couldn't resist. I got out of my hummer and motioned for Specialist Carr to join me as I walked toward the men.

"Carr, please ask these guys where they're taking this light pole?"

After a short discussion with the two men, she looked at me and said, "They are taking it home so they can have some light."

"What? How do they plan to do that?"

"They seem to believe that if they take it to their home and stand it up in their front yard, they will have light tonight!"

"Oh, well if they're willing to drag it home . . . please tell them I said good luck. Won't they be surprised when it doesn't light up when it gets dark tonight?"

I turned to Jim and we tried not to laugh.

Meanwhile, Captain Konz had seized two three-story buildings and was preparing to defend the university from the remnants of the library and administration building. As I drove closer to his position, a man who spoke fluent English approached my vehicle and began to provide me with specific information about people in the crowd and what had happened prior to our arrival, and he warned me about the armed Iraqi soldiers downtown. His name was Dr. Majorid Al Gomer. Dr. Gomer was a professor at the University who had been thrown out of his home a couple of days before our arrival. Three armed Iraqi army defectors who were part of a larger group had entered the University staff's housing complex, terrorizing them and forcing them to leave their homes. He was quite happy to see us and asked for our help in taking back their homes.

As we had learned in Hillah, each town, village, and city was different. Each had formal and informal leaders, and each had different needs. Saddam's regime, and local clergy had controlled each differently. Family feuds and hatreds had been suppressed under Saddam, and in some cases his fall signaled the time to settle old scores between villages and families. Even though each group, tribe, and city was different, they all had one thing in common: They all had lived in a social welfare state for over 25 years.

In the case of the Agricultural University, Dr. Gomer's claims were well-founded and we managed to peacefully return the university professors and their families to their homes on campus. By helping the professors, Charlie Company, principally Captain Konz, gained instant credibility with the university professors, staff and the local community near the vicinity of the campus. As Matt's credibility grew, he was able to get the people of the town to return looted university equipment. The largest theft was the hundreds of books from the library, which came back one truck at a time for four days.

THE CLASH OF SOCIALISM AND DEMOCRACY

After surveying the cities and villages in our sector, I had to develop a strategy: Not a plan of operation, but a strategy to establish the right conditions for the citizens in my sector to best govern and prosper from their newfound freedom. The dilemma would be suppressing old habits that prevented progress, while also dampening appetites for all the goodies they were just now discovering. The surge of satellite TV dishes in our sector was introducing Western culture and all the material goods it had to offer. Democratization was taking a back seat to the desire for material things. Freedom meant no law in their eyes, and that attitude was the genesis of the less-than-honorable push of the limits of the society, which had yet to define itself.

Unknown to most Americans, including Congress, every Iraqi man, women and child had a chit or ration card and was paid a salary based on their compliance with and support of Saddam Hussein and his brutal regime. The Iraqi people were conditioned to believe that all substance came from the government. This social dependence on the government, a mythical dependence, made even the simplest tasks hard for the battalion. The citizens of Iraq were used to seeing monetary reimbursement for compliance, which was not the way American forces planned to reestablish Iraqi leadership. Worse, Iraqis seemed to expect that since we were now in charge, we would soon begin disbursing money and showering goods upon them.

As the hot days of summer dragged on, what were initially requests for help and assistance from the Iraqi citizens began to grow into a numbing drone of constant demands and complaints levied on the soldiers of *No Slack*. These demands were not simple to solve.

Most were common services that we as Americans have all come to expect and take for granted. However, it was incredibly hard to deliver these services in a country that had never had them before our arrival. Suddenly, they demanded them because they now lived in a "democracy." Providing clean water, building new medical clinics, road construction, and completing power plants along the Tigris, begun but never finished by Saddam, became *No Slack*'s new priorities. It was frustrating for my soldiers to work night and day to provide these services while never seeing the Iraqis take any initiative to improve their own lives.

In an attempt to determine our priorities in the sector and curb the ever-growing appetite of the Iraqi sheiks, I decided to have my first regional meeting to find ways to work together with the Iraqis, combining our efforts between villages and tribes. During this first meeting my staff and I quickly learned that the war for Iraq was far from over. Not the current war to remove Saddam; rather, the problem was the ongoing war that had raged in this land for over 4,000 years, long before our arrival. This was a war that, when not repelling or resisting invaders, was among fierce people spoiling for a fight *with somebody—anybody!*

It was our first meeting and we decided to have it in the town of Ash Shurah, not for any particular reason other than its central location and the security of its police station. I already had Bravo Company guarding the police station and it had a perfect courtyard that we could use for the meeting. All was going well as the sheiks arrived and jockeyed for position in the row of chairs and couches we had managed to find the night before. Once the meeting began, all was cordial and respectful as we discussed the ongoing projects and the purpose of our newly developed Civil Military Operations Center.

As the meeting wore on and the questions from the sheiks continued to focus only on what would benefit them and their tribes, it happened. One of the sheiks in the second row suddenly took off one of his sandals and slapped a sheik in the front row in the back of his head. The fight was on, not just amongst the two sheiks, but with their sons who were along the wall in the background. For a tense five or six minutes, shoes were flying and men were yelling and pushing, but with no real physical contact or fighting, kind of like the World

Wrestling Federation. I stood in front of the gaggle waiting for a solution to present itself. With nothing else up my sleeve, I decided to whistle as loud as I could—and I have met few others who can whistle louder than I—to see if it would startle them enough to stop out of pure curiosity. It worked. They all stopped mid-conflict and looked at me. In the most disgusted fatherly look I could muster—one that withers my children and junior subordinates—I motioned for them all to sit down. Reluctantly they did and we quickly concluded the meeting to get them on their way before anything else stupid could happen.

Later that afternoon when all had settled down, I sat with Armer, the Ash Shurah police chief, and asked him what the fight was really about. He told me the son of the sheik who had started the fight was stupid and unable to work or raise a family because the son of the other sheik had hit him in the head with a shovel ten years earlier. I told him that seemed like a long time to hold a grudge, and today was an odd time to bring it up. He then told me that the shovel incident was only the reason the fight had started; as it continued the two sheiks had covered two entire centuries of atrocities their mutual tribes had levied on each other. Armer then looked at me seriously and said, "You don't insult someone with the sole of your shoe for just one son. You do it for your tribe and your beloved ancestors. Arabs never forget. They pay their debts and punish those who dishonor their tribe."

The incident took me back to Macedonia in 1994 when I first learned about historical hatred. While on patrol with a Macedonian captain in the hills along the Macedonian/Serbian (at the time) border, the captain stopped and pointed at a city along the border and said, "This conflict will not end until those Albanian squatters leave Macedonia."

Trying to understand the root of this conflict after the fall of the Iron Curtain, I queried the captain about the Albanians, their Islamic faith, and the wars they had fought with Christians in what I had always known as Yugoslavia. As we discussed his history and hatred for all things Albanian, I scanned the city of over 100,000 citizens with my binoculars in search of a tent city, a slum, or anything that looked like a concentration of Albanian squatters. All I could see was a rather modern city, like one you would see in southern Germany; it was actually a beautiful city considering the ongoing conflict. What came next would remain with me forever and become the baseline of my understanding of the hatreds in Iraq.

The conversation between the Macedonian captain and me went something like this: "What squatters are you talking about, I don't see any squatters?" "They are right there in the city . . . they are all over the city, can't you see them?" "All I see are the people who live in the city." "Yes, that's them." "You mean the whole city?" "Yes, the whole city." "Who built the city?" "They did." "When?" "Six hundred years ago after we lost at The Field of Black Birds [Kosovo Polje]."

"You're kidding," I responded. "You're still pissed about a battle you lost over 600 years ago . . . you have got to get over it."

"Never. They will either leave or my men and I will kill them all to avenge my family. Aren't you a Christian?"

"Yes, but I don't hate because of religion."

"Oh. I'm sorry. I thought that was why you came to Macedonia—to rid the land of the Albanians."

BRINGING IN THE SHEAVES—THE NATIONAL HARVEST

Understanding the hatred of the Iraqis amongst their religions, their tribes, the Kurds and Turkmen, and their neighbors in Iran and Syria was only aggravated and complicated by the scarcity of resources we discovered upon our arrival in northern Iraq. The one that became the most urgent, and also complicated, was the pending wheat and barley harvest. Within days of arriving in Mosul, Major General Petraeus and his division staff found themselves not only trying to form a government but finding innovative ways of reopening international markets and negotiating prices for the Iraqi grain we suddenly found ourselves responsible for with the Syrians and the greater Middle East.

General Petraeus' negotiations over the wheat and barley harvests were preceded by buying benzene and trading propane with the Syrian and Turkish governments in an attempt to reestablish trade and normalize northern Iraq. The propane and benzene would allow the Iraqis to cook their food and use their cars to move goods and provide services that had broken down during the invasion. I remember looking on in amazement and asking myself, "Can we do that? Our own country doesn't even trade with the Syrians, do we?'

It was mind boggling and fascinating to me that an infantry division was actually supporting a massive grain harvest, facilitating the reintroduction of Soviet-style collective farming while arbitrating land disputes between the Iraqi Arabs and Kurds. Never in my career did I ever believe I would be responsible for the livelihood of a quarter million people, and finding myself anxiously awaiting the grain prices from my division commander.

Although I had my hands full in my sector putting out wheat fires and facilitating the movement of combines between fields, my brother battalion commander, Lt. Colonel Marcus De Oliveira, had a far more complicated task to accomplish. Marcus' battalion was charged to find all the consolidated communal farming locations, account for all the regional combines, register the combine operators, license the combines, track the fields and ensure the crops were collected in the right order, measure the harvest when it was returned, store the wheat in these huge silos and holding pits, and lastly, yet most importantly, ensure that the Kurds were not coming south stealing the Arab wheat.

Marcus' battalion, 1-327th known as *"Above the Rest,"* straddled the Kurdish green line and required some innovative thinking and doing. And it was not the kind of innovation they teach at the Army Infantry Officers Advance Course . . . well at least not in the '80s when Marcus and I were young captains. I pray they do now.

When I first visited Marcus' massive operation I was immediately impressed, and being from Iowa I was a bit envious and homesick. But that quickly passed when one of Marcus' captains walked me through his operation. Marcus wasn't at the silos because he was up north adjudicating a dispute between some Kurdish officials and two Iraqi sheiks. I watched the grain arriving and being dumped into football field-sized concrete pits. Tons of wheat coming in by the truckload; it was as if the entire crop had come due at the same time.

It was then that I noticed Marcus' infantrymen around the compound. Here were America's finest infantry, honed to a razors edge, battle hardened, tending to the harvest. Yes, there were dozens of locals hired to assist, but this was still early in the war and we had to innovate. Marcus' battalion and the other battalions in the division had a distinctly American resource—plenty of Midwestern farm boys in both the officer corps and the enlisted ranks. Harvesting would be a form of creative play for our resourceful men after the stress of campaigning and combat. In the 101st we were all now demonstrating the genius of American creativity and improvisation.

Sorting out education majors, accounting degrees and agricultural degrees were just some of the new tasks we were forced to assign to our junior officers and our soldiers. We would ask who knows how to run a truck scale, ever paid wages before, how much is a metric ton? This was not soldier work, but only soldiers could do it. Our men knew that the quicker we got the job done the quicker we got to go home. Marcus' men were transformed into heavily armed farmers, truck drivers, scale operators, vehicle inspectors, crane and bulldozer operators and police. They were truly "Above the Rest!"

When I enquired about the wheat silos, a young captain told me they were not functional and would take over five million dollars and two years to repair. Fascinated by their size and puzzled as to why they were painted in a camouflage pattern, I couldn't resist going inside to inspect them, having seen more than a few in my home town of Red Oak, Iowa. I was shocked at what I found. They were completely gutted and in disrepair. It was typical of what I had seen in the oil pumping stations in my sector and with all the transformer stations and water production facilities. The destruction of the silos was not new, it appeared to be tens of years old, and despite their ominous appearance from the outside, they were worthless. It would have been cheaper to build new ones.

As I returned to the headquarters building two helicopters were making an approach to the grain warehouse. I thought it was Marcus returning from his meeting, but much to my surprise a group with two sniper teams exited the aircraft and moved to a small building in the compound. I stopped what I was doing and went to the shack to see who they were. When I entered the shack, they were surprised to see me and quickly introduced themselves as Marcus' scout platoon. What was next would stick with me for as long as I live. I asked their mission and why they were airborne with their snipers.

The young lieutenant explained their unconventional mission with much pride, despite the obvious disillusionment in the eyes of his snipers. Their mission was to conduct airborne sniper missions against the combines in their sector. They launched daily with their sniper

The author,
Colonel Christoper P. Hughes.

The late Master Sergeant
Dan Maloney.

The famous "Stitch and Bitch" in the battalion classroom. Marguerite
Hughes in the middle directing deliveries.

CSM Richard Montcalm raising the *No Slack* battle flag over Camp Pennsylvania in Kuwait, March 2003.

A squad from Bravo Company (Bayonets) in Kuwait before the invasion.

The all-too-common Scud Bunker drill in Kuwait.

Sandstorms became an occupational hazard while on the move in Iraq.

The enemy attempted to slow our progress with berms across highways.

Approaching the scene of battle at Najaf.

No Slack troops on the 54-hour ground assault to Najaf, March 2003.

Bravo Company preparing to move to the Mosque of Ali to negotiate a Fatwa to stop the fighting in Najaf and southern Iraq.

War Wagons arrive in Hillah behind the armor assault.

The effect of two Air Force 2,000-pound bombs.

Al Hadar, above, and Nemrud, right, 4,000-year-old Sumerian archeological sites, under *No Slack*'s control south of Mosul.

The partly reconstructed Babylon as it looks today.

A bathroom in one of
Saddam Hussein's
captured palaces.

Major Jim Crider and LTC Hughes with the ever-present embedded
reporters, Garwin McLucky and Stuart Ramsey of Skynews.

Issuing attack orders before the assault on Najaf.

A painting of the assault on Najaf by artist James Dietz.

Typical vehicle in a ground assault convoy—no wasted space.

This road intersection west of Hillah served as a 3rd Brigade rally point.

A warm greeting to *No Slack* from the children of Najaf.

Quayyarrah West Command Post.

101st Air Assault team in action.

No Slack Chemical Officer and NCO inspecting three captured Frog 7 ballistic missile systems to ensure they are not chemical warheads. The two photos were taken in May 2003.

First meeting with the newly elected government of Hillah, the first government established in Iraq after the fall of Saddam. *No Slack* formed the government without orders; later the process became standard.

One of the first meetings of the new Hillah City Council.

CW2 Bermia, the unsung hero of the Battalion as head of the vehicle maintenance team.

Bob Bevelacqua (right) and another member of the Iraqi Advisory Task Force, August 2004.

No Slack Lieutenants Bradford, Taylor, and Nati.

24 football field-sized warehouses of food were captured. Nothing had been distributed by the Saddam regime in over 6 months.

Just one of the thousands of stockpiles of Iraqi munitions found south of Mosul.

1LT Morgan, Battalion Chemical Officer, being greeted by Kurdish children and families north of Mosul, June 2003.

The wheat fields of northern Iraq.

LTG Richard Cody and his wife Vicki with their two sons, Tyler (left) and Clint.

Mr. Kadhim Al-Waeli, Senior Cultural
Advisor, Multinational Force Iraq.
Pictured above with Secretary of
Defense Robert Gates and Chairman
of the Joint Chiefs of Staff General
Peter Pace, and at right with Lt.
General Ray Odierno.

Below: Committee One, National War
College Class of 2005. The best
group of professionals I've ever been
honored to meet. We always had fun.

teams strapped into the floor of their Black Hawks, doors open, like a normal airborne sniper mission, yet their mission wasn't to find enemy troops. They were to scout out wheat combines and determine if they were friend for foe. "Friend or foe?" I asked.

"Yes sir, we track to see if they have clubs stenciled on all four sides and the roof of the combine cabs." The club was the regiment's recognition symbol from WWII, when the regiments of the 101st painted the suits of card decks on their helmets to distinguish units from one another from a distance after large airborne operations. (You'll note the 506th Parachute Infantry, depicted in "Band of Brothers," used the spade symbol.) We wore these club symbols on our helmets in Iraq and now Marcus was using this historic symbol to identify friendly or enemy combines. It was simple, brilliant and just one more example of military innovation.

This came in handy because we knew the Free Kurds had other combines under their control and suspected they would try to poach wheat and barley, just as we had caught them trying to poach oil and gasoline at Beiji. Sure enough, those helicopter-mounted snipers of Lt. Colonel Marcus' battalion did spot combines harvesting grain that lacked the Club stencil, and shot their tires out, calling over the radio for ground troops to drive over and arrest the grain hijackers. The contraband equipment—combines and grain trucks—were pressed into government service, repaired, stenciled with the 327th's club symbol and added to the legal harvesting team.

A NOTE ON THE HARVEST FROM
COLONEL MARCUS DE OLIVEIRA

Chris,
Bit of history about our little wheat harvest. Seems 13 years before our arrival, the land changed hands from the Kurds to Arabs. Arabs claimed the Kurds were compensated but not sure how much or whether it actually happened. As you remember the truth is a tricky thing to determine in Northern Iraq. As we came north, the Kurds moved south just short of the Tigris River and surprised all of us upon our arrival.

The issue, when we arrived, was that Arabs had planted the wheat and now the Kurdish militias had occupied the land—so who owned the wheat? The issue was further complicated in that there was an Arab "owner" of the land and an Arab "farmer" who leased the land, a Kurd who originally claimed ownership, and a loosely armed band of Kurdish fighters now claiming territory south of the green line. Oh, and lets not forget Iraq was a socialist country, so the Iraqi government provided the seeds, the fertilizer and further subsidized fuel for planting, harvesting and storage.

Given all that, some Arabs tied to a Sheik in Mosul started complaining directly to Division HQ about the wheat harvest and how it was now our responsibility to bring it in and equally distribute it.

I was on the Syrian border and told to go to Makhmour, and while en route back to settle the issue, I learned that my S3 Blain Reeves had already moved to Makhmour along with Ben [Hodges] to command and control this rather odd mission. Our first issue was to ensure the Arabs understood we could do things at our level so they did not have to go bother Division HQ and quibble about the price of wheat/barley and who should be the benefactors of the harvest. We could handle that at Brigade and Battalion level...I think?

An agreement was finally struck when Brigadier General Freakley brought down the Nineveh Governor or Deputy, the Arab Sheik and officials from the Kurdish Democratic Party in Irbil to negotiate a settlement. They met for about 20 minutes and signed a rather simple agreement (with our witnessing) that divided the harvest 50-50 between the Kurds who owned the land and the Arabs who planted it. The Arabs further had to split their share with those they leased from.

First task was to get all the claims straight. We developed a simple form that outlined the split of the harvest and responsibilities for actually bringing in the harvest, storage and sale. Blain and my fire support officer spent all day every day in the agriculture office adjudicating disputes, signing agreements and tracking down violations of the accords.

The second task was bringing the harvested wheat to our silos where we would weigh and give credits to the two parties involved. Sometimes a patrol would have to go out with disputing parties to settle the agreement. We did not have translators to do all this but young leaders could be seen sitting out in the middle of a field, groping for a means to communicate and finding solutions between the Arabs and Kurds. We had some very innovative and adaptive leaders.

The other task was how to control the combines. These huge harvesters had to be licensed based on agreements between the two parties involved with our sanction. Some of the combines were painted with our unit club so we could identify them at a distance. As you met the sniper team we had squads flying around checking on the harvest so a Blackhawk with a squad might come in on a combine and check on proper permission to harvest or get sent back to an impound yard at the silo.

I think where we really made money by instituting transparency and a requisite level of fairness (not everyone liked the decisions but they were fair) and that did much to keep the area safe. We did have one issue of an RPG shot at a convoy and some Kurdish police shot an Arab while we were there, but for the most part the year was violence free and the harvest went well. I truly believe we were able to make the area weapons free because of some of those early efforts and perceptions of fairness and cooperation.

We also agreed early on to stay out of land claims as that would have muddied the issue and gotten us down some tangents we wanted to stay out of. We deferred any talk of that until after a transitional government.

Bottom line—US soldiers are not taught how to do what we did, but they are a product of our society and the American system. The result is what we all saw throughout Iraq, soldiers who fought very well when necessary, yet agile and innovative enough to transition to doing things like getting two farmers with a long history of conflict, barely able to communicate with each other, to sit in a field of wheat and agree to split their harvest without fighting.

Couple things I was proud of:

Young American soldiers and junior leaders sitting down with Arabs and Kurds—finding solutions and brokering agreements in a foreign land. They did this without translators and with little guidance or supervision other than having a copy of the agreement and generally being told to be fair and get an agreement. Its my best example of the American spirit—we need to tell this story to our countrymen!

Marcus

DOGMA'S AFTERSHOCKS

The dogma of Saddam's regime was simple and effective: He leveraged Abraham Maslow's Hierarchy of Needs,[14] holy Islamic values, the Arab feudalistic system, and socialism to instill and reward compliance in the Iraqi people. The best example I can give is the plight of my favorite Iraqi Police Chief, Armer Al Jubari. Armer was four years younger than I and had four wives and 32 children, a fact that was a complete mystery to me, and that motivated me to continually read the Koran to understand his motivations as we slowly returned order to his region of Iraq.

During a trip to an archeological site in his sector, I finally thought I knew him well enough to ask about his large family. Somewhat jokingly, through my linguist Specialist Carr, I told him I understood his fourth wife, but it was his second wife that had me baffled. "How did you manage to talk your first wife into your second wife? That is something just unheard of in my country." After asking, Carr grinned at me because she was just a curious as I was, especially since we all teased her about her crush on Armer, who did strike an uncanny likeness to Tom Selleck. Looking at us somewhat bemused, Armer asked Carr to repeat the question; he did not understand. "How did you talk your first wife into your second?"

"I didn't," he replied. "She asked me for the second wife!"

Carr and I were both stunned. "Why did she want you to have a second wife?"

After hearing his answer, a bewildered Carr turned to me and said, "She had twelve kids and needed some help, so he went out and got permission for a second wife from his brother, the Sheik, and the local cleric"—all perfectly legal within their religion and society.

It was this very system that Saddam sought to exploit to maintain control of his people. By paying government salaries to every man, woman and child, encouraging multiple wives to men who were wealthy enough to care for their families, a direct result of the government salaries, and further rewarding such men with cars and bonuses for overt support and compliance to the regime, he exploited and pacified the bottom tier of his society by providing for their basic needs—food, water and shelter at no cost other than their loyalty. This form of control, also aided by the distribution of free subsistence from the food-for-oil program, free gas for cars and free electricity, leveraged the population and conditioned them to absolute dependence on Saddam.

This system took 30-plus years for Saddam to perfect and less than 21 days for the Coalition to dismantle with no real plan for how to fill the vacuum—a vacuum of power and logic so foreign to the Western world I'm not sure anyone could have predicted it, let alone planned how to remedy it. But there they were, the Iraqi people and military, in our faces with their tobacco-stained and out-stretched hands asking—no, demanding—back pay for the months leading up to the invasion because Saddam hadn't paid them. By default, was it now my responsibility to give them their back salaries since I represented the new government?

As I looked at them in utter disbelief, I wondered if ever in the annals of warfare had any defeated army had the courage or ignorance to demand back pay from their conquerors. It was this dilemma that finally put to rest, in my mind, the debate that rages in the classrooms of our universities, Washington think tanks and Congress today—is the United States becoming an Empire? I think my peers and I answered that question in the early days of the war when the Iraqi soldiers, despite their resounding defeat and surrender, were not executed for their audacity to demand back pay. Instead we treated them with compassion, dignity and respect like no other empire in recorded history. The answer is clear. The United States is not an

Empire, just a reluctant Superpower with a conscience—another first in recorded history.

THE TIGRIS RIVER VALLEY
COMMISSION

As the summer dragged on, the ambiguity of our redeployment time-line continued to nag at the men, their families and my ability to sustain morale. The demands and complaints Iraqi citizens made on our soldiers became a constant and increasing friction that quickly began to take a toll on each side. The only invariable we had was that our area of operation would continue to grow, and so would Iraqi demands on our soldiers, despite our limited resources available to help them.

I also began to tire at the constant complaints and demands from local leaders and their inability to take responsibility or accomplish even the simplest tasks. Years of oppression, socialistic conditioning, and an apparent lack of initiative at the individual and collective level would take time and patience to overcome. I no longer wanted to be the one to take the time to teach it to them. My task was made harder when senior US political planners decided they knew what I needed better than I did. The Coalition Provisional Authority (CPA) seemed to know what I should be doing to stabilize my area without ever visiting or even having the courtesy to ask for the opinions of those serving outside of Baghdad. What worked in the cities normally didn't work with the tribes. This was a lesson that haunted Saddam and now hindered the Coalition.

Iraq is a nation of many parts, all complicated with hundreds of different and conflicting ethical and moral interpretations of right and wrong, which was now suddenly governed by a Coalition force with very strict and well documented definitions of law and ethical standards. Most of the Coalition's precepts, in addition, were in direct contrast with the Arab world because our Western standards of law are man's law, not God's, as interpreted by the Koran.

I truly came to believe that "Iraq has a religion that allows for government; America has a government that allows for religion." These differences could not be more incompatible. In my opinion, this was the main root of the conflict in Iraq and the fuel of the insurgency. How can the Coalition impose order and security with a foreign concept of right and wrong that's a direct affront to the very religion that acts as the only means to unify the hundreds of tribes that make up Iraq, the Cradle of Civilization?

As the debate raged in Washington over the Army's new stability mission in Iraq, the 101st decided to plan a one-year deployment. My battalion was not happy, but we dug in and planned for the long haul. Even though the division was finding meaningful and innovative ways to get us resources and money (such as for reinstituting social salaries for teachers, doctors, police and utility workers), the constant meetings with mayors, sheiks, teachers, lawyers, farming guilds and medical personnel was starting to take a toll on me.

By late May, our area of operation had expanded to the south and now encompassed over 13,000 square kilometers, 52 towns and villages, 72 schools, the regional sulfur plant, two uncompleted electrical power plants, two 4,000-year old archeological sites, three regional markets, a propane plant, and close to 250,000 citizens. To drive to a meeting in my sector would take up most of my day. To see all four of my companies in our sector would take three days of driving, with only an hour spent at each location. If I could get use of a Blackhawk helicopter, I could complete my rounds in one long day.

At the end of one such day, I was returning from a meeting with Mayor Naji in Hammam. I remember it being so hot that I closed the windows in my hummer because the breeze blowing in the window made the vehicle feel like a super convection oven. As I considered my next set of meetings, I found that most of the topics were the same— the same complaints, the same promises, and the same urging of the mayors to step up, take responsibility and stop relying on the government-type meetings. *No Slack*, in their eyes, was the new government and responsible for providing everything their communities needed to survive.

After weeks of slowly being drawn deeper and deeper into what I perceived as gross irresponsibility on their part, I came to realize I needed a forum that would bring all my civic leaders together to coordinate their efforts, share their ideas, display equity, and most of all, inject some pride and competition between my mayors and their communities. The three-hour drive back to Qayyrah Airfield gave me time to develop a detailed concept for my staff.

Great ideas were a dime a dozen in Iraq. Selling them to the people was another story. I learned early in the process that selling an idea and naming it well was as important as the project itself. The Iraqis were conditioned to ignore mundane issues and ideas in order to fully engage with the grandiose. Even if a project was superficial, if it had an important and meaningful name the Iraqis would fight to participate in order to gain the requisite reputation and power that came with the project.

As I contemplated the concept and what I would call it, I looked out the window of my hummer and then back to my map. All these cities straddled the Tigris River and they all depended on each other; thus the name Tigris River Valley Commission (TRVC) was born.

As the battalion staff put the final touches on the plan, I embarked on a Public Relations trip to begin the groundwork for selling the idea. The PR campaign was very important and we felt we had enough information on our sheiks, mayors and clerics to get the program off to a decent start. Key to the PR campaign was our world-class Counter Intelligence Team (CI) and Tactical PSYOPs [Psychological Operations] Team (TPT) and their ability to leverage the numerous informal relationships they had developed outside of my formal relationships with the local leaders. Encouraging, coaching and manipulating, these formal and informal leaders became the main effort in our execution plan. The plan was simple—I would personally work the formal leaders and the TPT and CI team would work the clerics, tribal leaders and general population.

Selling the TRVC went quickly and surprisingly well. We had full cooperation in less than a week. The first meeting would be held in Ash Shurah because it was centrally located in the region and the police station was well suited to hold such a large gathering. The attendees included the mayors, sheiks and educational, medical and police representatives from each municipality.

To visually empower and legitimize the representatives, we launched ground teams to each town to mark off and set up pick-up zones for each delegation. Each pick-up zone was made into a spectacle of over-exaggerated preparation symbolic of the city's value to the

Coalition and the new Iraqi government. This was especially important in the towns and villages in our sector because of the oppression they had suffered under Saddam's regime.

"Town vs. Country" dynamics are both fascinating and important to understand, especially in the developing world and in reconstruction efforts. Saddam knew all too well how disciplined the tribes were and how much control the sheiks had over the young men in Ninawa Province. The local sheiks told me that Saddam had made Mosul the most modern city in Iraq to draw the young men out of the fields and into the city. Saddam felt that he could control the province if the young men felt more loyalty to the regime than to their tribes.

In the eyes of the sheiks, Saddam and their thirst for a modern Iraq were leading their young men astray. Saddam was in effect buying the loyalty of the youth and diminishing the power of the tribal sheiks at the same time. I was told on more than one occasion by my sheiks and mayors that they would "no longer settle for the crumbs of Mosul." Each wanted what Mosul had to offer in their own cities, towns and villages while maintaining traditional values and control over their tribes.

As expected, the pick-up teams made quite a commotion and drew large crowds. We sent Blackhawk helicopters with Apache escorts to pick up each city's commissioners. Iraqis were very impressed with our helicopters and always assumed that when they saw them the passengers on board were very important. Much of my initial credibility was because I could arrive in a hummer or a helicopter based on my own personal desire, which had previously been a luxury reserved only for Saddam and his top generals. Now these same instruments of power and prestige were circling their towns to pick up their leaders and ferry them off to this important commission. The effect fostered a pride in the Iraqi citizens we had not seen before.

The Apaches flew over the towns to announce the arrival of the commissioners' aircraft, and then the local Iraqi police and the American escort detail drove the commissioners to the pick-up zone. They were then ceremoniously loaded into the aircraft, as the American detail formed into ranks and saluted the aircraft as they departed. The extraction was modeled on the American President boarding Marine-One. In each instance, the crowds cheered and rejoiced at the sight—the consensus was that the Americans were high-ly interested in their city. It was clear that we had bought ourselves and our new commissioners' legitimacy and some time to make a differ-ence—but for how long?

6

CHANGING COMMAND
IN COMBAT

"Don't make me leave them here . . . please!"

LEAVING *NO SLACK* IN HARM'S WAY

As the mayors in our four provinces began to take control of their people, programs and institutions, I still had one unresolved issue that I had avoided but carried in my heart every day as I drove around our sector to see the men—my approaching change of command.

The Army had determined years earlier that battalion commanders should spend an average of 24 months in command. Any longer than that and commanders ran the risk of burning out and becoming, at best, an inefficient leader or, at worst, a dangerous one. Of course, no commander wants to hear that after nearly two years of command he is approaching incompetence, but as I later came to realize the extent of my own mental and physical exhaustion, I realized it is a pretty good rule. Still, no commander likes it and at the time I personally hated it.

Even under normal circumstances, a change of command is a highly charged and emotional event, at least for the commanders involved. But these were not normal circumstances: they involved an incipient combat situation. I was being told to turn over my men to a new commander at my 24-month anniversary with the battalion in June 2003. How could this be true? Surely no one would force me to leave my men here when I had promised them and their families I would bring them all home alive?

Months of heart-tugging dread and wistful hoping were confirmed when General Petraeus summoned the commanders of the division to a conference in Mosul in May of 2003. Using sound logic and decades of experience, General Petraeus told the collective group that he planned to rotate the commanders who were approaching the end of their 24-month command while the division was still in Iraq. Relating his own experience of taking command of a battalion after Desert Storm, he remembered how difficult it was to build his command because he was the outsider who hadn't served with the battalion in Iraq. He did not want this to happen to future commanders in his own division. Petraeus made the decision after reflecting on the bonds that develop between soldiers and how difficult it is for a new member to penetrate a team that has bonded in combat.

Leaving was not about us and how we felt as the outgoing commanders. Rather, the change was for the good of the men and our battalions. Very reluctantly, I agreed with him. The battalion was bigger than I was, and its cohesion in the unknown days ahead was more important than my personal feelings. Bringing the new commanders into the division while still in Iraq would give them and the men a chance to develop a relationship under harsh conditions.

The experience would improve the new commander's chances of building a sound command team based on a shared hardship to deal with the challenges ahead. Central to the general's plan was a belief that the division would return to the United States in September of 2003, giving the new commanders two months of maneuvering their new commands in northern Iraq, followed by a complicated relief in place and redeployment to the United States. It was an ideal situation for Major General Petraeus to train his new commanders, get them comfortable maneuvering their units, and develop a strong foundation for building their teams over the next two years.

When the conference was over, the other outgoing commanders and I informally discussed the peculiarities of our situation. How would we tell our men? When will and how will our replacements get into Iraq? How do you conduct a change of command in a combat zone? What would we tell the hundreds of family members we were responsible for when we returned to Fort Campbell without their husbands and fathers?

PREPARING MY REPLACEMENT

Being selected to command a combat battalion is the ultimate goal of any warrior, a selection that validates your competence as a soldier after eighteen years of deployments, education, hard work, and sacrifice. Most officers never see this day. It is a career goal that begins with the first class you attend at the basic infantry course at Fort Benning, Georgia, when the instructor tells the young lieutenants to look at their peers to their left and right, and then shows them the statistics confirming that less than three percent of them will become battalion commanders. One of the many truisms in the Army is that the centralized process for selecting battalion commanders is one of the fairest and most accurate selection processes in the United States Army, if not the free world. The men and women of the Army who are selected to command battalions are exceptional people, and for everyone selected for this position, there are five just as qualified and competent officers waiting in the wings as alternates to step up to the challenge if the need arises.

My replacement, Lieutenant Colonel James Johnson, was such an officer. A recent returnee from the war in Afghanistan, Jim arrived in Iraq in early June to begin our transition. He had returned from Afghanistan in January of 2003 and had taken a couple of days leave before he went on temporary duty to attend Air Assault School at Fort Campbell for fifteen days, in preparation for our change of command.

While at school, his wife had the movers pack up their household goods and prepared for their move from Fort Bragg, NC to Fort Campbell, KY. Upon Jim's return from Air Assault School this consummate Army family pulled up their roots and moved in the middle of the school year. Barely out of moving boxes and less than four months after his tour in Afghanistan, Lt. Colonel Jim Johnson said goodbye to his family, deployed to Iraq, and took responsibility for over 1,000 men. And just as deliberately, his wife began her transition with my wife, as she took responsibility for the *No Slack* spouses, their children and the battalion's rear detachment at Fort Campbell, KY.

The plan was to immerse Jim in the situation as quickly and as deeply as possible. He needed to understand the complexities of the sector, develop relationships with the sheiks, police and mayors, and understand why things were the way they were. We threw aside the normal protocol and courtesies between incoming and outgoing commanders—we had no time for pride, personalities or egos; the mission was more important and the men needed Jim to be successful from the moment he took command. Too many lives were at stake, American and Iraqi. Jim and I both recognized this and we quickly decided to coexist for two weeks to ensure a smooth and seamless transition. We could not afford a window of complacency or uncertainty to exist during our transition that the enemy could exploit.

THE CHANGE OF COMMAND SPEECH

There was no better way to describe leaving the men of *No Slack* than to simply include a copy of the complete transcript from my change of command on June 16, 2003. The change of command was conducted in the morning before the heat of the day and with less than 100 men from the battalion.

The ceremony was a much lower priority that morning than continuing our search for insurgents along the banks of the Tigris River, protecting the streets of Qayyrah and Ash-Shurah, guarding thousands of tons of Iraqi artillery ammunition in Al Hadar, advising our mayors on economic prosperity in their communities, and painting mosques and repairing schools. Although I had tried in vain for over two weeks to find each of my soldiers to say goodbye, I still felt like I was sneaking away like a thief in the night.

16 June 2003; Q-West Airfield:

Soldiers, non-commissioned officers and officers of 2d Battalion, 327th Infantry Regiment, *NO SLACK*, Major General Petraeus, Brigadier General (P) Freakley, Brigadier General Sinclair, Command Sergeant Major Hill, Command Sergeant Major Womack, distinguished guests and friends of *NO SLACK*

Sir, please forgive my breach in protocol by addressing my soldiers first, but I've always known that my fanatical loyalty to my soldiers was how I could best show my loyalty to you and Colonel Hodges.

Standing before you here and in the fields, towns and villages in the horizon are 981 of the greatest men I have ever had the honor and privilege to know. The men of 2d Battalion, 327th Infantry—*NO SLACK*.

A change of command may be a ceremony to officially pass the loyalty of the soldiers from one commander to the next, but the true purpose of a change of command is to fall out the rank and file and show what truly matters in an infantry battalion—its battle tested and hardened infantrymen! There will be no overflights in this ceremony, no armor pass and reviews . . . only the hard cold stare of the most lethal weapon that exists on the battlefield today. A man, his weapon and his will to close with and kill the enemy.

The men that stand before you today have grown into the boots they wear—by facing the enemy and accomplishing every mission I have given them. They have seen all that is good and bad in this world and they have done it with courage, iron clad discipline and honor.

To truly know the men of *No Slack*, you must walk a mile in their boots: Please know that:

These are the men that won 137 Expert Infantrymen Badges over the last two years, the same men who rolled out of the brigade motor pool, with live ammunition, and guarded the schools, hospital and gates of Fort Campbell less than an hour after the second plane hit the World Trade Center on 9-11—protecting our children and sick for over 42 days without relief.

These are the men who planned, built and executed the division's defensive live fire lane with only two days notice, a lane that was used to prepare the division for combat in Afghanistan.

These are the men who prepared to deploy to Afghanistan, yet selflessly pulled themselves off division ready battalion and pushed their brothers from 3rd Brigade Combat Team to the airfield, guarded their HQs, helped them with their maintenance, and assumed all their post-wide duties without complaint or whine.

These are the men who prepared for the second rotation to Afghanistan who went into the field on the 21st of January 2002, ending with the *Bastogne* Sh'mal training exercise in April of 2002, only to learn that the 82d Airborne Division would assume the Afghanistan rotation and *No Slack* was to field a new Anti-tank (TOW ITAS)

Missile System and prepare for an unannounced rotation to the Joint Readiness Training Center in August 2002.

No normal JRTC, the battalion took all its assigned equipment by sea, testing the division's deployment process, and attached to the 2nd Armored Cavalry Regiment for the rotation. During the rotation, these same men fought seven battalion battles, executed three company live fires, and three battalion air assaults in the August heat of Louisiana.

Upon their return to Fort Campbell, they ran headlong into vehicle recovery and post-detail cycle. No leave for them or their families; there was no time, the division was preparing for war—-again!

On 3rd Jan. 2003, these men conducted multiple live fire exercises, rifle ranges, road marches, urban warfare training exercises, four deployment exercises, new equipment fielding and training, assisted sister battalions with anti-tank missile fielding, and during a significant snowstorm, ran the Fort Campbell rail load facilities to help the division deploy to Iraq.

In Iraq these men fought in five major combined arms battles, dozens of company, platoon and squad level firefights, three battalion ground assault convoys, crossing over 1,200 kilometers, two battalion combat air assaults, and countless company level air assault operations—all without a single combat casualty.

All of these accomplishments are testament to the caliber of soldiers, noncommissioned officers and officers of *NO SLACK*.

A few short weeks ago I wrote a letter to the wives and parents of *NO SLACK* and told them that there were no longer any boys in this battalion—they are all men now. Their husbands and sons have faced all that is horrific and good in this world and they have been triumphant.

Many times, I have told these men about the incredible yoke of responsibility that I have felt from the battalion colors as they look down on me each day in my office or on a run—the countless faces represented in those colors: our fallen comrades, our veterans and our heroes. The men of *No Slack* trained hard to prove themselves worthy to carry these colors into combat, and I now believe that there is no doubt they have earned that right. These are now your colors men! As future members of this battalion carry these colors, it will be **you** that they are trying to impress and aspire to be like. Remember that you are now the example, others will look up to you, you will have instant credibility, you are a leader, and you will be sought after for your experience and your guidance . . . all because you now wear the Screaming Eagle Patch of the 101ST AIRBORNE DIVISION on your right shoulder!

Colonel Hodges, I want these men to hear me tell you, that I consider myself the luckiest man in the world to have been a *NO SLACK* soldier. These men have done everything we have asked of them and they have done it with honor and style. Yes, they are proud and cocky, but they are also compassionate and respectful. I did not deserve to be their commander, but luck, God and timing made it possible, and I have given them my heart and soul. They have been and always will be first in my prayers every night as I ask for God's protection and wisdom.

I think General Eisenhower said it best when he received the ancient honor, "The Freedom of the City of London," after WWII. Gen. Eisenhower said:

"Humility must always be the portion of any man who receives acclaim earned in blood of his followers and sacrifices of his friends. The only attitude in which a commander may with satisfaction receive the tributes of his friends is in the humble acknowledgement that no matter how unworthy he may be, his position is the symbol of great human forces that have labored arduously and successfully for a righteous cause."

Nothing could be more righteous than our mission here in Iraq. As evidenced by my friends from the Shurah District who have joined us today. Mr. Hussein (the mayor of Shurah), Sheik Athal Al-Jubari, and Major Amer Al-Jubari.

These men have stood up and taken control of their communities and are willing to do what it takes to ensure the freedom and prosperity of their people and their nation. I commend them for their courageousness—they are true patriots and I honor and respect them for being here today.

Lt. Colonel Johnson, I know these men will give you their complete and total loyalty. LTC Johnson is preceded by an exceptional reputation, he is a combat warrior, and I know he and his wife Kris

will find a home here in *NO SLACK*. Jim, YOU ARE NOW THE
LUCKIEST MAN IN THE WORLD.

Good Luck *NO SLACK* and God Bless you all—

Remember your history, men—-and remember you are now history as well!

No Breather from Work

No Relief from Combat

No Request for Respite

No Slack!

Bastogne!

Air Assault!

THE TRIP HOME TO FORT CAMPBELL

Protocol dictates that the outgoing commander leaves the ceremony as
quickly as possible, pausing near the podium to shake hands as the
new commander takes the division leaders with him to a formal reception. In this case, Jim Johnson had managed to pull together some
sodas and local desserts to entertain those leaders who were able to
attend our change of command. As the last well-wisher shook my
hand, the battalion personnel NCO, Staff Sergeant Reed, escorted me
to a supply hummer for the long ride to Mosul. After relinquishing my
body armor, 9mm pistol, M-4 rifle and ammunition to the company
supply sergeant, I was suddenly Lieutenant Colonel Chris Hughes, former commander of 2d Battalion, 327th Infantry Regiment.

As I climbed into the back seat of the hummer, I glanced over at
the long reception line going into the former Iraqi air force hanger and
caught a glimpse of the new *No Slack*-6, Lieutenant Colonel James
Johnson. The cycle was complete and it was time for me to leave.

As luck would have it, the battalion Chaplain, Captain Scott
Brown, was also being forced to rotate out and we had the opportunity to redeploy together. Scott was more than my chaplain; he was my
friend. His company and counsel during the long trek home was com-
forting and therapeutic.

Every aspect of the trip home was a series of contradicting emotions. For every euphoric surprise of comfort, freshness and taste,
there was an equally despairing twinge of embarrassment, guilt and

heartburn. Everything that tasted good quickly soured and tore at my stomach as the guilt over my departing while my troops were still in harm's way ripped at my heart. How could I have left them back there in that shithole while I sit here munching airplane food? The emotional weight of my departure made every moment of my trip miserable.

Had I aggressively argued my point for staying in Iraq to my boss? Had I made my desire to stay in Iraq in any capacity known to all the right people at division? Had I given in to my desire to see my own family too easily? Had I really fought General Petraeus' decision to send me home as passionately as I could have? The answer to all these contradicting questions was yes, but it didn't help. I was now sitting on a commercial plane watching "When Harry Met Sally," enjoying a hot meal, while my men were still sweating in 100 degree heat, drinking hot water and dodging bullets. I began to hate myself.

THE FAMILY READINESS GROUP

Nine days and five flights after leaving Mosul, I landed at Nashville International Airport, and my tour in Iraq and in the 101st Airborne Division had ended. Anxious and apprehensive to see my family at the airport, I stopped in the nearest bathroom and composed myself. Looking in the mirror, I noticed that I was much slimmer than when I'd departed, and my eyes were sunken deep into my head. Furthermore, my hair had gone another stage grayer. I felt old and tired.

As I approached the end of the terminal, I could see my wife Marguerite and youngest son Michael. My older two children were at camp and work. They both ran to hug me. We embraced in the middle of the hallway without words. It felt great to be with them, but the thought of *No Slack* tugged at my heart and dulled the moment. The guilt of leaving my men wouldn't let me enjoy what should have been one of my happiest moments.

The first topic my wife and I discussed was my pending meeting with the wives of the battalion: the Family Readiness Group. Before leaving Iraq, Marguerite had coordinated for me to meet the wives, give them a briefing on the status of the battalion, and try to answer as many questions as possible. I knew the wives were craving information and it was my responsibility to ease their yearning for anything I could tell them about their husbands. Marguerite told me the wives were excited to meet with me and had arranged for a large auditorium so they could bring the older children and a number of parents who were in town.

"They must hate me for coming back . . . I wouldn't blame them if they tarred and feathered me," I confided to my wife. She looked at me and assured me they were not upset. "They know you were ordered to leave." It helped that five commanders in my same situation had returned before me, so I wasn't alone. Despite Marguerite's assurances, I was preparing for the worst. I was sure there would be some negative emotions focused on me.

The wives met me at the door that night with hugs, tears and smiles; it was all I could do to keep my composure. The auditorium was packed and the mood was jovial with the kids, parents of my younger soldiers, new and seasoned wives, and some of my wounded soldiers who were on convalescent leave recovering from their injuries.

The brief was simple; the staff had put hundreds of pictures together on a CD before I left Iraq, as well as a few maps. I put the CD in the computer to give them something to watch as I put up a map on an easel so I could retrace our attack into Iraq. As the pictures scrolled across through the screen show, the crowd grew quiet.

"Look, it's daddy!"

"Oh my God, it's Kevin."

"Hey, isn't that Sergeant Wilson?"

I turned to see the whole group fixated on the slide show, wide-eyed, smiles, and hands covering their mouths, and tears of joy and fear.

After tracing our actions across Iraq until the day I left, the group asked questions for almost an hour. Out of courtesy, they managed to avoid the primary question—"When will they be home?"—because they knew I didn't have the answer. The wives of *No Slack* were the first to ease my pain and guilt. They didn't make me feel guilty for leaving their loved ones; they made me feel proud to be an American. They thanked me for caring for their loved ones and getting them through the major combat phase of the war. And just when I didn't think I could feel any better, a mother of one of my single soldiers opened my eyes when she said, "I'm proud my son served with you. He loves his squad and company. You need to take your love for my son and give it to your boys now. They need their father and you have nothing to feel guilty about. God Bless You." She kissed me as I left the auditorium with a lump in the throat and my heart on my sleeve.

In order to make room for the incoming battalion commanders and their families, Marguerite and the kids were forced to clear out of our government quarters and move to the Fort Campbell Inn. She had painted and cleared our military quarters without me. This was not unusual for her, a military wife of twenty years, but peculiar to this move was a spare room we had built into our garage. Military housing is a "one-size-fits-all" deal, and our house at Fort Campbell was too small for our family. We had the garage professionally remodeled as a family room at our own expense to give us room to entertain my visiting officers and accommodate three teenagers. I was shocked to learn that the installation clearing team had forced Marguerite and the kids to turn it back into a garage when they moved out. After the experience, my son Michael swore he would never paint or drywall again. He told me, "You better get promoted or retire because I'm never doing that again, DAD!" The waste involved in ensuring strict conformity and compliance to regulation baffled me, but after twenty years in the Army, it failed to surprise me.

Three days later, we departed Fort Campbell, and after three weeks leave in the Midwest visiting families, we made our way to Washington, DC to continue the war effort from the halls of the Pentagon. I was determined to make good on my promise to Sheik Al Jubari and the men of *No Slack* not to let the Army's senior leadership forget them, and to get them the resources they needed to get the job done.

PART II
A FOOTSTOOL AT THE SEAT OF POWER

7

THE PENTAGON

"This is not business as usual—soldiers are dying!"

WAR, BUREAUCRACY, FRUSTRATION AND PROGRESS

It was an odd feeling walking into the Pentagon in my new battle dress uniform. In typical Pentagon style, everyone was scurrying about transfixed on his or her particular troubles and avoiding eye contact as they passed others in the halls. If being in a hurry meant being busy, then this was a very busy place. I silently laughed at their attempts to look important and overworked, considering how nice it must be to work on military projects where there was little to no chance of being killed during the workday. This self-induced stress was mystifying. I just wanted to grab one of them by the neck and explain eye-to-eye that he just needed to stop sweating the small shit and enjoy life!

The urge to beat the crap out of one of these poor fellows passed when the smells of the cafeteria slapped me in the face like a wet-wool blanket. Starbucks, McDonalds, Burger King, and Subway! After a half-year in Iraq, I quickly deviated from my planned route and head-ed straight for the food court. The aroma of the cafeteria made me feel safe and unchallenged. It was definitely a pleasant feeling to sit and enjoy a cup of coffee without worrying if someone in this throng around me would pull a gun or shout *Allahu Akbar* and try and stab me in the back. I rubbed my right thigh and longed for my sidearm in the cafeteria, but the vente almond mocha was helping!

The deeper I passed into the bowels of the Pentagon, the more I began to think that the last six months hadn't happened in the eyes of these people—no war, no casualties, no pain nor sacrifice. It was business as usual here and I was expected to make a smooth transition and re-enter American society without missing a beat. How does one recover from combat? Does anyone ever fully recover from combat? I couldn't get the faces of my men left behind in Iraq and the tears of their wives out of my mind. This was definitely not where I was supposed to be. Leaving my men while they were still in a combat situation was the hardest thing I had ever done and I was having a tough time coming to terms with it. I also knew the war had profoundly changed me. No one seemed to know how I felt, or really gave a shit. Yet when asked, my first reaction was to push them away and shake it off as if nothing had happened in Iraq; a joke, a smile, a superficial comment, but never the truth. The war and guilt were mine and I wasn't going to share it with anyone.

As I approached my new office, my head began to spin and the increasing beat of my heart became physically noticeable. Spotting another eatery at the edge of the Pentagon's Army corridor, I sat down to compose myself. After a moment, I began to take notice of the cafeteria crowd. It was a hodgepodge of military officers, defense department civilians and military contractors of all shapes and sizes engaged in eating and bitching about everything under the sun. I had lost 35 pounds in Iraq and my mind was conditioned now to notice everything associated with food, especially how overweight everyone looked as they shoveled food into their round faces. Working on my composure as I sipped my drink became more difficult as I inadvertently eavesdropped on nearby conversations—traffic sucked, the project budget was insufficient, and mortgage rates were on the rise. All of which was such trivial babble. To me, they seemed to be insignificant topics that did not warrant such passionate attention.

"What about the war?" I thought. "This is the Pentagon isn't it? Don't these people realize we are at war? How can they be so engrossed in their personal lives?" I wanted to jump up and scream at them to skip their lunch (God knows most of them could skip a lunch or two) and get their fat asses back to work! But, I kept silent, stood up and meandered to my own office—resisting the slight temptation to appear hurried and busy. Taking my own advice, I threw away my drink. It did not seem right to finish it when the soldiers of my former battalion were definitely not getting designer coffee. This was a recurring feeling that would haunt my consciousness until my former command returned to Fort Campbell seven months later. It was funny how my attitude immediately softened once *No Slack* returned from Iraq, and I now think that my initial feelings about my Pentagon co-workers may have been too harsh.

When I turned into the E-ring, the outer ring of the Pentagon, where the senior leaders of the Department of Defense maintain their offices and which most junior officers avoid, I hoped I would see a friendly face. I didn't, but was relieved to see other Army officers in camouflage uniform going about the business of managing the Army. At least I had worn the right uniform. Two years earlier, I wouldn't have worn a field uniform while conducting business in "the building."

During my last tour, we wore dress and semi-dress uniforms at work everyday; we were expected to look professional and business like—not warrior like. Yet to my surprise and delight, I could feel a new sense of urgency as I entered the Army corridor. It was different than the rest of the building; the Army Staff was at war and their deliberate pace in the hall, their warrior appearance and attentiveness to each other gave me a proud feeling inside. They cared, and I admired them for their dedication.

THE PENTAGON'S LEADERSHIP

My pay-grade or rank in the Pentagon did not allow me personal contact with the Secretary of Defense, Donald Rumsfeld, upon my return from Iraq. However, since this subject appears to be an endless source of curiosity I can relate some earlier impressions.

When I was an operations officer in 2000 working in the Combating Terrorism Division on the Joint Staff in the Pentagon, I had two occasions to develop impressions of how the building was being run.

The first was when the 2000 election was still in debate and the Pentagon yearned for new leadership, one that would quickly recognize how broken the military had become in terms of manning, equipment, and most notably, quality of life. The cuts of the '90s had caused the Army to use more and more of its R&D dollars and Base Operations budgets to train its soldiers. The thought of a Republican

administration that would work quickly to reenergize an under-
funded and tired Army was all the buzz. Never had I been so involved
in the debate and never was I in a position to see the Constitution
being implemented at such close proximity—in Washington, DC.

The process was complicated by the apparent tie in the national
election and, for those of us who lived their lives in the shadow of the
Constitution it was a no brainer—the House of Representatives
should convene a special session and pick the next president. But the
debate never got that far and it was settled with the Supreme Court.

While this drama unfolded, the Rumsfeld team had already head-
ed to the Pentagon and dry-walled half the cafeteria into makeshift
offices. As you can imagine, as we passed the newly forming offices we
wondered if the debate was over because one of the camps was already
setting up shop. Shortly after the declaration of President Bush's victory and the conciliatory remarks of Mr. Gore, I was working my way
to a meeting when I noticed Mr. Rumsfeld and a team of suits entering the new office area, which was now inaccessible. The doors, which
had once been glass, had been covered with large sheets of white
paper, and written on the paper were the words "NO MILITARY
ALLOWED." I remember thinking that this was an ominous sign, but
of what I didn't know.

The second was in April of 2001 when I was attending the Army
Pre-Command Course (PCC) at Fort Leavenworth, Kansas. PCC is
designed to expose incoming brigade and battalion commanders to all
that was new and developing in the Army to prepare them for their
next two years in command. And in the process, every senior leader in
the Army came to Leavenworth to share ideas and command philoso-
phy with the newly selected leaders. During this PCC I was excited to
listen to the issues that faced the Army Chief of Staff, General Eric K.
Shinseki, because I was seeing them firsthand. After he spoke and finished discussing his now infamous decision to put the entire Army in
the Black Beret, I had my chance.

"Sir, I'm sure you've seen the Secretary of Defense's transition
team's office that says "NO MILITARY" on the door, and the rumors
that they are preparing to cut the Army by two divisions [almost
35,000 troops]. My question, Sir, are they asking you for your
advice?" General Shinseki replied (and here I must paraphrase): "I

have no idea what's going on behind that door and no one is interested in my advice or opinion."

Later, Paul Wolfowitz, the Deputy Defense Secretary, would state that estimates from General Shinseki that several hundred thousand troops would be needed to secure postwar Iraq were "wildly off the mark." Pentagon officials put the figure closer to 100,000 troops. But who in the building said this? It certainly wasn't the Pentagon's senior and most experienced Army officer. By now it's apparent that time has proven General Shinseki most accurate.

Upon my return from Iraq in 2003, much to my chagrin, I found I would be working every day under a microscope, since my new office was directly across the hall from the Army's senior Operations Officer (G3), Lieutenant General Richard (Dick) Cody. To those who feared and loved him, he was known as "Commander Cody."[15] In 2002, during a pre-Iraq rally at Fort Campbell, KY, President Bush had addressed the 17,000 men and women of the 101st Airborne Division and called Cody "Commander Cody" a number of times during his speech, drawing vast cheers and applause from the troops each time they heard the phrase. In my experience, few commanders were as well known and as well loved as Cody. He was truly a soldiers' soldier.

General Cody had personally changed my assignment from the Army War College in Carlisle, Pennsylvania to the Army Initiatives Group (AIG) in Washington, DC. All I knew about the AIG was that it was normally manned by a select group of smart guys who worked on new concepts and initiatives for the G3 and the Chief of Staff of the Army. By diverting me to the Pentagon, Cody had purposely taken advantage of General Petraeus' decision to allow some of us to leave the theater early before the division returned to Fort Campbell. Former brigade and battalion commanders across the Army who had fought during the invasion were brought to the Pentagon in a number of key roles to help the Army, the Joint Staff and the Secretary of Defense. I hoped that by working in AIG I would get a chance to make good on a promise I'd made in Iraq to a local sheik to help Iraq more from Washington, DC than from Ash Shurah. However, would the Department of Defense really listen to a mere Lieutenant Colonel?

Commander Cody was famous throughout the Army for firing the first shots of the Gulf War in 1991, when he led the first air attack against Iraqi air defenses in southern Iraq. His Apache battalion blew a hole in the Iraqi air defense network that cleared the way for the Air Force and Navy strikes on Baghdad at the beginning of the air campaign. As the Army's senior aviator, Commander Cody had flown every aircraft in the Army inventory and had commanded at virtually every level of the Army, including an Apache battalion in the 101st Airborne Division, the elite Special Forces aviation unit, Task Force 160, stationed at Fort Campbell, Task Force Hawk in Kosovo, and the 101st Airborne Division during Afghanistan. Arguably, the toughest commander in the Army, Cody enjoyed a good chew of tobacco, tough language and had a reputation for cutting through the bullshit and fixing what needed to be fixed, normally through personal presence and passion. I was excited to get an opportunity to see him navigate the treacherous and unforgiving corridors of power in Washington, DC.

My previous Pentagon assignment taught me that candor and character were a dangerous mixture of qualities for an Army Officer in our nation's capital. Men of Cody's caliber and frankness are normally sealed in a glass case with a large sign affixed above their heads saying, "Break only in a case of war!" Well, we were at war—maybe candor and character would work this time.

The office was nicer than I expected. I had a personal desk, two computers and a window. Proximity to power and importance in the building is signified by windows—only the most powerful have a view of the world outside the Pentagon's walls. As I met my new peers, I quickly realized I was in the company of some exceptionally intelligent officers. As I sized them up and tried to determine my role, I quickly realized that what I lacked in formal education I could compensate with operational experience. I was not assigned to this august organization because of my Masters Degree in Business Management from Webster University in St. Louis, but because of my antiterrorism training and time in Iraq.

Things happen. If being on the E-ring wasn't intimidating enough, I learned quickly that I would be privy to numerous private forums and conversations that I hadn't experienced before in my career. During one such conversation, I discovered that the simple act of going to the latrine could result in overhearing a sensitive conversation between senior Army leaders pressed for time and constantly working.

When I finally found a latrine in the E-Ring, I did notice it was small-er than I expected, but pressure and timing made the observation irrel-evant, until I was joined by two gentlemen who entered behind me deep in conversation. The first gentleman occupied the urinal to my right as the other entered the stall to his right.

Attempting to mind my own business, I attended to my business and avoided eye contact, but as their conversation continued, it dawned on me that this latrine was small because it was the private sanctuary of the Chief of Staff of the Army.   As I stood there realizing my mistake, the Acting Chief of Staff, GEN Jack Keene, was on the stool discussing the piss-poor tactics of an officer, senior to myself, during the invasion. I kept my head down trying not to listen, but I could feel the man to my right glaring at me. I sheepishly glanced to my right and immediately recognized retired General and former White House Drug Czar Barry McCaffrey staring at me.

General McCaffrey smiled and shot me a get the hell out of here look. I stopped myself midstream and moved quickly to the sink in an attempt to maintain some decorum as the two discussed relieving this officer or at least ending his career. As I turned to see the Chief exit the stall, all I could muster was a good "Hooahh, Sir" and I got out of the latrine with as much dignity as possible. I glanced back at the door, making a mental note to keep it off limits. It was at this moment I truly realized I was sitting on a footstool at the seat of power!

Later, as I was talking to my new deskmates, the office door sud-denly swung open with a bang and in walked Commander Cody. Cody doesn't enter a room, he consumes it with his personality, instantly stopping every conversation, telephone call and email. In other words, the room stops and all attention is focused on him. Unlike the others, who were comfortable with his presence, I immedi-ately stood at attention. With great fanfare, he yelled "Chris" and quickly crossed the room, grabbed my right hand and pulled our right shoulders together, which pulled our Screaming Eagle Combat Patches together. Squeezing my arm above the elbow, he said, "Welcome to the combat club brother." If there was any doubt in the minds of my new peers that Cody had personally picked me for this job, it was erased.

There are some benefits when you work for a senior officer of the Army. The first of them is expedited in-processing. Normally an arduous and drawn out process that justifies civilian jobs in the Pentagon, mine was streamlined so I was on the job in less than three days. Once settled in, I had an immediate audience with Cody and started to receive phone requests from across the Army Staff to provide lessons and observations from Iraq. Unfortunately, the two most important offices I had hoped to visit were vacant; the Army was at war without an Army Secretary or Chief of Staff.

Both Secretary Thomas E. White and Army Chief of Staff General Eric K. Shinseki had either left office or been fired during the war. There was obviously a lingering tension in the E-ring between the Army leadership and the Secretary of Defense's office. I did not really grasp or understand this friction since most of it had originated while I was preparing for and fighting in Iraq. I was determined to ignore this tension. As one of the very few officers at the Pentagon who had actually served in Iraq, I hoped to stay above the bureaucratic battles and be in a position to help ease tensions and continue to help the troops who remained in harm's way. Having Commander Cody in charge made that possible.

THE ARMY STRATEGIC PLANNING BOARD

At our first private meeting, General Cody and I discussed everything from the performance of our equipment on the battlefield to my attempted meeting with Grand Ayatollah Sistani. During the meeting, Cody gave me my duty description and my additional unofficial role as his primary Iraqi Advisor and Scout within the building. As his Iraqi Advisor, he wanted me to help the Army Staff cut through antiquated and bureaucratic processes to get the troops what they needed rather than what the bureaucrats or the beltway bandits thought they needed. He gave me carte blanche to throw the "bull-shit flag" whenever something didn't make sense to a soldier on the ground. As his scout, I was to immerse myself in any and all meetings, forums, and conventions, and report when I saw that the Army community was straying from the war effort. He made it plain to me that anyone conducting business-as-usual causing unnecessary pain and suffering on our soldiers in combat would not be tolerated. He then gave me authority to act on his behalf by allowing me to use his name whenever I felt the actions of the staff were contrary to his intent. I did not accept this responsibility lightly and rarely used it because, as I would eventually learn, the Army Staff was at war and doing everything possible to win.

Armed with this unorthodox guidance and mission, I started to physically explore the unique environment of the Army Staff. It was not long before I stumbled upon the Army Strategic Planning Board (ASPB), which was easily the most innovative and influential forum in the building. I had never heard of the board before, but I instinctively knew it was something I wanted to be part of. This was clearly "the" planning board that set the tone for all others within the Army bureaucracy, and I literally had to push my way into my first meeting. True to form, the ASPB had not existed until Cody became the G3 in June of 2002. In a moment of frustration with the glacial pace of new initiatives, Cody established the board in order to quickly prioritize resources within the Army in an effort to better support the war and to help sustain current and future operations.

The genesis of the ASPB came after an August 2002 meeting General Cody organized with the division commanders who were preparing for war in Iraq. The purpose of this summit was to ask the commanders to prioritize a list of all the equipment and weapons they needed to fight a mid-to-high intensity conflict on a chemically contaminated battlefield. After two days of discussions and presentations by a number of technology and equipment experts, Cody had what he needed to accelerate the Army acquisition process and rapidly purchase what the field commanders wanted and needed to fight in Iraq. The ASPB gave General Cody a weekly forum to personally prioritize, track, and anticipate the needs of an Army at war. It also gave him the ability to cut through an Army establishment that desperately needed overhauling. The Army acquisition process, with all its laws and bureaucracy, was designed for administrative efficiencies but not effectiveness in war. It simply could not keep up with an Army engaged in day-to-day combat. Commander Cody was a master at finding legal ways to work the system and give the warriors what they needed to fight and win.

The primary problem with the acquisition process was the Army's inability to simply buy a commercially available item right off the shelf. To streamline the antiquated process of Army acquisition, Cody hired an Army scientist, Colonel Bruce Jette. Jette was an exceptional out-of-the-box thinker who understood the acquisition process, but more importantly he knew how to legally use or bypass the unresponsive bureaucratic machine. He also had the industry contracts that proved invaluable in getting what the field commanders needed—and getting it NOW.

Jette and his team of ten soldiers and civilians were called the Rapid Equipping Force (REF). By the fall of 2003, they had pushed dozens of technologies and innovations to the men on the ground. Remote control toy cars with video cameras used to look down streets and in buildings; devices to lower into wells in Afghanistan to look for weapons and tunnels; small unmanned airplanes to scout enemy positions; innovations in body armor to include lung and rib protection; and acoustic sensors to determine sniper locations by sound. Colonel Jette was a hands-on warrior who constantly returned to Iraq and Afghanistan to talk to his teams and the field commanders. He traveled to test sites and constantly pushed the system to satisfy the commanders' needs.

The REF team was knee-deep in the war and nothing was going to stop them from getting anything the soldiers needed. No other group of unsung heroes did more to help our soldiers on the ground. They tirelessly rebuffed the naysayers and bureaucrats, which made them very unpopular in the Pentagon, but loved by those in the field who knew what they did. As Cody's scout, I watched this process to identify the obstructionists in the Pentagon who had their knives out waiting for a chance to destroy this team. The internal enemy was everywhere, wearing both civilian clothes and uniforms, and I had to resort to unconventional means to identify them; it was strikingly similar to finding the *Fedayeen* hiding amongst the rioting crowds in Najaf. Over the course of the year, we either converted the naysayers or removed them.

THE IMPROVISED EXPLOSIVE DEVICE TASK FORCE

On August 1, 2003, General Peter Schoomaker was sworn in as the 35th Chief of Staff of the Army. Schoomaker[16] was a Special Forces

Officer well known for his coolness under fire and extensive combat experience. He walked into the building with his now famously dry and unassuming persona. He was confident in his skills as a warrior, his duties as an officer and his role as the Chief of the United States Army. In one of his first meetings with the Army Staff, Schoomaker was rumored to say, "I know a number of you are wondering why the Secretary of Defense would hire a man who has been retired for three years? Well rest assured that I came to DC in my '72 pickup truck, with my gun rack and my honor. In two to three years, I will leave DC in that same pickup with my honor intact."[16]

His unsubtle message was clear to me; don't worry about why General Shinseki was gone and why he was here . . . our job and his job was to serve our soldiers and country. Politics is best left to the politicians; we had a war to fight and for now that was all that mattered. With that statement, he started to pull slips of paper out of his pockets and give them to his aides. Those slips of paper represented his thoughts and goals for the Army. He had jotted them down on napkins and notebook paper during his long drive to DC. They eventually became the Chief's sixteen focus areas for the Army's future.

While the Army dived headlong into Schoomaker's sixteen focus areas, the chief added a new worry—Improvised Explosive Devices (IEDs) and the effects they were beginning to have on our forces in Iraq. Simply put, an IED can be made from almost anything with any type of material and initiator. It is a "homemade bomb" that is designed to cause death or injury by using explosives alone or in combination with toxic chemicals, biological toxins or radiological material. IEDs were by no means a new weapon and have been the documented weapon of choice for terrorist organizations for over a hundred years. Easy to make, they can be produced in varying sizes, functioning methods, containers and delivery methods. A child could be taught to make an IED in less than a day. Most worrisome, with all the military munitions scattered about Iraq's countryside after the invasion, an IED could be easily fashioned utilizing commercial or military explosives, homemade explosives or military ordnance and ordnance components. There was an endless supply in Saddam's storehouses, schools, and strewn about the farm lands. IED materials and components were everywhere.

Although the use of IEDs was limited during the major combat phase of the war, this tactic was gaining momentum in the post conflict period. Their use was an indicator that the conflict was entering a new phase and that the enemy was morphing from a conventional military force into a terrorist group, an insurgency, or both. This was an unscientific assessment based on the fact that IEDs were the weapon of choice for just about every known terrorist organization and insurgency in the world.

While serving in the Combating Terrorism Directorate (J34) of the Joint Staff Operations Center from 1999 to 2001, I had studied and trained with IEDs in laboratory and field conditions to understand their effects and help develop simple low-tech countermeasures for commanders in the field. In that capacity, I was part of a project that capitalized on lessons learned from the British Army and Israeli Defense Force gathered during their conflicts with the Irish Republican Army, Islamic Jihad, Hezbollah and Hamas. The result was the merging of a number of similar organizations within the Department of Defense charged with rapidly purchasing off-the-shelf force protection equipment, rapidly prototyping anti-IED technologies, and developing tactics, techniques and procedures to help forces on the ground safely identify and combat vehicle and roadside IEDs. My participation in this earlier project, as well as the 2000 U.S.S *Cole* Commission, helped the Army Staff identify the organizations and programs we would need to leverage as we formulated the Army's first response to the growing IED threat.

I decided to go to my old directorate, J34, to find out what the Joint Staff or Office of the Secretary of Defense for technology was doing to fight the emerging IED threat worldwide. I thought that I would find a tremendous effort in progress which I could then easily tap into and secure a vehicle for getting the technologies and experts into the field to help the Army. Much to my surprise, I found an organization that had been neutered by the Department of Homeland Security and was sitting atrophied and dormant after losing its General Officer and operating under the command of a retiring Air Force Colonel. The organization apparently lost most of its key personnel, oversight authority and funding as the Pentagon reacted to initiatives to stand up a Homeland Security organization immediately following 9/11. I tried on numerous occasions to tap into what apparently didn't exist anymore. I reported back to General Cody that if we wanted to take the IED fight to the enemy we would have to do it without much help from the Joint Staff.

As usual, Cody's response to my report was swift. He ordered me to develop an organizational structure for a Task Force that could directly confront the IED threat in Iraq and Afghanistan. He said, "I want a team of experts who can get to the sand box and save lives!" I immediately went to work building a straw-man organization by tapping into former members of the Technical Support Working Group, the Physical Security Equipment Action Group, and a private corporation I'd worked with in the past—Wexford Group. This corporation was pivotal; without them, we would never find the former operators we needed to build the field teams. The Columbus, GA, branch of Wexford was headed up by a former boss and friend of mine, Retired Colonel Hank Kinnison. The corporation had managed to retain former Special Forces and Delta Force warriors who possessed special skills for use within military contracts.

I had decided to start with Wexford to find a corps of experts the IED Task Force would require because just about everyone on active duty who possessed the required skills was deployed and fighting. The skills we needed limited us to a finite pool of men—and we needed them immediately to stop the casualties we were taking in Iraq. I contacted Kinnison and presented my idea over the phone. As we spoke, I could tell I had gone to the right man and the right team. No hemming or hawing; his responses were quick, precise and positive; he expressed the sense of urgency that I needed. Kinnison quickly offered to pull his experts together to develop a timeline and feasible solutions for forming a first class Field Team. I sent him my manning diagram, mission statement and intent. Within hours, he sent me a stronger proposal with a feasibility statement and possible timeline. This was just what I needed to go back to Cody for a deskside decision.

My access to Cody was unprecedented. In my career, I had never before worked so closely with a senior general officer. All I had to do was walk to the entrance of his door, look at him and he would stop what he was doing and ask me in. This day I had a packet of slides in my hands named IED Task Force. I told him we had the potential to tackle the IED issue within 45 days. He then motioned me to his desk and I knelt down to his right and briefed him on the slides. Our problem could not be solved by technology alone—success was a matter of training. We needed to teach Tactics, Techniques, and Procedures (TTP) for preventing, finding and destroying IEDs. More importantly, we needed to train soldiers to detect an IED and use the active device to track, hunt down and kill or capture those who emplaced it, built it, financed it, and finally those who were actually responsible for it.

To complement the field teams, we would need a command element at the joint headquarters in Baghdad. This would ensure the field teams had unfettered access to the field commanders and freedom to move about the battlefield. Finally, to capture what the field teams were seeing on the ground, we would need to establish electronic and digital connectivity to the Army's Center for Army Lessons Learned (CALL) at Fort Leavenworth, KS. This connectivity would allow the command team to pass lessons and training vignettes to our training centers for Army and Marine forces preparing to deploy.

We needed to educate our troops on the IED threat before they arrived in Iraq. To do this, we would have to build our own team of experts at CALL dedicated exclusively to analyzing and disseminating information about IEDs. They had to be credible former officers and noncommissioned officers who would travel across the Army and teach IED Defeat Procedures. The Army has a strong tradition of self-critique, better known as the After Action Review (AAR) process. This process, developed in the 1980's at the Army's combat training centers in the Mojave Desert and eventually the swamps of Louisiana, placed Army units in unwinnable wartime scenarios, forcing them to learn battlefield lessons through tough and realistic force-on-force missions against the best enemy the US Army could field.

This enemy, or Opposing Force (OPFOR), rarely lost and taught our forces fierce lessons that would forever shape how the Army trained, manned, equipped, fought and learned—most importantly learned. In essence we were blooding the force just short of combat and hardening our leaders to take the hard right over the easy wrong. If you lost a battle, you learned how the enemy beat you and if you won, you learned that despite your win, you still needed to improve, do it better, do it faster and with fewer casualties. This process of teaching our leaders how to think was the very system we needed to tap into if we were going to defeat the IED threat. The concept was a holistic approach to fighting IEDs, not a silver bullet to be manufactured in a favored Congressman's district.

To give the team the ability to defeat an IED incident, we would need six distinct skill sets within the team: a team leader, combat tracker, a school-trained man-hunter, SF explosives expert, two Delta operators, a communications specialist, and an SF medic. This mix of disciplines would enable the team to approach an IED with a trained eye toward complex ambushes.

This is how we envisioned it would work. Once arriving at an incident, the operators would quickly assess the ambush site and establish security to prevent continued injury from the IED. The explosives expert would examine the device from a distance to determine the type and provide the combat tracker an approximate range to the enemy who was watching the IED. Two operators would join the combat tracker, who was simultaneously determining the number of insurgents, time they spent on location, their approach and exit direction, and their potential observation point. The operators would use the distance provided by the explosives expert to begin their hunt for the insurgent. Once the insurgent was killed or forced to withdraw, the SF explosives expert would neutralize the device and conduct a battlefield triage to exploit the device in order to add to his analysis and to eventually track and find the bomb maker. He would then provide technical data and pictures to the team's communications expert who in turn would digitally send the technical data and frequencies to the Combined Explosives Exploitation Cell (CEXC) in Baghdad for immediate assessment and exploitation. If all went as planned, the medic on the team would rarely be needed.

Commander Cody smiled at me and said, "Perfect. I know just the man to lead the Task Force—Joe Votel." I didn't know who Joe Votel was at the time, but I quickly met him and became a fan. Colonel Votel had just given up his command of the Army's elite 75th Ranger Regiment and was the new Director of Information in the Army's Operations Center in the Pentagon. Votel had already been selected for promotion to brigadier general and carried the requisite level of prestige and credibility that would be necessary to pull off recruiting, equipping, training and deploying an untested Task Force into a combat zone in less than 60 days.

After meeting Colonel Votel, I gave him the original concept and allowed him time to digest and become comfortable with it while at the same time getting used to the pace at which the project was moving. The sudden shock of being volunteered to lead a nonexistent unit, his unfamiliarity with the Pentagon and a sudden reliance on me (someone he didn't know) was a bit overwhelming. As it all soaked in, I used Cody's authority to have Hank Kinnison send his planning team to Washington to help Votel and me further develop the concept and begin recruiting the right men for the Task Force. The planning team arrived without a question or a request for funding. Kinnison once again proved his worth as a friend and dedicated citizen.

The planning team consisted of two former Delta Force planners who had over 40 years of Special Operations experience both in and out of "the unit." As I would eventually learn, elite operators who had actually served in Delta always referred to Delta as "the unit." For twenty years, operators from "the unit" and I had crossed paths in training and in foreign countries, but now I was going to have the special privilege of getting to see them in action. I would not be disappointed.

The two former operators Kinnison sent, Rick and Eric, were consummate professionals. Since my first phone call, they had worked overtime to develop, war game and fine tune options for Colonel Votel's consideration. Rick had been instrumental in the development of the assessment and training program for the unit, so he was focused on the types of men we would need. Having his former teammates on a rolodex was certainly convenient. Eric was the skunk works and weapons guru, and as such, determined not who we needed, but what we needed. If the Army didn't have it, Eric would buy it or make it. The four of us worked around the clock for three days to finalize the Task Force make-up and deployment plan. Cody was pumped to see the team and periodically gave us input to keep the planning moving. We didn't waste time with briefing multiple courses of action and remained unconcerned about stepping on toes.

At the end of three days, Cody blessed the plan and the team moved out to make the Task Force a reality. Eric and Rick started to hire the team members and Colonel Votel and I went about finding the money. Throughout this period, the Wexford Group committed substantial monies and resources to this project before we had secured funding. They did so knowing that if we failed they wouldn't be paid.

I suddenly found myself learning a lot about contracts, "colors" of Congressional dollars, contracting officers, and how to leverage existing programs to make things happen in less than five years! General Cody then directed me to go before the ASPB to secure the funding. Although it seemed like a formality since Cody chaired the ASPB, he felt that he needed to do the right thing in the eyes of the Army Staff by exposing the IED Task Force to the same rigor and scrutiny any project faced at the ASPB. However, he left it to me to face down the full ASPB. After two more all-nighters, and finding the best spots to grab short naps on my office floor, I was ready for the moment.

The rigor of the ASPB process ensured that the IED Task Force became a reality—a legal and fully funded reality. We managed to eventually secure about $20 million to create the IED Task Force and in time to create the foundation for a new Army organization called the Asymmetric Regiment, which would continue to explore innovative methods to fight terrorists. Within twenty days of securing the funds, and within 25 days of creating the straw-man concept, the task force was prepared to deploy, but we had one last hurdle to overcome. Since this project was not solicited from the field, we would need to contact Combined Joint Task Force 7 (CJTF-7) in Iraq and ask for their support. As luck would have it, the CJTF-7 Operations Officer (J-3) was a former boss of mine. I had worked for the general in a number of jobs and hoped to use our relationship to seek an audience aimed at convincing him to accept tactical control of the Task Force and deploying them within Iraq. Field commanders are justifiably cautious when teams from Washington, DC call and offer free help, but he immediately expressed his willingness to accept our offer to fly to Baghdad and personally explain the composition and intent of the Task Force, serving as a testament to his professionalism. I hoped it also had a little to do with his trust in me as one of his former subordinates.

On December 12, 2003, the first two field teams deployed to Baghdad and were further deployed into the sector with the 4th

Infantry Division and 1st Armored Division. The teams had an immediate and profound impact on reducing the number of combat casualties caused by IEDs. In the first six months, the teams surveyed as
many IEDs and incidents as humanly possible. The data collected and
lessons derived from their efforts influenced in-country and pre-
deployment training, helped units formulate new and innovative tactics, fine-tune search techniques, improve targeting procedures, and
drove rapid development of improved body and vehicle armor by the
defense industries. I knew we were on the right track when, as I was
seeking some additional information from one of my British counterparts, he confessed to me that he could no longer help me because,
"Mate, you've [the U.S. Army] become the world's expert on IEDs.
Your teams have seen and defeated more IEDs in the last six months
than we have seen in the last 30 years . . . we need your help now."

Despite the initial success of the IED Task Force on the ground, we
still faced a bloody and uphill battle within the Pentagon. After pur-
posefully bypassing the Joint Staff to get the field teams deployed in a
hurry, we now had time to work with them and the Office of the
Secretary of Defense (OSD) to make the Task Force a "Joint" effort
and not just an Army one. Putting the cart before the horse was necessary to save lives, but now the right thing to do was to seek proper
Pentagon backing and authority. Without Joint and OSD support, the
Task Force would never have the requisite long-term power and funding needed to accomplish its mission. We never considered this an
Army-only issue—it was an American issue. We also knew the IED
problem wasn't going away anytime soon and it was our responsibility to build the right institutional solution, which would be capable of
sustaining itself after our departure to other duties. Besides, we all
knew that even the best ideas had very short existences in the
Pentagon unless they could rapidly secure Joint authority and funding.

While the field teams were in the Iraqi trenches fighting the hor-
rific battle against IEDs, the Army's IED Headquarters, led by Colonel
Votel and his executive officer, started a second front in the Pentagon.
This second front was designed to coordinate IED efforts between the
Services, the Joint Staff and OSD.

Although the Army counter-IED effort in Iraq and Afghanistan
was reducing the killing and maiming of our troops, the Army had not

been an original invitee to meetings on IED program priority, funding, and decision-making within the Department of Defense. Again, we were forced to barge our way into these meetings. For the first couple of months, every meeting Votel and I attended exposed us to yet another forum or office that was working, or thought they were working, the counter-IED issue in the Pentagon. There was a vast, slowly materializing network of offices throughout the Pentagon charged with working some aspect of the counter-IED threat, and accessing the funding to combat IEDs was now flowing to work the IED issue. These so called experts, scientists, and acquisition gurus were all seemingly set on avoiding us in an apparent effort to protect their multimillion dollar institutions. All of these fiefdoms were more then willing to discuss, analyze, study, and debate IEDs. However, none of them seemed to show any urgency in getting solutions to our soldiers in combat. As our frustration grew, so did our determination to identify and determine the functions these dispersed and inept organizations actually served. Eventually, the light of day either forced them to play ball with us or scurry away to a dark corner to die.

Using Cody's mandate to slice through the bullshit, our efforts to coordinate with every IED forum and office in the Department of Defense slowly paid off. In very short order, we went from pushing ourselves into the room to sitting at the head table and controlling the agenda. Additionally, Colonel Votel began to coordinate and share information with the FBI, Secret Service and CIA, using the same contacts we had established with the Combined Explosive Exploitation Cell in Baghdad. Our gradual control and prominence in these forums happened and was solidified because the field teams were feeding us first-hand data and ground truth from Iraq and Afghanistan—no one had more current data or exploited IED information better than our Task Force. The field teams had become so efficient that they were able to send us IED incident reports in less than 24 hours followed by detailed reports, with lessons learned and recommended solutions within 72 hours. No other organization had access to this type of information; what we lacked in authority we compensated for with dynamic information and knowledge.

As the IED Task Force gained recognition in the building, over 27 separate IED organizations within the American government began to seek our advice, access our information and request membership on our teams in Iraq and Afghanistan. It wasn't long before Votel was able to host the first Pentagon IED forum. For the first time, all the disparate IED organizations in the Pentagon were sharing critical information, coordinating and combining similar efforts and, informally, prioritizing technology and test programs. However, despite the synergy, Votel and the Army still had no authority to direct any other organization within the government to do anything. The Task Force still lacked the authority and funding necessary to take the fight to the next level.

Before long, the IED Task Force became the center of the counter-IED world in the Pentagon, and quoting the Task Force suddenly had cachet for those who didn't have the vaguest idea what an IED looked like. General Cody was fond of saying, "You can never find the father of an ugly baby, but a cute baby has a thousand fathers." The IED Task Force was suddenly the cutest baby around with a thousand doting fathers.

One morning I was sitting at my desk researching the details of an IED attack that had taken the life of a National Guard soldier from a Midwestern state. The young soldier hadn't been directly killed by the IED, but the blast had disabled the truck he was riding in, and during the ensuing gun battle, he was killed by a rocket propelled grenade (RPG). General Cody had received a letter from the soldier's family asking for any details he could release on the death of their son. Cody always took time to write the families of our soldiers who had lost their lives in the line of duty. When their letters asked for details, the AIG would help General Cody understand the circumstance surrounding the loss. What most people didn't realize was that General Cody and his wife Vickie had two sons flying Apache helicopters in Iraq with the 101st Airborne Division in Mosul. His love of soldiers was as much personal as it was professional; every time a helicopter went down, he turned ghostly white.

As I was writing the report for Cody, I periodically glanced up at CSPAN to see how General Schoomaker was doing in his open hearing before the House Armed Services Committee (HASC). Since the AIG was normally involved in helping the General's personal staff prepare for his hearings, we always watched to see if our notes and charts helped. We also needed to be current because his staff, the guys who sit behind him during these sessions, would constantly send us requests from their Blackberries for additional information during the hearings to help the chief when the information was not at his finger-tips.

During this particular hearing, the Congressmen were grilling the chief about IEDs and what the Army was doing about it, and the chief openly credited the IED Task Force for facing the threat on the ground and coordinating IED efforts within DOD. I was shocked, not from what the chief said, but that the Committee members also acknowl-edged the efforts of the IED Task Force, crediting it with making a profound difference in the war. Then a senior Congressman pressed the chief for DOD's plan to institutionalize the Task Force since the IED threat wasn't going away. The chief told the Congressman the Army was preparing to make the IED Task Force a permanent Army organization—hopefully with Joint and Inter-Service participation. I grinned at my deskmate, Captain Paul Weyrauch, and yelled, "He did it!" OSD would have to respond—they would have to fund us now!" The Task Force was no longer a Band-Aid fix to a long-term problem. We were actually going to create a new unit to fight IEDs.

Only three days after these hearings, General John Abizaid, the Commander of The United States Central Command, sent a message to the Department of Defense asking for a "Manhattan Project"–like effort to seriously develop technologies and tactics to defeat the use of IEDs in Iraq and Afghanistan. The message quickly passed through the Joint Staff, to the Army Staff and to Army Operations. I was sum-moned to General Cody's office with Colonel Votel and handed the message. We spent the next two hours discussing our plan for briefing the Chairman of the Joint Chiefs the next morning.

The chairman's corridor is adorned with white pillars, dark mahogany walls and glass doors etched with the Joint Staff symbol. It was a far cry from the bare and sterile Army corridor; the chairman's corridor is intimidating and formal. We entered the small, yet elabo-rate, conference room prior to the arrival of the chairman and vice chairman, giving General Cody an opportunity to introduce Colonel Votel and me to the senior members of the Chairman's Staff and make some pleasantries. The room could only seat 12, so it was hard not to be noticed or to participate in the discussion. I hadn't seen the chairman since 2001 when I last worked in the Pentagon, when he was the vice chairman. He looked relaxed, but worn. I couldn't imagine how difficult his job must have been since assuming the chairmanship from General Henry H. Shelton—9/11, Afghanistan, Iraq, and now the scrutiny of the pending Presidential election. I wondered if he ever got any sleep or took any vacations.

The Chairman, General Richard B. Myers, always an attentive listener and gracious man, looked around the room and shook the hand of everyone he didn't know or work with every day. He started the meeting by telling us about the Abizaid message and acknowledged that he had heard of the IED Task Force but didn't have a complete picture of its work. He wanted to know if we could meet the Abizaid request for a Manhattan Project for IEDs. General Cody asked Colonel Votel to give the chairman a quick rundown. Although I wasn't trying to collect any intelligence, I was in a unique position to watch the Chairman's body language and see the key notes Vice Chairman General Peter Pace wrote to himself—the room was too small for much personal space or privacy.

When Votel had finished, the chairman looked relieved and impressed. Pace's notes included three bullets: funding, authority, and jointness. The three notes were the exact questions that needed to be asked and answered by the senior officers in the room. The chairman settled the issue and said he would support the Army's current effort and recommend to the Secretary of Defense that the Army be the Executive Agency (EA) within DOD for countering IEDs. We were further directed to begin coordination with the other services to determine their desired involvement and to prepare to brief OSD in two days. As with most victories in the Pentagon, the associated work resulting from it is normally three times the original effort. We were all sleeping in our offices again.

Based on the ease of our meeting with General Myers I really thought we were prepared to brief the Deputy Secretary of Defense, Mr. Wolfowitz and the Senior OSD Staff, but I was wrong. What I saw at this briefing was the single greatest disappointment in human character I've witnessed in my entire military career. When Colonel Votel began the brief, I scanned the room to assess the body language. All of a sudden the Secretary of the Air Force, James Roche, at the head of the table, caught my attention. Despite Col. Votel's briefing, he was still talking loudly with another civilian. As respectfully as possible, General Cody leaned toward the Secretary to let him know the briefing had started. I was shocked when the Secretary waved Cody off like a mere peasant.

Unfazed, Colonel Votel continued while the Secretary began shuffling his notes, which appeared to be well prepared. He soon started interrupting Votel and systematically destroyed his attempts to reach the end of his presentation. Yet, despite the Air Force Secretary's unprecedented rudeness, Votel pressed the brief with a vengeance because he knew his embarrassment was outweighed by the gravity of the topic and its effects on our troops in harm's way. I'd seen great acts of courage in my career, but many of them paled in comparison to the composure Colonel Votel displayed during that meeting.

Of all the parties present during this decision brief, the Air Force had the fewest troops in harm's way. Their attendance, in my opinion, was for information. I didn't think formalizing the Task Force would be perceived as a threat to any service, but evidently this individual strongly disagreed. Secretary Roche became the squeaky wheel in the room; he argued that there was no need for an Executive Agency for IEDs—-the services were already working together to solve the problem and consolidating their efforts would only act to slow the incredible progress that "we" had already realized. Each time he made his feeble and uninformed arguments, he would lean forward and look down the table at General Cody and say "right Dick—-isn't that right Dick?" General Cody respectfully responded at first, but eventually kept silent. I'm not clear when and how Colonel Votel finished his brief, but before it was over the whole head table had digressed into a half dozen sidebar conversations caused by the Secretary's protests. On three separate occasions, the Chair of the meeting regained control of the discussion and asked intelligent and thoughtful questions, only to be interrupted and challenged by Secretary Roche who was now advocating something called an IPT. I didn't even know what an IPT was, or at least what the secretary wanted it to be.

Secretary Roche singlehandedly stopped our progress in its tracks. I could not help but be impressed with his ability to control the room.

However, I grew very angry when I considered how many soldiers and marines would die because of his seemingly selfish single-mindedness.

In the end, the Air Force Secretary's agenda prevailed and Mr. Wolfowitz tabled the issue until the Army had time to research the difference between an Integrated Production Team (IPT) and an Executive Agency. I never understood why it was our responsibility, but we got the task to determine which would work better to realize the synergy we needed to beat IEDs. In the end, the Army became the Executive Agency for IEDs within the Department of Defense, but only after agreeing to give up control of the Research and Development dollars the Air Force would apply to the problem. This compromise made Secretary Roche's agenda clear—the Army can be the Executive Agency as long as the Air Force did not have to surrender any money or man-hours. In other words, IEDs were not Secretary Roche's problem. His behavior at the decision meeting acted as a stark reminder to each of us what happens when institutional culture and duty collide. It's an everyday occurrence in the Pentagon and those who cannot recognize it or learn to work the system eventually fail the men and women in harm's way. It is tough to compromise on basic principles, but if you don't do it from time to time, things grind to a halt and soldiers die. Because Secretary Roche was willing to kill a project and endanger thousand of lives rather than part with a few budget dollars, the Army compromised.

THE CANCELLATION OF THE COMANCHE HELICOPTER

An Army Initiatives Group Officer attended every meeting General Cody held to capture notes and taskings for the staff to tackle. We directed most of the taskings with suspenses for the Army Staff in order to help Cody keep the organization moving forward. In this capacity, each of us on the AIG was exposed to dozens of different programs and projects that fell under General Cody's purview. One of those programs was the Aviation Task Force (ATF). ATF was headquartered in the Pentagon with the sole purpose of assessing Army Aviation and its ability to support the current war as well as other existing war plans.

I was not a usual attendee at these meetings because I wasn't an aviator, and when I was present, I found my lack of aviation expertise, outside of being a passenger, made the meetings difficult to follow. My mind wandered when I found myself stuck in these meetings, which were always replete with acronyms, avionics and massive egos. Yet, the issues discussed were dear to my heart, having just left the only helicopter-borne air assault division in the world. So I did my best to stay engaged in the process of determining if Army aviation was in trouble and I could clearly see that it was. The total number of aircraft the Army had in the active and reserve forces, multiplied by the intense number of flying hours they were logging in Iraq, Afghanistan, Bosnia, Kosovo, Korea, and in the United States for homeland defense, multiplied again by the horrific environmental conditions to which they were being exposed, and divided by the size of the budget allocated to sustaining them, equated to a looming disaster.

I wondered if General Cody hadn't been an aviator would anyone have noticed what was going on and the magnitude of the problem? It took an aviator to recognize the true danger and to keep the issues on the front burner despite all the other urgent and competing priorities facing the Army. With no outside pressure or guidance, Cody decided to tackle this problem within his own organization to ensure it didn't fall into obscurity until it became obvious to all when aviation units could no longer do their jobs. By leveraging the experts within the Army Staff, the Department of Defense, and the aviation schools and centers within the Army, Cody went in search of a solution. When the dust settled, he found himself looking at one of the most difficult and emotional decisions of his life.

Previously, General Cody had visited Boeing Corporation where they had let him fly the first Comanche helicopter, billed as the future of Army aviation. When he returned, a baseball bat delivered to the side of his head could not have removed the ear-to-ear grin on his face. He was now officially the first active duty aviator to fly the Comanche. Although he had flown only a prototype, it was a fully functional aircraft and he was in love with it. At first, he could barely contain his excitement. The Comanche was everything he had dreamed it would be and would carry the Army's aviation branch through most of the first half of the 21st century. For aviators like Cody, it was a dream come true.

Less than three weeks after Cody's return from Boeing, the ATF recommended killing the Comanche program and redirecting the programmed dollars for a variety of other efforts, such as: purchasing over 400 additional older model helicopters desperately needed to fight the war on terrorism; refitting and repairing the current fleet; and transferring technologies from the Comanche to the Apache fleet. The recommendation, while not totally unexpected, was still an exceptional recommendation. Killing off a fully funded project was not a usual practice in the Pentagon and one only has to look at the bloody political war over dropping the Crusader Artillery System to see how ugly such a move can get. What impressed me the most about the recommendation was that it was coming from officers who all wore silver aviation wings with stars, and stars with wreaths on them (indicating they were senior pilots with thousands of flying hours).

These individuals were all senior and master aviators, the most experienced the Army possessed, and they were telling the ranking aviator in the Army that he could not afford to continue to fund the Comanche program and effectively fight the war on terrorism. They were advocating ending a project most of them had waited and worked for for almost two decades. It was a practical example of men of honor taking the hard right over the easy wrong. As I looked around the room at the bowed heads and disappointed faces, I thought of the men of my old battalion and smiled knowing that the men in this room were willing to make the hard decisions necessary to ensure the U.S. helicopter force in Iraq and Afghanistan would remain safe, deadly and ready to support *No Slack* and the dozens of other battalions fighting that day around the world.

Once General Cody was presented with the recommendation and reasoning behind it, he wasted no time getting the decision brief to the Army Chief of Staff so it could get to the Secretary of Defense in very short order. The airframes in Iraq were rapidly deteriorating and we were beginning to sustain combat losses from shoulder-fired missiles. We needed replacement aircraft quickly. It didn't take long to convince the chief that the recommendation was sound, and his staff coordinated a decision brief to the Secretary of Defense who also agreed with the recommendation and prepared to brief the President of the United States.

The decision brief to the President was scheduled for a Saturday morning in the oval office. General Cody was the main attraction, armed with 26 slides justifying the cancellation of potentially the most sophisticated helicopter in history. The ATF had done an excellent job of preparing the boss to describe the situation, the problem and the recommendation. But this brief had a fourth dimension I wasn't familiar with—Congressional fallout. Despite a soundly reasoned and well justified recommendation to cancel the Comanche, the staff had to show the President the second- and third-order effects of any possible decision. These included job losses, industry impacts and possible Congressional reaction; yet the ATF had thought through these political issues and the presentation articulated the positives of building the 400 plus airframes, transferring the new technologies, etc. It seemed all was set; everyone had done their homework and the boss was ready to take action—-we must kill the Comanche.

While the briefing team left the Pentagon and crossed the Potomac, the AIG and ATF remained in the dugout and tried to stay busy, feeling a bit helpless. Once the briefing was complete, there was nothing more for them to do. It was up to Cody to sell it. About 45 minutes after the briefing team left, the phone rang. Cody was back and it was over. We could hear him talking loudly as we jogged toward his office. When we got to his office, he was laughing and telling the story of how he, the Army Chief of Staff, Secretary of Defense, and the President hunched around the briefing book in the oval office. Apparently, General Cody was only three slides and five minutes into the brief before the President interrupted and asked, "Is canceling the Comanche the right thing to do Dick?" Cody looked him in the eye and said "Yes sir."

The President asked the same question of each person in the room and got the same response. He then looked back at General Cody and said, "OK, approved. Cancel it." With that, Cody reached for the tabbed portion of the brief and flipped to the slide titled "Congressional Fallout" and tried to show the President who would be upset by his decision. The President stopped General Cody mid-sentence and again asked, "Is canceling this helicopter the right thing to do?"

"Yes sir, it's the right thing to do"

"OK, I don't care who gets mad, it's cancelled."

In a display of enlightened staff work, the ATF had prepared a letter of intent with the President's signature directing that the savings from the cancellation of the Comanche could only be used to fund the Army aviation priorities outlined for the President that Saturday morning. If this hadn't been done, there would have been a mad scramble for those funds and much of it would have gone to other Pentagon programs, worsening the aviation shortfalls.

With the President's approval and his letter of intent for the reallocation of the funds, there was still one major hurdle left to negotiate—the aviation industry. General Cody felt it was important to explain his rational for the Comanche cancellation to the industry and get their acknowledgment of its necessity, if not their approval. He also felt it was necessary to get their input on how to minimize the impact of the cancellation on the industry and ensure that his shift in priorities wouldn't face any unforeseen friction in the near and long term.

I was nervous when we entered the chief's conference room. The room is always dark because of the mahogany table, red captain's chairs, and forest green rug. The table accommodates twenty, and there was another twenty filling back row seats. Being a soldier, I own one suit and one blue sports coat, so I'm no expert when it comes to pricing a suit, but I can confidently say there wasn't a suit in the room from JC Penny's. These were not the kind of guys I was used to being around—pin-striped, Rolex wearing, power types. The fact that they had come, personally, helped to further emphasize the significance of Cody's decision to recommend the cancellation of the Comanche. No one could ever accuse Cody of planning to get a job in the defense aviation industry after retirement—these guys were not happy.

The General stepped up to the front of the briefing room and detailed his rationale and vision that lead to his difficult decision. Cody was calm, precise and logical, and before long, they began nodding, smiling and agreeing with his proposals; even when he suggested that the defense aviation industry had failed America's most important military resource—the soldier. The Comanche, no matter how impressive, had become an industry for the sake of itself, not for winning the nation's wars. Boeing appeared to have forgotten why they were building the Comanche, but it was the Army's fault for allowing them to forget. No longer was this business as usual. Soldiers were dying and we needed to remind each other of that fact every day.

KADHIM RETURNS TO AMERICA

In early September 2003, I received an email from Kadhim (my interpreter and cultural advisor in Iraq) telling me that he had completed his tour with the 101st and that he was writing from his empty apartment in St. Louis. He had lost everything—his job, his car, and his girlfriend—because he had gone off to war with us. He was picking up the pieces of his life and wanted some advice on what to do next. I told him if he had enough money to come to DC; he should get here as soon as he could. His skills were in great demand and I thought it would be easy to find him a job. For all Kadhim had done to serve and protect my battalion, I assured him I would stop whatever I was doing to help him find a job that would allow him to stay engaged in the rebuilding of Iraq.

When he arrived in town, Kadhim had just enough money to stay afloat for two to three months. He had managed to find a distant cousin to live with, and was good at cutting corners when it came to day-to-day expenses. Yet I still felt a strong sense of obligation to help him find work. The bond soldiers form in combat is like no other in the world, and it doesn't fade with time, distance or age. Kadhim was one of my men and his actions in places like Najaf and Hillah had saved an untold number of lives. There wasn't anything I wouldn't do to help him.

Once Kadhim started interviewing with the numerous defense contractors who were hiring Arabic linguists in DC, I couldn't help but feel he was much more valuable to the Global War on Terrorism than merely as an interpreter. During the war, he had made me successful with his keen insights, knowledge of Iraqi history and uncanny ability to take not just my words, but also my body language and intent, and interpret them to those I needed to influence. It was this combination of skills that had forced me to introduce him to my brigade commander, who in turn knew he had to introduce him to our division commander. His skills were invaluable and we needed him in a position where he could use his skills to the best effect. Hence, I decided to introduce him to General Cody.

The day Kadhim met General Cody was the same day Kadhim and I were scheduled to conduct an interview with Jamie Macintyre at CNN. The purpose of the interview was to tell the world the story of Kadhim and how he and other Iraqi nationals like him were proud to participate in the war and how ecstatic they were about the results thus far. In classic CNN style, Macintyre managed to turn the piece into a "Gee, this guy helped us and we dropped him like a hot rock" story. I never took another story to the CNN team in the Pentagon again.

When the interview was over, Kadhim and I went to Cody's office. I only intended to introduce the two so the boss could get a feel for Kadhim. Commander Cody was a quick judge of character and I would normally hear what he thought of someone during a follow-up visit to his office. The moment Kadhim walked into the office, the two became close friends. What was supposed to be a quick meeting between two strangers became a tribal family discussion that spanned four countries, three generations and two continents. I was surprised to learn that Cody was second generation Lebanese and knew much more about the Middle East than those of us who advised him.

The next day I was in General Cody's office for a different topic when he asked me if I had hired Kadhim yet. I turned puzzled and said, "You want me to hire him?" As Cody pushed the speed dial on his phone, he smiled and said, "I have the perfect job for him." The duty officer in the Army Operations Center answered the phone and Cody told him to get Lieutenant General Thomas Metz, the commander of the Army's Third Corps, on the phone as quickly as possible. In a moment, General Metz was on the other end of the line. The two jokingly jabbed at each other for a moment and then Cody interrupted with, "Tom, I have the ability to hire a first-class cultural advisor to work for you in Iraq. His name is Kadhim al-Waeli and he was Chris Hughes' Freedom Fighter in Iraq."

Metz quickly responded with a resounding "yes," telling Cody he had been racking his brain and driving his staff crazy trying to find someone to do just that—be a cultural advisor that speaks Arabic.

Cody smiled and swung a fictional baseball bat in the air—a home run. "I will send Chris and Kadhim out to see you so you can interview him and make your own decision," Cody said, "but, I'm sure you will find him a valuable contribution to your team in Iraq." General Metz agreed and they concluded their phone call.

Ms. Kathy Condon, the deputy G3, was also in the room during this call. Commander Cody, very satisfied with himself, stiffened his brow and tone, and told Condon and me to find a way to hire Kadhim and get him out to interview with Metz as soon as possible. As I walked out, I looked at Ms. Condon and asked her how in the hell do I hire this guy? "We don't hire people, this is the Army."

Then she said, "If the Commander wants it, we would find a way. Now go find Kadhim and tell him to stop interviewing to be a dammed linguist."

Kadhim had interviewed as a linguist with a number of companies and was excited by the dollar figures they were quoting him, but the thought of sitting in a room reading documents or teaching intermediate and advanced Arabic in Monterey, California at the Defense Language Institute didn't sit well with him. Kadhim was a man of action; he was already antsy to get back in the fight. When I told him Cody wanted to hire him as General Metz's cultural advisor, he jumped at the chance. Then he turned and asked me how much it paid —"more than a dishwasher I would assume?"

I told him not to worry about that, "we're going to get you back in the fight!"

General Metz was hosting a commander's conference at the end of the week in San Antonio, TX, and wasted no time inviting Kadhim and me to attend. The goal was to give Kadhim and the General some time to get to know each other and for me to provide Iraqi lessons learned to the command group. The conference was a great success for the leaders of Third Corps. Kadhim made an excellent impression on the General, while I had an opportunity to meet Major General Peter Chiarelli, the commander of the 1st Cavalry Division.

General Chiarelli was hard to miss with his button-down polo shirt, LL Bean slacks, and reading glasses hanging around his neck. When I was in college, we called people dressed like that preppies. But what drew my attention was his unique and exceptional intelligence. He was keenly interested in every experience and lesson I had brought with me from Iraq. Between meetings, he would pull Kadhim and me aside and continue grilling us on the Iraqi psyche, Maslow's Hierarchy of Needs, and innovations Kadhim and I had used successfully in Iraq. Chiarelli was one of those rare officers who believed there were no new ideas, just forgotten ones. His mind was engaged and I watched him plan out his division's entire tour in Iraq in his note book. He wasn't satisfied with good enough; he wanted more than the rest. He wanted fresh and innovative ideas for rebuilding Iraq—he wanted to win.

As the conference progressed, General Chiarelli told me he wanted a "Kadhim-like" capability down to the platoon level. He didn't just want linguists, he wanted Iraqi advisors who could help his soldiers do more than just the minimum—-he wanted help accomplishing the mission. He promised me I would get a formal request through the ASPB process, but in the meantime he challenged me to find a way. I liked this man very much as he struck me as a true warrior who wasn't afraid to use his mind and thrive on innovation. I would happily spend the next eight months fighting to get him his "Kadhim-like" capability in Iraq.

In January of 2004, Kadhim deployed to Iraq as the Multi-National Force Iraq Cultural Advisor to Lieutenant General Metz, the commander of all combat forces in Iraq. As Metz's advisor, Kadhim was instrumental in brokering numerous ceasefires, warning of the pending second battle for An Najaf, and providing weekly country and international level classified intelligence and cultural assessments for the senior leaders of thirteen different armies, the United States Marine Corps, three heads of State and the Department of Defense.

In November of 2004, Kadhim returned to the United States to brief the Vice Chief of Staff of the Army and to prepare Lieutenant General Vines, the commander of the XVIII Airborne Corps, and his staff to relieve Lieutenant General Metz and the Third Corps in Iraq. As a result of this trip and upon the strongest recommendation from General Metz, Kadhim would remain in Iraq as General Vines' Cultural Advisor to facilitate the transition.

Kadhim rotated back to the US in late 2005 for some home duty and returned to Iraq in late 2006 for another tour of duty, advising Lieutenant General Ray Odierno, now the Multinational Ground

Force commander in Baghdad. Of all the men I have met in my life, Kadhim is one of the very best I know—an American, an Iraqi.

THE IRAQI ADVISORY TASK FORCE

Leveraging the sheiks in Iraq was doable when I was on the ground and surrounded by close to a thousand armed soldiers, but how could I recreate the same synergy I had in my local area for General Chiarelli in Anbar from the Pentagon? The idea that I could somehow develop a strategy to give Chiarelli a fighting chance in one of the worst provinces of Iraq was a stretch, but I was driven to find a way. General Chiarelli had made an impression on me and a man like him deserved a full court press.

As I disengaged myself from the IED Task Force, I reengaged with a number of my former Iraqi contacts, plus the interagency and contractor community in an effort to float the idea of developing a corps of local Iraqi linguists that would have the ability to speak English, operate in close proximity to their home villages, and have either business ties or blood relations with the local sheik. I envisioned that every patrol walking into a small town would be led by a lieutenant and accompanied by an English-speaking Iraqi who knew the people of the town and who was known by them. A young Iraqi man would know what "right" looked like and would carry a banner of protection by being the sheik's son or nephew. Such a situation would be a win/win for the coalition and the local Iraqis.

Although General Chiarelli liked the idea, no one else did. The question most frequently posed was, "Can't we just hire these guys when they get to Iraq?" The response was yes, but this concept was bigger than just Iraq. The Army should figure it out and develop a program to support Major General Chiarelli and the other division commanders in Iraq and Afghanistan. The only other advocate of the concept was Ms. Condon, the deputy Army G3. Ms. Condon was friends with Chiarelli and believed in his ideas. She provided me top cover as I once again strayed into uncharted territory in the corridors of the Pentagon.

After a number of false starts and ridiculous proposals, I met the team of experts who had created the Bosnia Training Program (BTP).

A CD-ROM they had produced ended up in my personal files, and one night when I was trying to find a briefing I came across the unopened CD and decided to watch it. To my surprise, it had a section that discussed Army unit relationships with local communities in Bosnia. The video encouraged the local Army commander to engage with the community and to seek local linguists who were familiar with the area and could help to identify different ethnic groups violating restricted areas and zones of separation. I immediately contacted the contractor and asked to meet with the project manager.

A couple of hours before the BTP project manager arrived, I asked Mr. Gary Williams from the Strategic Studies division in G3 to attend the meeting. He agreed and asked if he could invite his desk mate, Mr. Bob Bevelacqua—why not? The meeting was interesting, but fell short of the mark I was looking for to engage the sheiks in the Anbar Province of Iraq. I was disappointed at the BTP's failure to fully grasp the size of the project I envisioned and the overall price they would charge. Their option was a lot of buck and very little bang. I thanked the project manager and left the meeting, still standing on square one. As Gary, Bob and I were returning to our office area, Bob turned to me and said, "When you get a chance, I would like to give you my pitch on how to skin this Iraqi Advisory issue of yours."

I said, "Sure, who are you anyway?" As we continued to walk closer to the Army corridor, Bob talked and I listened. The quicker he talked the slower we walked until we came to a standstill outside Cody's office. What I was hearing was so innovative, so far fetched, so risky—it might actually work. What did you say your name was? "

"They call me Major Bob."

Bob was a former Special Forces officer who was working on the Army Staff as a strategy specialist, and his desk was less than twenty feet from mine. Unbeknownst to me at the time, he was also a Fox News Military Analyst who had gained quite a reputation for being a straight-shooter by giving some excellent field reports during the war and on more than occasion calling Osama bin Laden a "pussy" on national television. Since I had not seen his reports, I was unaware of his local fame. I'm not sure if knowing would have tainted my first impression of him, but I felt I was a quick judge of character and I admired his passion and desire to help win the war.

Bob's proposal was to leverage the 52 sheiks in the Anbar region through a group of Lebanese businessmen working under a loose confederation led by a man named Charles. Bob explained to me how the Lebanese and the Iraqis had maintained open trade routes for thousands of years, but these were disrupted by the Saddam regime. The Lebanese were anxious to reopen their business relationships in Iraq. Charles was confident the sheiks were willing to engage with us and was prepared to arrange a meeting when we were ready. In fact, he had already done so when Bob was in Iraq covering the invasion, but Bob and Charles couldn't convince the Coalition Provisional Authority to participate in the discussions.

If this Lebanese businessman really had the ability to mobilize and negotiate with the Anbar Sheiks, then we had a real chance of pulling this thing off. For the next week, Bob and I fine-tuned the plan and presented our desired outcome to Charles, who in turn would determine support from the sheiks. The concept was not simple and would require a leap of faith by the Army and General Chiarelli to make it happen.

The plan called for Bob to become the project manager, using an existing contract within the Army to hire an American team to support Bob and his headquarters outside of Baghdad. This team would be composed of Middle Eastern experts with managerial, administrative, linguistic, security and medical skills. Charles would hire a team of 10–20 Lebanese businessmen who would establish liaison with the sheiks, hire and oversee their sons and nephews as advisor-linguists for the American forces in Anbar, and facilitate trade with the Iraqis from Lebanon.

My first feasibility test was with Ms. Condon; she was close to the project and could easily shoot holes in it before we took it to Cody for approval. Bob and I sat with her for less than twenty minutes before she stood up and said "follow me." We walked into Cody's office and she reminded the General about General Chiarelli's request for me to develop a Kadhim-like capability for his division in Iraq. General Cody remembered and asked us to sit down. As Bob spoke, Cody got that look—that deviant, innovative, outside-the-box look—in his eye. He liked what he was hearing. Here we go again, I thought. A lot more work lay ahead, but hopefully a lot more American lives to save also.

The concept had all the makings of *Lawrence of Arabia II*—money-hungry businessmen, third country nationals fighting to open trade routes, an active war in the former Ottoman Empire, rogue sheiks exerting their power and influence, a former Army Major with hopes of uniting warring Arabs, and a General with a grand vision. Cody looked at me and asked, "What do you think?"

I replied, "I think we should send him to Fort Hood and see what General Chiarelli thinks."

"Roger that, approved. Bob, you go to Fort Hood; Chris you figure out how much this is going to cost and find the money." Cody was finished and we were dismissed.

As ordered, Bevelacqua flew to Fort Hood, TX, to see Major General Chiarelli while I went to the Army Budget Office (ABO) to determine the degree of difficulty in obtaining the money needed for the formulation of the Iraqi Advisory Task Force (IQATF). Bob's meeting with Chiarelli went well. As expected, the general liked the concept. Furthermore, the chemistry between the two seemed compatible, which was good because their relationship and trust in each other would be crucial to the overall success of the mission. As with Kadhim and Lieutenant General Metz, they would have to have absolute confidence in each other to ensure the Task Force maintained the requisite authority, innovation and freedom of maneuver it would need to be effective on the battlefield.

My meeting with ABO didn't go as well as I had hoped. To fund the concept for one year, we would need $15 million to recruit, man, equip, train, deploy and sustain the American side of the team and subcontract with the Lebanese to screen and hire the Iraqi advisors. The Iraqi advisors would provide insight on political, cultural, social, economic, religious and security related issues—this was not a spy network, it was an advisor network, a distinction that haunted Bob in-country on several occasions. Bob spent many hours convincing people that he wasn't running sources for the Agency and that this was a legitimate community outreach program that could provide valuable insight for American commanders. Charles' Lebanese team formed the Senior Advisor Council (SAC) for General Chiarelli. Unlike the typical American Arabic speakers, the SAC were able to do more than interpret Arabic; they were able to read body language, decipher dialect, and ask tribal questions that would validate or expose an applicant's assertions and intent; plus they had extensive pre-existing relationships with prominent Sheiks—that was the real vetting network. Using them to hire, vet, fire and control the Iraqi advisor teams was invaluable. They were Kadhim-like.

This was a significant shift from the norm and would require detailed planning, but this new arrangement lowered the overall cost of the contract, decentralized the activity away from the Americans and, most importantly, reduced the possibility of the Iraqis and Lebanese being attacked while standing in long lines outside of the bases. Bob and I were acutely aware of the force protection steps we needed to take to prevent advisors from becoming insurgent targets or a point of infiltration for insurgents and suicide bombers. In addition to being good stewards of the American taxpayers' money, we had to find innovative ways to protect the members of the Task Force, whether they were Iraqi advisors, Lebanese businessmen or American contractors and soldiers. To do that, we decided to keep the IQATF outside the American bases and maintain a low profile.

Despite the logic of the concept, I still had to persuade Combined Joint Task Force 7 (CJTF-7) in Baghdad to supply the funds. The budget supplemental for Operation Iraqi Freedom was outside of the control of the Army Staff, and using those funds required me to coordinate directly with CJTF-7. The real difficulty in selling the project to them was that its strongest proponent, General Chiarelli, had not yet deployed his division to Iraq. It was a real Catch-22.

Chiarelli was preparing to deploy and wanted the Task Force in place when he got there, but the guys in Iraq currently running things controlled the money and did not acknowledge Chiarelli's request. For three frustrating months, I worked numerous options—workarounds—and innovations to legally acquire the money to deploy the advisors. On three separate occasions, I thought I would fail, but then I would stumble on another way to keep hope alive. When all hope seemed lost, CJTF-7 transitioned to Multinational Force Corps (MNF-C) placing Lieutenant General Metz in command of all combat forces in Iraq. Metz's staff in Baghdad acknowledged General Chiarelli's request for the IQATF and sent us the funds we needed to deploy the team.

The IQATF began operations in Iraq in the summer of 2004 and continues to successfully operate as this book is being written. Although their activities and accomplishments remain classified, it is safe to say the advisors extended the operational envelope in Iraq and provided General Chiarelli and his division a unique capability that greatly aided their mission.

8

ON TO THE NATIONAL WAR COLLEGE

"We had just fought an invasion—who gives a damn what Karl von Clausewitz wrote?"

LEAVING THE ARMY STAFF

Much as I felt I had made good my promise to my troops and the Sheiks of the Tigris River valley to represent their needs in the Pentagon, I was ready to take a needed break to charge my batteries, specifically by attending one of the service war colleges I had been destined for before diverting to the Pentagon in 2003. Despite the need to rest and gather my thoughts and to reengage with my family, the need to attend a war college carried with it the possibility of having to move the Hughes gang a third time in less than four years.

Uprooting the family within the US military is almost a tradition, one with as many tangible attributes as negatives. For the soldier, this constant movement helps to keep them in a constant state of learning, growing, experiencing different surroundings, conditions, environments and cultures. The same is true for the officers, except they move more frequently because once a job is learned and mastered, the officer is promoted out of it and is on to the next job.

The Army educational system for the first twenty years of an officer's career is a constant series of ever-increasingly difficult jobs, sandwiched by developmental schools lasting between four and ten months. Most officers' careers consist of a series of three-year assignments with schools in between until they reach full Colonel. After Colonel, moves gradually increase to once every other year as there become fewer and fewer jobs for senior officers on military installations or in the field.

What most civilians would consider a miserable lifestyle is in fact one that produces a soldier and family that is accustomed to adversity and appreciative for the small things in life. I have always detested the idea of homesteading, or staying in one base for a whole career, which has been advocated by numerous leaders during my career. Having grown up in the military, I believed that my upbringing as a military brat had made me a better and more appreciative person. The idea of joining the military and staying at one base is counterintuitive to one of the core competencies of the Army—flexibility.

To homestead would stagnate the force and stifle its learning, flexibility and agility. When others hear about, discuss or study the incredible agility of the US Army—able to mobilize and deploy hundreds of thousands of troops, thousands of vehicles, tons of ammunition and material across the globe in mere weeks—-they always marvel and ask how? When I'm asked this question, I enjoy seeing their reaction when I turn and ask my wife to answer the question—Marguerite has moved our family and our household 21 times in 24 years! The culture of the Army, including its incredible families, is to prepare to deploy, practice deployment, and stay ready to fight in any environment against any foe, taking only what you need, and learning to live without when you get there and win.

This same lifestyle is shared by those who make up a soldier's family: our military spouses and Army brats. Army families are tough teams, worldly, and the best of friends. They serve and sacrifice for their country as a team; soldiers do not do it alone. The United States asks much from our military families, including missed family reunions, birthdays, births, sporting events, high school graduations, a child's first love, Christmas and anniversaries. No medals or no extra pay for spouses or children, just a strong sense of commitment for something bigger than themselves—the American people.

When the War College orders finally came, the worst was realized when I opened the email attachment and read the assignment for Carlisle Barracks, PA—the Army War College. This would mean another move or I would have to live in Pennsylvania, three hours away and commute home on the weekends for a year. To this point I had worked hard trying to get assigned to the prestigious National War College (NWC) at the National Defense University in Washington DC. Not only because it was the best college in my opinion, but because we wouldn't have to move or be separated.

I learned from a friend of mine that I wasn't selected for NWC because I was "overqualified"! This had never happened to me before; I had never been overqualified for anything I had ever done, and found the term comical. Even if I was "overqualified" it didn't seem logical to force me to make yet another move or leave my family because I didn't fit the computer model for NWC.

The "fit" problem was based on the fact that NWC was a Joint College, meaning all the Military Services attended, as did many of the interagency folks like the CIA, FBI, State Department, USAID and others. There was also a large contingent of foreign students, making NWC unique in comparison to the other Service Colleges. The Army decided it needed to assign officers to NWC who had little or no experience serving in Joint Commands manned by officers from multiple military services and other US governmental agencies. The obvious advantages of having Army officers working with the other services to enhance and synergize all our military resources was not only an Army goal, it was a Congressional mandate called the Goldwater/Nichols act of 1986. Goldwater-Nichols ordered the Department of Defense to force the services to train their officers to work with each other and operate seamlessly within these consolidated staffs called Joint Task Forces.

Since I had already met the letter of the law of Goldwater/Nichols when I was an operations officer on the Pentagon Joint Staff working for the Combating Terrorism Directorate (J34) before 9/11, I was already knighted as a Joint Qualified Officer. Therefore, over-qualified to attend NWC! Because of a little letter designator on my official military records, 3L (joint qualified), the computer model never even considered me for attendance at the NWC during the selection process.

I stared at the email for three days before I talked to Marguerite. My daughter had just graduated from high school after being forced to complete her senior year at a new school in Virginia after our last move. My son was now going into his junior year in his fourth school in five years. How could I ask them to sacrifice again; or how could I separate from them for a year in an attempt to stabilize them, when I had only been home eight months, if you call working fourteen hour days six days a week being home?

After mulling it over for about a week, I finally did something I had never done before in over twenty years of service—-I asked for a favor. For those outside the military this may seem like a simple choice, but in the military we are taught mission before soldier, service before self, and as a result, we normally don't ask for what we wanted; we dutifully executed the needs of the Army. But in this case, my selection for the Army War College was not for the needs of the Army, it was because a computer model didn't consider my family's needs as a field in its database. I needed to act selfishly for the first time in twenty years . . . so I asked my boss Lieutenant General Cody if he could help. Four hours and two emails later I was going to the National War College. Once again I learned that loyalty was a two-way street. I had earned the General's loyalty and he would forever have mine.

THE NATIONAL WAR COLLEGE

The NWC is located at Fort McNair along the scenic waterfront along the Potomac River at the gates of Washington DC. The mission of NWC "is to prepare future leaders of the Armed Forces, State Department, and other civilian agencies for high-level policy, command, and staff responsibilities. To do this, NWC conducts a senior-level course of study in national security policy and strategy for selected U.S. and foreign military officers and federal officials."

At first glance the school, the base and the faculty are most intimidating. When I first walked on the campus, I quickly realized I was not overqualified and had positioned myself for quite a challenge. School had never been one of my strong points, but I had had an epiphany while attending the Army Command and General Staff College (CGSC) ten years earlier: That I needed to get off my butt and read, read, read. At CGSC, I learned that I was more experienced than my peers, but I was missing a most critical element of my training as an officer—-reading, about history, economics, politics and leadership. And while I was on the Pentagon Joint Staff in the late '90s, riding the train to work every day for three hours, I had finally found the time to read, realizing what had been missing in my personal development as an officer. Just read. Anything, everything . . . never again would I be field smart and book stupid. I would need both to survive in the future, and Iraq would eventually confirm that belief.

In particular, while working for Commander Cody, a friend coaxed me into reading T.E. Lawrence's *Seven Pillars of Wisdom,* giving me his own notes for the book (like a *Cliff's Notes*), and Lawrence's "27 Articles of Conduct" for his advisors to the Arab Revolt. When I looked up the passages he had flagged as important, I xeroxed the pages, highlighted the passages, and passed them on to Cody. Lawrence had impressive insights into insurgency and the character of Arabs and their societies. He was also the first to use command detonated IEDs, and likened counterinsurgency to "learning to eat soup with a knife."[17]

The friend also gave copies of the book, notes and articles to Kadhim in Baghdad, and Article 15 in particular has been widely adopted by our forces:. "Better the Arabs do it tolerably than that you do it perfectly."[18]

He also pointed out that the classic movie, *Lawrence of Arabia,* could be very useful as an introduction to Arab culture, as it addresses all the important points of their lifestyle's rules. It should be shown in a structured way, with Q&A discussions to be useful. He was right.

So when I walked into the college, found my name on the committee assignment board, and walked into my committee home room, I was relieved and laughed to myself when I looked at my desk. Erected above each desk or cubiclel was a two-tiered shelf full of books, 42 to be exact. I smiled because in a glance I recognized more than 75 percent of them. If this was what I was supposed to accomplish this year, I would be home for dinner every night, something I hadn't managed to do in over three years.

MY CLASSMATES

My overconfidence was quickly dampened as I met my new committee classmates and listened to their conversations, read their biographies, and attempted to understand their jokes. This was an intellectual yet colorful group; they were the overachievers from the top one percent of their military service, department, embassy, or country. After all, this was the college that had produced the former Secretary of State and Chairman of the Joint Chiefs of Staff, Colin Powell, and eventually the current Chairman, General Peter Pace. I had much to learn, but I also realized I had much to share.

As we socialized at the famous Joint Pub in the basement of the school after class, sweated it up together on the sports fields, and interacted in class, the incredible legacy of this class began to emerge. My classmates were the best and brightest our country had to offer; each had made a significant contribution leading, planning and debating those issues most important to the survival of Democracy in the 21st century. I was in the right place and at the right time to become a better officer and person.

Just a small sampling of these exceptional people included one of the lead commanders from the "Thunder Run" into Baghdad; the Marine commander who personally helped to fight off two Iraqi ambushes against his headquarters; the first military member of the Coalition Provisional Authority; a special assistant to Lieutenant General Newbold, the former senior operations officer in the Pentagon who resigned over the invasion; senior planners from the Pentagon and Central Command staffs; the commander whose battalion parachuted into northern Iraq; and countless officers who had been to my front, flank, rear and defending the skies over my battalion during the invasion.

Additionally, there were CIA operatives who had ridden on horseback in Afghanistan, senior State Department negotiators, and FBI counter- IED experts and analysts. This was arguably one of the most famous and talented classes to attend the college in a long time, and I was in the middle of what would prove to be a controversial, difficult and outstanding year for the college, its faculty and students.

MY MISSION

By the time I reported to NWC I had written about 30 pages of the book you're now reading. While on the Army staff I had accidentally discovered that writing down my experiences from Iraq was a simple way of wrestling with and defeating the mental demons that still haunted my dreams and idle moments of the day.

I had learned this while producing information papers, responding to letters from families and politicians, and developing lessons-learned briefs for the Army and the Department of Defense. Every time I put a good idea, lesson or best practice on paper, I didn't have to think about it anymore. All the good I had learned was now captured so my mind wouldn't constantly repeat the event over and over again in my head. The same was true for every mistake, misjudgment and failure. I found that when I wrote down what was haunting me, my mind slowly let it go, allowing me some peace. Instinctively my mind had put my whole war experience on a mental CD so I couldn't forget what had happened. This mental CD would play over and over again, never allowing me to forget; writing the stories down from this mental CD stopped the torment.

Even so, now that I was in school, my mental demons returned with a vengeance, because my mind was no longer occupied with a fourteen-hour work day in the Pentagon. The anguish this caused forced me to make a pact with myself: I will use the NWC as an excuse to write a memoir about Iraq and kill these demons once and for all.

But how do I do this without sounding like an egotistical careerist who thinks he has all the solutions? There is a stigma with active duty military officers writing a book—it is always assumed a unit or staff suffered while the book was written. So in this case, I felt if I could do it while I was at school I wouldn't be patronized by my peers. Despite my fears, I would eventually learn that my peers, my instructors and former subordinates in *No Slack*, and my family encouraged me to write the book. So I did and did it for them.

CLAUSEWITZ 101?

We had just fought an invasion—who gives a damn what Karl von Clausewitz wrote about war in the early 1800s? What I want to know is: "What were you thinking when you jumped into Tal Afar? How many men did you lose at the intersection? Did you really use an anti-tank Javelin to kill snipers? What the hell was Bremer thinking when he disenfranchised the Ba'ath party; what a stupid move?" These were the discussions, no matter the professor, the course or audience—the students wanted to discuss and debate the war. It wasn't an attempt to avoid the homework; it was a passion, a quest, an uncontrollable desire to piece together what happened and why: "This is the National War College, right?" I'm not sure the professors, Doctors, and Military instructors at the college were prepared for our collegiate *coups de main* but it happened in the most ostentatious way; we simply ignored the instructors and discussed the war amongst ourselves.

Rude as it was, ignoring our prestigious and brilliant professors, we had to talk about the war with each other, and the NWC curriculum wasn't up to the challenge. The curriculum was for a peacetime class, a class without the depth of experience that the NWC Class of '05 had. Another significant factor contributing to the coup was that most of my peers were still suffering from their own mental CD war reruns and were not yet as lucky as I was to discover the power of writing down one's thoughts.

So when confronted with the uninspiring prospect of having to read and write about the same old military strategists we had read and reread over our years of schools and developmental courses, we became rebellious and openly obnoxious. We wanted and demanded to discuss the war, including what worked, what didn't and how we could improve. A good majority of the class knew they were going back to Iraq or Afghanistan at the end of the year and needed to prepare. Screw Clausewitz, Jomini and Machiavelli—what the hell do they know! Eventually we would learn that the professors at the NWC knew a great deal and had much to offer each of us, but our passion to discuss the ongoing war would have to come first. We had to vent about the present before we could study the past.

WARRIOR COMBAT LUNCH BRIEFS

Realizing our growing frustration with the school, a school designed to teach national strategy and not how to maneuver a tank battalion or an infantry brigade, some of the NWC's exceptional instructors, Dr. Lani Kass, Col. Gary West, Col. Jeff Harris and Mr. Harvey Rishikof, acted to ease our pain through capturing our experiences and new-found perceptions by seeking and receiving permission from the faculty for the students to present lesson briefs during lunch. This eventually became known as the Warrior Combat Lunch Series. These luncheon briefs quickly became a very popular program at the National War College and my favorite activity for the entire year.

On their own, and helping to still their demons, my peers began to put together presentations about their missions, operations and accomplishments in Iraq and Afghanistan. I remember being mesmerized listening to their stories and seeing the videos and pictures. I hadn't seen anything like this since late 1993 when Lieutenant Colonel McKnight from the 75th Ranger Regiment came to the Joint Readiness Training Center to give us a presentation on what happened on October 3, 1993, when the Rangers lost 18 soldiers in Mogadishu, Somalia.

These combat briefs were emotional, unvarnished firsthand accounts of war at the very tip of the spear, normally ending with a list of fallen comrades and a commander marginally able to answer questions from an emotionally drained and hypersensitive audience. These presentations generated heated discussions, fascinated those who hadn't been deployed yet, validated observations by other commanders, highlighted shortfalls, confirmed failures, and provided raw, relevant and timely lessons that the Department of Defense needed—needed now to sustain the fight! Yet, all this value and interaction would be stopped by the faculty, because we always ran out of time at lunch, and we had to go to class. We were all trying to come to grips with this war, and we wanted the college to help us in the effort. We felt the war college needed to change, and it was our responsibility to compel it to do so while preserving the best of the institution. It was our duty to share what we had learned with each other and with those who had yet to deploy.

When I first returned from Iraq, I had wandered the Pentagon looking for the agency charged with the responsibility of capturing what had happened and producing the lessons learned for those who were yet to deploy. What I had learned had value and it wasn't mine to hold close to my chest; it belonged to the big Army, yet I couldn't find a venue to release it. Why not here at the National War College? Why are the instructors disinterested in capturing this information and providing it to the Services, the Department of Defense, Congress and the American people? An incredible opportunity for the institution was passing quickly and we wanted to do something about it. A number of the faculty, especially our committee chairs, decided we had valuable input, and worked with us to develop our stories and the lessons we had to relate. We wanted our experiences to impact how our nation looked at strategy, and how the War College taught it.

We had vital information, although raw and unvarnished, that needed to be captured, studied and used, now and in the future. We represented that future.

THE COUP

At first my fellow committee mates and I discussed the stupidity of writing three, five and eight-page papers on people we had written about and discussed our whole careers. When we had brought this up to the Commandant early in the course, his response was that neither the US students from the interagency student body nor our foreign students had grown up in the same educational systems as the military students, so NWC needed the first half of the year to get everyone on the same sheet of music before we could get into the graduate level discussion in the course. We should take the time to relax and do some outside reading. In shock, my classmates and I couldn't believe NWC was going to force us to regurgitate papers on irrelevant topics for four months while others caught up? What a waste of time and loss of an opportunity to do something relevant with the experience of the class.

In frustration I continued to write my book and produce mediocre papers for the college and steer classroom discussions off the 12th, 17th, and 18th centuries to 2001–2004. It didn't take long to realize I was not alone in my quest; Colonels Stef Twitty, B.P. McCoy, Jeff Bailey, Renn Gade, P.J. Dermer, Mike Kershaw, Harry Tunnell and many others were all actively staging their own coups, one classroom and instructor at a time. And to the credit of the faculty at the NWC, a handful of instructors were beginning to realize that an opportunity was about to be lost and they began to engage the institutional leadership on our behalf.

THE NEGOTIATIONS

The process of figuring out what to do with the depth of knowledge that existed in the class bogged down our initial discussions. In other words, the process got in the way of the product. What would it be— a book, manuscripts, group information papers, deployable briefs— and what do we do with all this related and unrelated information once the students produce it? Most of us students looked at each other and shrugged . . . not our problem; the college needs to figure this out!

I remember one discussion during these after-class meetings with the faculty when the question was finally asked, "Why can't the product we produce take the place of our mandatory class work?" We were going against the standard practice, and the impasse of what to produce and what credit the students would receive for it remained in debate, under advisement, and in staffing with the commandant till the Christmas break. The original group of interested students began to wane because the discussions had no visible end in sight and the regular course papers were still coming at us fast and furious. Yet a core of students remained determined to produce something of value despite the institutional pushback, continuing to force the topic without fear of rank or discipline. We were prepared to give the college complete credit for being at the forefront of learning and taking the lead over all the other War Colleges by producing this "lessons learned book," produced by their students and edited by some of the most talented instructors in the nation. It was a win for everyone involved and we were still at an impasse. Institutions are hard to change; it requires work and some very hardheaded individuals. The war had made us obstinate and willing to risk all for what was right. This product was the right thing to do and we were prepared to finish it with or without the college. But if we did it without them, we were going to ensure the world knew it. The college relented.

THE BOOK

After the Christmas break, the group met the first day and the students were given the opportunity to produce one 30-page paper about their experiences in the war. Further, they were to pick faculty members to mentor their progress, and were to turn in their paper during each elective to get yet another look from a faculty member.

We still didn't know what we would do with the final product, but we were given the green light to proceed and not to worry about any other papers. The 30 pages for me was an instant relief considering I was quickly approaching 80 pages on my own, but I was now more inspired than before. The idea that I would get help from some of the brightest Professors and Ph.D.s in the nation convinced me I could actually publish a book, and on my own time. But most importantly the institution had changed. The NWC had stepped out of their norm and, although reluctantly, decided to usurp the status quo and transform. Journalist Jim Lacey and Sharon Tosi Moore, a 1990 West Point graduate, signed on as editors and eleven students, including me, provided chapters to the anthology, entitled: *Fresh from the Fight: The Invasion and Occupation of Iraq.*

Change is hard for any institution, and the National War College was no exception. Our class is still remembered as "that class."

Three years after this experience I visited the War College and was impressed and proud at how the institution had expertly retooled to capture lessons from its students. The school offered Islamic and political culture electives, produced timely and relevant books by its students and faculty, and helped lead the way for the Department of Defense and greater Washington, DC by providing key papers and articles adding to the national debate on Iraq and Afghanistan as well as military issues beyond the Global War on Terrorism.

Reporters and students have asked why I have criticized the National War College in forums and discussions since graduating, and I must profess that I get much enjoyment telling them they have missed the point of my criticism. "My passion for learning, and willingness to openly critique and question systems and institutions are a direct reflection of what I hold most dear about my education at the National War College—specifically, my willingness to think critically using history, current events, culture and politics. The War College taught me *how* to think, not *what* to think." I can pay the National War College no greater compliment.

HOW DO CONGRESSMEN LEARN TO WORK IN CONGRESS?

In the end, the NWC was one of the best academic experiences of my life, and I wouldn't trade that year for any other, but I did walk away with one burning question after seeing scores of briefs and presentations by our national leaders in Washington, from the President on down. What training or schooling do Congressmen or Senators attend to prepare them to run the most powerful nation in the world?

In my experience, whether during senior leader testimony on Capitol Hill concerning the invasion of Iraq, or presenting the results of the USS *Cole* Commission in 2001 to the Senate Armed Services Committee, or eventually briefing Congress on the timeline for the use of US military forces during Hurricane Katrina in 2005, I have always found the questions and experiences of our national representatives lacking in depth and understanding—not just an ignorance as to my role as a Department of Defense employee, but to their own role as Congresspersons on Capitol Hill.

Despite respecting the process for their selection, during the NWC I finally found myself and most of my peers disillusioned at the role of Congress and their ignorance of their own laws, most specifically their role in the 1986 Goldwater/Nicholls Act, raising the question, "Why doesn't Congress attend the National Defense University for a year like the rest of the US Government?" Or where is Congress' National College that teaches them constitutional law, their role as congressmen and their responsibilities within the US government and her subordinate agencies? How can a middle school teacher from Small Town, Missouri possibly know or appreciate her role as congresswomen, the impact of her vote, and the negative impact of her uninformed and ignorant questions to senior military leaders live on CSPAN? (Reference the production of body armor and up-armored hummers.)

This ignorance is not their fault and my comment is not meant as an insult. It's simply a question: Why don't we train Congress? This is an issue that needs to be addressed soon to ensure that the men and women who represent the great people of the United States are prepared for the challenges of the 21st century. Congress, as it should, holds the Department of Defense and other agencies responsible for shedding dysfunctional and outdated Cold War systems and processes, constantly pushing for change and transformation. Yet who holds Congress accountable for its own transformation? If I understand the document I have pledged my life to defend, the US Constitution, it's the people of the United States. The American public needs to ask the question: How will Congress transform to meet the challenges of the long war on terrorism and the 21st century? May I suggest they attend or at least monitor classes at the NWC or an equivalent college?

9

THE GREATER WAR ON TERRORISM

Bin-Laden's 1998 fatwa reads like an al-Qaeda Security Strategy (AQSS) and is arguably his plan for the near future.

CENTER OF GRAVITY

In hindsight, it's easy to debate what went wrong in Iraq, point fingers and blame the neoconservatives for a flawed concept of warfare. But in my opinion, the continued partisan debate in Washington is not healthy, a waste of valuable time for study and intellectual discovery, and is impeding the rapid implementation of key lessons and best practices. Our focus should be on what we have learned—from failure as well as success, and applying these lesson to the greater war on terrorism. Our immaturity as a nation is exposed by our sheer lack of understanding of other cultures that stand in stark contrast to our own. The United States has a propensity to brush aside societies steeply rooted in traditions and beliefs, viewing them as flawed, ignorant and inefficient without realizing why they have evolved within a region or a people. It is our own ignorance that feeds into the hands of fundamentalist groups, including al-Qaeda, who have used Arab and Middle Eastern history to paint the United States as the next great western empire that seeks to destroy Islam, oppress the peoples of the Middle East, and exploit and steal the wealth of innocent Muslims around the world.

Western colonization and foreign influence in the Middle East over the last 200 years, the annexation and enslavement of Muslims by empires in the last 900 years, and genocide through invasions over the last 2,000 years have left Arab leaders, scholars and their people distrustful of America's desire to "ignite a new era of global economic growth through free markets and free trade and [to] expand the circle of development by opening societies and building the infrastructure of democracy."[19]

Of our eight vital National Security Strategy goals, five specifically mention economic growth and expansion, international trade, anti-terrorism, global power, and the export of democracy as American vital interests in preserving domestic security. As stated earlier, to expand the circle of American influence and to open all societies to newfound democratic infrastructures directly threatens bin-Laden and is seen throughout the Arab world as an affront to basic Islamic values and laws. Fundamentalist Muslim organizations are quick to point out that democracy is a sin. It seduces Muslims, erodes their religious values and leads them astray because it stipulates the separation of church and state. Such a separation in governance is apostate and a direct violation of Islamic law.

Simply put, a large majority of Muslims believe that Western democracy imposes the arrogance of man's law over Sharia Islamic, or God's, law. Muslims detest and condemn any governmental construct that advocates majority rule, because it implies that man is equal to God. To accept man's laws over God's laws is to commit apostasy, the abandonment of one's religious faith. According to the Koran, anyone who leads a Muslim from his faith has committed a crime, even if the perpetrator is a Muslim as well. The Koran further dictates that the punishment for such a crime is death, especially for the perpetrator. It is this "indivisibility of politics and religion" that bin-Laden used in 1998 to declare armed jihad against the United States, even though he was not legally authorized to do so in accordance with Sharia Islamic law.

More than 1,500 years of history has taught the Arabs one inalienable truth: foreign occupations lead to exploitation, misery and death. The succession of foreign occupations, tyrannical empires, nefarious treaties and criminal international business deals over the past centuries only help to fuel the hatreds and goals of the insurgents in Iraq, empower and legitimize al-Qaeda, and stall the US-led war on global terrorism.

When America comes to realize that the key to the future of the Middle East lies in its past, then, they will understand why phrases such as "winning the hearts and minds of the Iraqi people" humiliate and enrage Muslims around the world. To understand Islam is to know that only God can win the hearts and minds of the Iraqi people. Do Americans truly believe they are above God? Taking the question one step further, is it ignorance, arrogance, or both, when these same Americans criticize and ridicule themselves on satellite TV for not winning Iraqi hearts and minds in twelve months. It took the Prophet Mohammad almost 40 years, and he had God's help.

Muslims see no differences between the US occupation of Iraq in 2003 and the British occupation in the early 20th century. Consider the proclamation the British commander, General Stanley Maude, made after entering Baghdad on March 18, 1918, when he said: "In the name of my King . . . Our military operations have as their object the defeat of the enemy and the driving of him from these territories. In order to complete this task, I am charged with absolute and supreme control of all regions in which British troops operate; but our armies do not come into your cities and lands as conquerors or enemies, but as liberators."[20] I think Edwin Black captures Islamic sentiment best when he contends, "In the West, we will not give up the future. And in Iraq, they will not give up the past."[21]

Despite US presidential rhetoric blaming the attacks on the American embassies in East Africa, the USS *Cole* in Yemen, and the World Trade Center in New York City as the work of a radical network of terrorists, "the fact is that the attacks against America on September 11, 2001, [were acts] of consummate religious devotion. Those who committed it were deeply pious . . . and they expressed their motives in indisputably religious terms, and they saw themselves as carrying out the will of God."[22] This is a war of religion to bin-Laden, and al-Qaeda draws its strength from the belief that:

"Islam is in mortal danger from the West [and] jihad [against the United States] is a duty."[23]

Quoting apocalyptic Islamic literature, bin-Laden predicts the final conflict with "world infidelity" by identifying the United States as the anti-Islamic Zionist-Crusader who intends to destroy Islamic values, control Middle Eastern oil, and impose an American empire on the Middle East through apostate dictatorships. He goes further when he warns Muslims of their pending doom in the eyes of God when they accept western values, foreign armies in the holy lands, and consume American products by quoting Hadith scripture in his 1998 *fatwa*, which states: "The people [of Islam] are close to an all encompassing punishment from Allah if they see the oppressor [United States] and fail to restrain him."[24]

. The attacks on 9/11 gave bin-Laden an opportunity to claim responsibility for turning the Islamic world from "the extreme division," a time of confusion, chaos and lost souls, to the period of "shared epiphany"—a return to the time of the Golden Age of Islam. If bin-Laden can sell his prophetic role in saving the sole of Islam, he could claim the right of succession to caliph. He would thus return the Arab world to "the golden age: one God, one prophet, one scripture, one people, and one ruler. The Caliph symbolizes the indivisibility of politics and religion, and he exercises his authority through the enforcement of Sharia and his pursuit of jihad to enlarge the realm of Islam."[25] It is this "indivisibility of politics and religion" that bin-Laden uses to flame resistance to democracy . . . in the name of God.

Bin-Laden has declared America the enemy of Islam and seized the offensive by attacking American citizens across the globe in armed jihad. The key to winning a limited war against al-Qaeda is to understand that it's not a war on Islam, but a war against the false prophet Osama bin-Laden and his apostate organization al-Qaeda. To regain the initiative and assume the offensive, America needs to relearn that "the best policy [in war] is to attack the enemy's plans; the next best is to disrupt his alliances, for to subdue the enemy's army without fighting is the acme of skill."[26]

Bin-Laden's 1998 *fatwa* reads like an al-Qaeda Security Strategy (AQSS) and is arguably his plan for the near future. The AQSS draws its legitimacy from Koranic, Sunnah and Hadith scripture and the narration of the Prophet Mohammad. Bin-Laden's interpretation of the word of Allah, and his Prophet Mohammad, is al-Qaeda's greatest strength as well as its single point of vulnerability. Islamic justification for al-Qaeda's war against America is its "dominant characteristic," providing organizational legitimacy, moral courage, power projection, and financing. Without the legitimacy of Islam, al-Qaeda would lose its "center of power"[27] and render itself irrelevant. Al-Qaeda's ability to convince the Arab world that God has justified their jihad is its Center of Gravity (COG).

If uniting Muslims into a single Islamic state is al-Qaeda's justification for jihad, then they need to communicate this to Muslims throughout the Middle East and across the globe through both public and clandestine means. Failure to harness international Islamic commitment to this global struggle will result in al-Qaeda's defeat.

As the CIA and the US military continue direct action missions against terror cells worldwide, hunt the Taliban in Afghanistan, and destroy foreign fighters and Iraqi insurgents in Iraq, the American administration must update its war plan to attack this al-Qaeda COG and its flawed use of Islam through a deliberate overt and covert information campaign plan. It will be designed to separate moderate Muslims from bin-Laden's most infamous misinterpretations of the Koran and his nefarious attempts to apostate millions of innocent Muslims for personal greed, pride and power.

Targeting a national information campaign at al-Qaeda's COG with the above mentioned theme, while sustaining military and economic efforts against bin-Laden's terror cells and fundraising activities, will have an immediate impact on al-Qaeda's strategic reach by calling into question its motives and self-interest. The focus of this information campaign should target three groups simultaneously: Middle Eastern government officials, Muslim religious leaders and academics, and the American public and Congress.

There are dozens of options for overtly engaging the three groups mentioned above. The following three provide only a start-point for consideration and discussion:

(1) The world deserves, and America should facilitate, a public debate and discussion between Muslim clerics, muftis, ayatollahs, academics, and Islamic historians in the Middle East to educate the masses about the teachings of the Prophet Mohammad, the Koran, and the legitimacy of armed jihad. Such a debate could provide a forum for Muslims to openly discuss their views, educate the West on their history and its significance to their future, ask pointed questions without fear of retribution from within their governments, and share

ideas on the peaceful return of the Golden Age of Islam.

(2) There are numerous Sunni and Shiite clerics, imams, and Grand Muftis across the globe, who confront terrorism daily on the internet and in the mosques, without coercion or intimidation from governments, kingdoms or fundamentalist groups. They are speaking out against terrorism because they fear young Muslims are being lead astray, misinterpreting the teachings of the Prophet and forsaking their families. In July of 2004, the imam of the Grand Mosque in Makkah (Mecca), Sheikh Abdul Rahman Al-Sudais, issued a *fatwa* stating, "Terrorism and extremism must be stopped and the organizations that promote terror should be dismantled."[28] This brave imam and hundreds of others like him are the true believers in the Koran and the keepers of the teachings of the Prophet Mohammed. They are fighting for their beliefs and their fellow Muslims, much to the detriment of bin-Laden and his justification for terrorizing the West.

"He who makes peace between the people by [presenting] good information or saying good things, is not a liar."[29]

If the United States were to simply help these Muslim leaders get their *fatwas* heard by more of their followers, the greater Arab world, the United States and its allies, America could directly and indirectly expose bin-Laden's legitimacy and question his use of religion as justification for war. Essentially, America could help to normalize and educate a whole generation of young Muslims by facilitating the resurgence of peaceful Islamic values through an already existing religious hierarchy. The key is the resurgence of Islamic values through Islamic religious institutions, not actual or perceived American propaganda through apostate dictatorships.

(3) Recently, National Public Radio asked a small group of Americans to "rank order Islam, Christianity, and Judaism from oldest to youngest." The overwhelming majority of Americans interviewed listed Judaism as the oldest, followed by Islam, then Christianity. Much to their amazement, they learned that the Muslim religion was nearly 700 years younger than Christianity. Ignorance of Islam in America has done more to empower al-Qaeda than the combined efforts of its attacks on America since 9/11. Sun Tzu keenly criticizes those who fail to "know the enemy and know yourself."[30] The Chinese philosopher leaned this truism at the tactical and operational

levels of war over 2,000 years ago. Yet, the lesson is still true today and with the advent of mass communications and the internet, warring nations can no longer assume that understanding the enemy is exclusively the responsibility of a soldier, a general, or a statesmen. The new reality of globalization and American hegemony across the planet dictates that American citizens must understand the threats that exist outside their borders as their economy becomes interdependent with foreign governments, peoples, and religions. As the world grows smaller, the risk of misinterpretation, violation of sovereignty, religious and international law, and the unintentional fallout of ignorant policies between American executives and foreign states can thrust an unsuspecting world into an otherwise avoidable conflict or war.

The use of information and education as force multipliers in the war against al-Qaeda could expose and cripple their radical agenda of jihad and Osama bin-Laden's desire to become the next great caliph. Easing of tensions through debates and public forums would further open the diplomatic and economic discussions regarding Islam's tolerance for individual freedoms, interaction with foreign governments, and regional stability and growth. Religious war is upon us and we must find ways to increase the use of information to facilitate the emergence and acceptance of a moderate strain of Islam with which the United States can peacefully co-exist.

CAN IRAQ CHANGE?

Historians rightfully argue that the ongoing cycle of violence in Iraq since the invasion should have been expected by the Coalition and was openly predicted by her neighbors in the months and weeks leading up to the war. Those who've studied Iraq realize that hatred and sectarian violence has been a way of life in Iraq since its first claim to be the Cradle of Civilization over 6,000 years ago. In Europe, Persia, and the Middle East, it's a well known fact that Iraq has never had a time of peace, or a government or leader that has protected her people, or an era without an invading army exploiting her resources or using her as a land bridge to the riches of Africa and the Far East. They know this because in most cases they have been the nations that have tried to steal and control the riches of Iraq for over a millennium.

Somehow civilization in Iraq had been stopped in its infancy. It had never matured. Instead, it became a mere cradle fit for robbery and abuse by the greatest forces in history: by the most murderous barbarians, by the most powerful nations, by the greediest corporations, by the onslaught of progress that sprang from its midst and took root elsewhere, continents away, and by the ravages of cultural self-wounding that ensured Iraq would remain a prisoner of its own heritage. Indeed, for nearly 6,000 years, Iraq has been shackled to unspeakable violence, toppled pride, cruel despotic authorities, and an utter lack of self-governance. The unbreachable continuum of its legacy inculcated bitter alienation as a birthright. Rather than becoming an intersection of the most splendid and accomplished, as ancient European civilizations ultimately became, Iraq has become a crossroads of conquest and conflict. [31]

So how did the 2003 invasion of Iraq and the invaders themselves differ from all the rest? Mainly because none of the preceding invading armies attacked Iraq to liberate her people and free her from a dictatorship. This was our stated purpose and I'm still convinced, as are thousands of my fellow Soldiers and Marines, that we went to Iraq to liberate her society and break the cycle of terror that existed prior to March 2003 under the hand of Saddam. And yet despite breaking that cycle of terror, we gave birth to yet another time of violence and sectarian hatred—could it have been avoided?

Could a Western power like the United States or Great Britain have truly believed that 6,000 years of hatred could be subdued in a matter of years by using terms like liberty, justice and democracy? The answer is simply . . . no. The key to winning, for both the Coalition and the Iraqis, is our willingness to look to the future and protect the past in the eyes of the Iraqis and the greater Middle East by dropping democratization and globalization, and instead focus on attainable goals that are designed to incrementally help Iraq to lift herself out of the past and regain her position on the international stage as a regional leader and international partner. Unlike others nations such as Haiti, Rwanda, Somalia, and the Balkans, Iraq has the natural resources necessary to achieve rapid improvement and modernization, both internally and within the region. This potential is exciting to the West and at the same time horrifying to those in the region who see their regimes of power challenged by freedom and progress in Iraq. Yet despite the different goals in this invasion than those of the past, the retaliation of Iraqis and her neighbors is the same: the repulsion of the occupier through armed conflict and attrition.

Anyone who has been to Iraq knows the secret to her future is understanding and leveraging her past. Iraq had a 2,000-year head start on Western society; Babylon was the uncontested nucleus of scientific discovery, including math, astronomy, literature, and art in 600 BC. But this golden age of greatness was destroyed by wars and foreign occupations, reducing Iraq to what it is today—a diverse grouping of people who long for the past and fear for the future. This loss of prestige and position in the new world has long haunted modern Iraq and has motivated multiple dictators and false prophets to rise to power, only to loot and further exploit Iraq's resources and delay her entry into the first world—a world she created over 2,000 years ago. Nonetheless, Iraqis are still a strong a proud people who proved to me their willingness and courage to join the 21st century.

Once you peel back the history, religion, feudalism and socialism, you find a people who simply need to be shown a path to the future— a path that considers their environment, acknowledges their pride in their heritage, and accepts the inevitable violence that has always been an intricate part of their politics and governance. The solution in Iraq is communication; this society values the written word, methodical documentation and an articulation of a critical path. Providing the Iraqis with a plan that lays out a path that they can see and influence will quickly turn the tide on those who wish to see the country fall back into a state of chaos and arbitrary exploitation.

A SOLUTION FOR IRAQ?

A year after returning from Iraq, while attending the National War College in Washington, DC, I offered a solution to the Iraq War to my instructors. This paper reflected my views then and today. I wrote the following:

While foreign and Iraqi insurgents in Iraq continue to initiate hostile contact with the Coalition and the Iraqi Army at a rate of 10:1, the Iraqi government continues to struggle for national and international legitimacy and sovereignty in the eyes of the world. Despite winning 99 percent of these contacts, continued fighting acts as a constant reminder to Coalition and Iraqi forces that the insurgents are on the offensive and unafraid of the results. Yet even without a stated objective, these insurgents do seem to agree on one shared goal: the end of the American occupation of Iraq.

As the continued use of US military force and economic coercion in Iraq appears unlikely to resolve this impasse alone, the Iraqi National Government (ING) should aggressively develop, negotiate and publicize a detailed phased military withdrawal of US forces from Iraq in order to defeat the insurgency. Such a plan could facilitate the acceptance of the new Iraqi authority and help to solidify its legitimacy within Iraq and gain acceptance in the Middle East, the United States and the world.

As al-Qaeda and other radical Islamic fundamentalist organizations have made clear, "its not if we win or lose, its how well we fight and how we die"[32] when fighting the great infidels that occupy their holy lands. Rarely in the history of warfare has a conventional army faced an opponent that gauges success solely on defiance through armed action, action that rarely has a tactical or operational purpose or meaning within a strategic or national construct. The stated goal of al-Qaeda is to sustain its ability to act in defiance of any American lead policy in the Middle East, resist unconditional US support for Israel and erode US support for corrupt governments within the Middle East (i.e. Egypt and Jordan).

To counter the insurgents' ability to use hostile action as a means to disrupt the ING, the Coalition should help the ING to regain legitimacy by placating the insurgency with a planned Coalition withdrawal that is contingent on a dramatic reduction in insurgent violence and an aggressive reconstruction plan for Iraq's infrastructure.

The use of hostile action by the insurgency to speed the withdrawal of Coalition forces from Iraq is their center of gravity (COG). Since August of 2003, the Coalition has recognized this COG and has attacked it with military force, economic incentives and sanctions, diplomatic truces and ceasefires, religious intervention and martial law with marginal results. In truth, the level of violence against the Coalition has increased proportionally to the coercive use of these instruments of power, thus limiting the Coalition's ability to rebuild Iraq.

The Coalition is at a critical juncture in Iraq, with a new Iraqi constitution, national elections complete and an ever-growing military— yet spiraling deeper into civil war under the shadow of continued kidnappings and beheadings, countrywide car bombings, unchecked sectarian violence, and the ING's occasional declarations of martial law throughout Iraq. To reverse these negative trends and regain the initiative, the Coalition should explore combining every instrument of power at their disposal to attack and destroy the enemy's COG.

What is currently missing in the ING's overall campaign plan is a publicly stated end state for the Coalition occupation. This lack of a clear event-driven timeline or checklist is causing frustration and anxiety in Iraq and the rest of the world. It is time the ING considers placating the insurgency's primary goal for a total withdrawal of Coalition forces from Iraq by publishing a plan to do so with a declared event-driven schedule. Such a plan is possible within the stated goals of the Coalition and the United States if they can agree that targeting the insurgency's legitimacy is more important than the face of the insurgency.

> *To give an insurgent what he wants, as long as it is not contrary to your central goal, is to steal his legitimacy for continued resistance against the government.*[33]

This plan would include two primary objectives: first, the establishment of a detailed plan for withdrawing Coalition forces, contingent on a methodical reconstruction plan for Iraq's government, infrastructure and economy. Second is a quantitative security force plan for the Iraqi army, police and border guards. Both objectives are subject to a measured tracking system designed to monitor a reduction in insurgent hostilities within Iraq. Simply stated, if the insurgents stop attacking the ING's reconstruction efforts, the Iraqi security and army forces and Iraqi citizens, the Coalition will begin an event-phased withdrawal of occupation forces from Iraq.

THE CONCEPT

Decisive to this operation is the ING's ability to place the burden of proof for peace on the insurgents. The ING must present a clear and precise plan for reconstruction, security and the Coalition withdrawal to the Iraqi people and the world. This plan must focus on a direct correlation between the Coalition withdrawal and a reduction of hostilities initiated by the insurgents.

This is not a timeline. It's an event-driven sequence of events that leads to a legitimate withdrawal of US and Coalition forces in order to return Iraq to the international community of nations.

This is a six-phase operation.* Phase 1: The ING will appoint an Iraqi Sovereignty Council (ISC) to develop the plan. Phase 2: The ING will approve the ISC plan and present it to the Coalition to confirm feasibility. Phase 3: ING will publicly present the plan to the Iraqi people and the world. Phase 4: ING will publicly monitor and track the progress of the plan and present weekly progress reports to the Iraqi people. Phase 5: Coalition forces will begin a phased withdrawal as key ING milestones are met in accordance with the plan. Phase 6: Reconstruction projects complete, hostilities at acceptable levels in accordance with the plan, and Coalition force withdrawal complete.

The plan must include both top-down and bottom-up programs that build support from the grassroots at the local and provisional levels, consistent with national programs and goals. In the end, an event-driven withdrawal of Coalition forces from Iraq may take years to complete and any reduction in the violence will take as long, if not longer. Nevertheless, if the Coalition and the ING ever hope to gain public support, both in Iraq and in their member states, a public plan is necessary to defeat the insurgency by returning Iraq to the international community of peaceful states.

---

*See Appendix I for detailed suggestions for the phases.

10

THE WAY FORWARD:
LESSONS AND BEST PRACTICES

Americans have a government that allows for religion.
Muslims have a religion that allows for a government.

THE SHEIKS IN IRAQ AND THE PEOPLE

The way I see it, there are two ways to rule people. There's ruling by inspiration, and there's ruling by fear. It's harder to achieve inspiration, but if you can get there, in the long run it's easier because you inspire people to take initiative to do things for themselves. Ruling by fear is easier until that day that people stand up to you, and all your power goes away.

We're trying to help the Iraqis find their inspiration. The insurgents are trying to rule by fear. They want to terrify people into thinking that their children are not safe, so that they stay at home and don't get used to this new life under democracy. They want to attack the things we build, like schools, so that the people see them as temporary. We can give them, but they want people to believe that they'll come along and take them away.

I'd rather be on the side of inspiration.

—*An unnamed Army Specialist E-4; 28 April 2007*[34]

It's about as simple as that Army Specialist put it so nicely.

"Money talks," right? When you inject cash into a post-war situation, activity picks up. Most importantly, if you use the cash to get young men working at clean up and repair, you reduce tensions very quickly. And we found that the tribal Sheiks knew just how to get the young men going. But as the Coalition Provisional Authority took control, inertia set in and conditions continued to deteriorate.

We are finding out how the traditional tribal leaders, the sheiks, are an important segment of society to align with. Our political scientists view tribalism as antithetical to a patriotic nationalism or constitutional state, but in fact they are a natural element and the keepers of order in their communities and districts. Culturally, they are part of the natural order in society—"the thesis"—and religious fanaticism is their antithesis, always seeking to replace secular tribal-based order with their vision of religious purity.

Tribes and their leaders are organic and integral: organic in that they are native to the soil and integral in that their structure maintains social order and protects property rights. The sheiks dispense local justice under known rules of the social contract.

We can see this struggle between sheiks and their opposing religious radicals in the large numbers of tribal leaders who have been murdered by al-Qaeda and Taliban fanatics in Iraq, in Afghanistan and the neighboring Waziristan provinces of Pakistan's Northwest Frontier. A friend counsels: "If you follow the purely Tribal model, you may impede and oppose Nationalism to some extent." But that may not be entirely bad. In our experience, working with the sheiks and other societal leaders led to local peace and some restoration of civil order, because everybody knew the rules of the game.

"If you preach Nationalism, you must destroy Tribalism" is the conventional wisdom in nation-building and large cities tend to facilitate the reduction of tribal ties and influence. But if you follow the natural marketplace, where Free Enterprise and The Invisible Hand rule and reward all ambition and aspirations, you can build up from the rubble of collapse without further destruction and use both the tribal system and urban populations to rebuild. You will want to negotiate the balance (synthesis) between Tribalism and Nationalism (Thesis and Antithesis).

In a multi-ethnic State, Nationalism and Tribalism often lead to Dominance and Slaughter as we saw in Rwanda, Bosnia and Kosovo. But in a Commercial State, The Invisible Hand of the Marketplace leads to prosperity and a healthy competition for primacy and prosperity."[35] And Iraq has been a hub of commerce and trade for 7,000 years. These people know how to trade among themselves and with their neighbors.

Now, a Kurd doesn't have to love the Sunnis or Shi'a. He only has to appreciate the value of their money and trade goods in the marketplace. Exchange salves *almost* all wounds. The marketplace and its access routes, have been the core of civilization since 5000 BC, and therefore, they represent the central purpose of "government" (which is tasked with establishing a fair medium of exchange, currency and the Media of Value—weights and measures—in the market, and security along its approaches).[36] The other tactical activity insurgents commonly pursue is to "decapitate" local society by butchering its leaders, teachers, physicians, lawyers and other educated elites, including the tribal sheiks. Ironically, Ambassador Bremer had decaptitated Iraq's economy, government and educational system through his now-infamous "De-Ba'athification decree."

Routes and marketplaces are the central targets of terrorists and insurgents for good reason: discredit the safety of the market and you discredit the government. I highlight this because General David Petraeus has, in "The Surge" of 2007, devised a plan that protects, in particular, the marketplace and its approaches.

So in counterinsurgency, you must build credibility for the host government. Charm and then enfranchise the sheiks and other elites and these problems start to solve themselves.

In the marketplace the "value of money" is equal to "the value of dominance," and deals get struck between the establishment and the nimble entrepreneurial class. This is good for improving quality of life, support for the government and developing information about the terrorist cells still operating. It is to be fostered.

Foremost, we must understand the central importance of the marketplace and protect it. And that is why, in watching General Petraeus' command of the surge, it is most heartening to see that his team is taking vigorous measures to protect the open markets of Baghdad and other cities to prevent mass suicide bombings in those spaces. Protect the marketplaces, their access routes and transport.

By Spring 2007, in Anbar Province, the Sunni Sheiks, seeing the wanton violence perpetrated by al-Qaeda in Iraq (AQI) against *everybody* in its attempt to foster civil war, have swung over to the side of the Iraqi government and now serve as our valued allies. Intelligence continues to improve and we are now able to capture or eliminate major AQI leaders and IED factories because Iraqi citizens have greater confidence that US, allied and Iraqi forces will take down the killers. It will take time, but time is on the side of a competent government that can give its people what they need to get on with their lives.

I also learned in my campaign in negotiating with sheiks and *sayyids* and in tours of service in Haiti and Latin America, that somebody has the "franchise" over every important *something*: *Somebody* controls the wheat and milk, *somebody* controls the religious order, *somebody* controls City-A and City-Z. And s*omebody* else controls a rival franchise.

A case in point: The competing *Sayyid* Ayatollahs of the Shi'a. Grand Ayatollah Sistani, the murdered Ayatollah Khoei, Ayatollah al-Hakim of the Badr Brigades and of the Supreme Council for an Islamic Republic of Iraq (SCIRI) and the younger Moqtada al-Sadr are all *Sayyids* –claiming descent from the Prophet's family. Each of these families has been practicing their religion for some 1,400 years and each has a particular city as its seat of power—a "franchise." And they are well-capitalized as well, with the Khoeis and Sadrs maintaining outreach libraries in London and Rome, as well as in their home cities. Grand Ayatollah Sistani has an internet website and has built hi-tech academies in both London and Qum, Iran.

Saddam had murdered most of the senior al-Sadrs before Operation Iraqi Freedom, but for the immature Moqtada al-Sadr to allow the murder of Ayatollah Khoei was an unpardonable act and a naked attempt to grab power that should have been punished. He turned co-equal franchises into a violent rivalry and should have been swiftly shut down after the murder of Khoei in April 2003. He wasn't, and thus remains one of our biggest problems four years later.

A friend advises, and I agree: "Avoid rivalries when you can; exploit rivalries and rival franchises when you must!" None of this is dishonest or a violation of the Geneva Conventions; it is a recognition of the legitimate power of the Law of "Divide and Rule" that we can find in our own *Federalist Papers*, and there is almost always a way to exploit in a positive way, as we in the 101st showed in 2003.

The most successful model for engaging the tribal sheiks was developed in the Ninawa Province, Mosul, by the 101st Airborne Division. The 101st was able to empower the province's sheiks through legitimate improvement projects. These projects were executed within their traditional tribal areas, gaining the Sheiks legitimacy and authority—authority that had been reduced but never totally eliminated by Saddam Hussein. Once these sheiks were credited with creating jobs, caring for their families, returning children to school, getting clean water to their newly refurbished medical clinics, and any number of other projects, they were able to return their tribes to a state of normalcy.

This state of normalcy afforded our ground commanders the security they needed to begin rebuilding Iraq. It also gave them the ability to work through their sheiks when there were problems, issues, or non-compliant forces or insurgents in the area. Essentially, by empowering these sheiks, our commanders could hold them responsible for the actions of their tribes, while keeping an Iraqi face on law enforcement, punishment and information gathering. This 4,000-year-old system works very well. It worked for the British in the early 20th century, and it worked well enough for Saddam Hussein to exploit and leverage following the first Gulf War. Saddam knew if he lost the sheiks, he would loose the people.

Historically, the sheiks are less effective in the larger cities. Islam is challenged in these modern cities, as traditional values begin to erode and so does the influence of sheiks. Saddam knew this and did everything he could to draw the youth into the city to reduce the influence of the tribal leaders. But he was unsuccessful in a vast majority of the country. The influence of the sheiks and the imams are crucial in returning normalcy and growth to Iraq. More than 75% of Iraqis still identify with their tribes.

To further the engagement of the sheiks, we should have decentralized the distribution of money from the CPA to the lowest possible levels within the civilian and military forces in Iraq. Immediate and timely access to money used for reconstruction, civil projects, and in some cases, simple compliance with the Coalition, helps significantly to reduce the influence of the disgruntled former Iraqi leaders, radical religious organizations, foreign insurgents, and terrorists like the late Abu Mussa al-Zarqawi. This decentralized distribution of money helps commanders to be more responsive with the sheiks and the needs of their people.

FILLING THE VOID

Most Americans, including those in our government, don't seem to realize that every man, woman and child in Iraq received a salary during Saddam's regime. Saddam's government was a socialistic dictatorship. This salary, similar to the sharing of the oil profits in Saudi Arabia, was based on a family's level of compliance with the regime and its programs.

When we severed Saddam's government from the people, they suddenly had no income. The people, including the former military, civil service, farmers and business owners looked to the Coalition to provide these salaries and their pensions (especially military once Saddam's army was disbanded). During the months of May and June 2003, the sheiks held their tribes together with their family/tribal wealth and kept them compliant while waiting to see if the Coalition would fill the gap created by the fall of the regime. Proactive military commanders found ways to generate income for these tribes in an attempt to avoid the inevitable violence of a nation struggling at the bottom tier of Maslow's Hierarchy of Needs. Captured regime money, unit operational funds, and eventually reconstruction dollars helped to fill the void, but the chasm was too wide to sustain in many of the larger cities.

TALK ABOUT JUSTICE AND FREEDOM INSTEAD OF DEMOCRACY

Western democracy specifies a separation between church and state. This is the single largest fear that transcends the entire Middle East about America and Western democracy. The average Arab is taught that Western democracy exists only to dilute and eventually destroy Islamic values and law. When we say we are going to give the Iraqis US-style democracy, it goes against the very fiber of their existence and infuriates the Arab world.

The concept of "Justice" does resonate with Iraqis, and other Arabs and peoples of the Middle East and the Islamic world. We need to talk about Justice and Freedom and let the Iraqi people determine the form of government the Iraqi people need. If we do that, we will truly be liberators and not conquerors!

Americans have a government that allows for religion. Muslims have a religion that allows for a government.

IMMEDIATELY REINSTATE THE NATIONAL SALARY SYSTEM

This will help those who are in need and also help to gradually transition the Iraqi public to whatever form of government they choose. For lack of a better term, Iraq has been a welfare state for the last 22 years. Asking them to suddenly and abruptly adopt a capitalistic form of democracy, realizing this was a forbidden topic in their schools and universities for 30 years, without understanding how that system violates the five pillars of Islam is unacceptable and arrogant.

A National Salary System (NSS) will help to curb the violence and drain the pool of unemployed and disgruntled men who are being recruited for the insurgency. Money is motivating the insurgency, as many of these men are not concerned about self-esteem or nationalism—they are desperate to secure, feed and shelter their families.

In their eyes, prosecuting jihad to save their families is currently their best and most honorable option. If they can care for themselves and their families, words like justice, freedom and liberty will begin to have meaning. But when their families live in fear and fight to live from meal to meal, freedom and liberty are meaningless rhetoric. The NSS will give the Coalition time to rebuild and, in the long-run, it will be less expensive than building infrastructure only to have it destroyed by the insurgency. Then, somewhere down the road, as the Iraqi government begins to meet the basic needs of its people, they can begin to create jobs and wean themselves from this program. It's worth noting that Hezbollah and Hamas legitimize themselves because of their social and economic programs in, respectively, southern Lebanon and the Gaza Strip. The *Wahhabis* in the entire Middle East also use this proven system.

RE-ENGAGE FORMER BA'ATH PARTY MEMBERS IN IRAQ

If you were to carefully track the beginning of the insurgency, you will find it happened within days of the Coalition Provisional Authority's (CPA) announcement that the top four tiers of the Ba'ath Party had no future in Iraq. Once again, it's a matter of understanding Maslow's Hierarchy of Needs. You cannot decapitate a group in a society that has obtained self-esteem by telling them they have no future in their homeland, especially millionaires who have a unique understanding of their country, its bureaucracies, infrastructure, history and the religious flashpoints that can incite their own people against each other. Placating these mid-level leaders is crucial for returning the country to a level of normalcy.

These are the recruiters and financiers of the primary insurgency. If we can engage them and make them a part of the solution, they will regain their self-esteem and no longer have a need to fund the insurgency. As we dry up the pool of disgruntled young men and placate these former leaders, we will gradually delegitimize the Iraqi insurgency in Iraq. This will allow the dust to settle, whereupon we can identify and focus on the foreign insurgency. Meeting the most basic needs of the Iraqi people will begin to expose al-Qaeda efforts within the country.

Before his death, Zarqawi had given us his plan and the method of his own destruction and eventual defeat.

If we deprive him of basing and unite the Sunnis and Shi'a, "[he] we can pack up and leave and look for another land, just like it has happened in so many lands of jihad." "By God, this is suffocation."

Despite Zarqawi's death, al-Qaeda has held on in Iraq because we have yet to steal its legitimacy with a clearly articulated strategy for ending the occupation of Iraq—the root point of the insurgency.

STOP TREATING AL JAZEERA LIKE AN OPPOSITION NETWORK

Al Jazeera is the most popular news agency to come out of the Middle East in the last 40 years. It features hard-hitting news, something the Arab community has never had before. The Arab world is instinctively suspicious of Western news agencies and, by default they're watching Al Jazeera in record numbers. We desperately need to engage with Al Jazeera.

To date, Al Jazeera has engaged both sides of the Israeli/Palestinian conflict and has attempted to engage the United States in Iraq. Currently we are not providing them our side of the story. The fighting in Falluja in the spring of 2004 is a good example of how we have failed to understand the power of Al Jazeera and how to use it as an information source and force multiplier at the strategic, operational and tactical levels of war. At almost every level of our military and civilian chains of command, you will find CNN and Fox News running 24 hours a day in our offices, command posts, and crisis centers, but no one is tuned into Al Jazeera. For the first time in history, we have the ability to stand behind our Marines shooting their weapons at the enemy in Falluja, live on CNN, and on the other screen we can stand behind the enemy and watch them shoot their weapons at our Marines on Al Jazeera.

We have complete situational awareness in our homes, offices and gyms, but do we have it in our command posts? Why don't we conduct interviews on Al Jazeera? Why didn't senior American officials go on Al Jazeera, where it would be translated into Arabic, to talk to the people of Iraq, and tell them our plan for helping Iraq return to Iraqi civilian control? We need to get our story to the people who need to hear it. The American public is in this for the long haul, but the Iraqis don't see their governing counsel on TV. They don't understand the road to peace; they don't understand that when the violence stops we leave, not the other way around. We don't have an effective communications strategy that targets our allies and the marketplace of Iraqi hearts and minds.

Using former Ba'ath leaders, Ayatollah Sistani, the local sheiks who are working to secure their tribes, and former Iraqi military leaders as our spokesmen, we can do much to gain the support of the populace and legitimize our publicly stated goals. A full-fledged information campaign is needed to get the word to our client, the Iraqi man on the street—or better, the man in the café watching Al Jazeera (see Appendix II for details). "Know your customer, know your people, know your territory." Saddam did and Osama does.

THE WAY FORWARD

Having spent July 2004–June 2005 at the National War College, I reported back to Army G3 in June 2005, newly promoted to Colonel. Commander Cody immediately put me back to work, through G3, as a scout involved with finding good people to assign to key duties in Iraq and in working with the AIG, IED-TF and IQATF initiatives.

By the time of my departure for command of Joint Task Force Bravo in Honduras in June 2006, those initiatives were decidedly more influential. Commander Cody and G3 had me and many other capable people working on the "nuts and bolts" of our efforts. At the same time, other officers and thinkers, under Lieutenant General Petraeus, were working furiously away at improving the theory and practice of counterinsurgency, producing a new manual that captured an intelligent doctrine which has now been approved and is being implemented with notable results.

Our experiences in the 101st showed that the "bottom-up" approach to stabilization and security operations is even more critical to success than the "top-down" course pursued by Ambassador Bremer and his team in the CPA. Bottom-up efforts are spread among the people and can be individually and personally observed by millions of onlookers, while top-down efforts are contained in high places and are only remotely observed through the media by captive tube-watchers. Bottom up initiatives tend to engage the people faster and better than top-down decrees.

It is important to note that to succeed we must attack problems from both the top down and bottom up. Further, it is in the bottom-up that you provide the essential services that the people desperately need when abandoned by their bureaucracies. And it is at the bottom-up level on the ground, as well as the top-down from the palace, where you can, with the least mistake, turn uncertain and disgruntled populations into actively hostile insurgents. Nation building "up from the rubble" involves creative destruction of traditions, and "stabilization" does not capture what's really going on. Bottom-up change does not elucidate the intellectual process but does illuminate the physical process of transition, and can tend to give comfort—build confidence—as the process of profound change unfolds.

Oddly, the experience at Najaf and Hillah and on, in contrast to Ambassador Bremer's mistakes in the CPA, underscore in my mind, that our civilian and OGA experts do not have the same sensitivity and determination to improvise that is inherent in our military ranks of "ground-pounders." And this is for many reasons, including the inability of civilian government agencies and departments to commit civil servants to long tours—which they did have back in the Vietnam era. So we in the military have to cultivate a culture of innovation and improvisation at every level, and in Iraq the 101st, and other units since, have proved that concept.

As this book attempts to show, our young men and women in uniform are capable of extraordinary achievements at every level of government and in the provision of services. As you see, junior officers and NCOs are involved with establishing governments at every level, while also restoring water, electricity, communications, and even superintending the national harvest. Not having direct military training, they fall back on their civilian education, training and skills, as well as the knowledge of their communities and of civics, and then bring all that out in a "Can Do" manner, exemplifying the best of the American spirit.

We are in the midst of a long commitment to countering Islamist fundamentalist extremism. Though serving in long, multiple deployments, our veteran troops will not falter. They are all volunteers and periodically have the opportunity to re-enlist or to resign from service, knowing they have performed a job well done in service to our nation. Don't worry about morale so much, as soldiers wallow in privation and tease each other out of any incidental misery or funk. And they don't much worry about what grandstanding politicians tell the media: our troops know the real story.

And young men and women will continue to step forward to fill the ranks and continue the mission until we have exhausted and contained our enemies. The troops and all our country's "first responders" will stand guard to prevent terrorist strikes and to pursue our enemies to the farthest dark corners of the world where we know they will continue to plot and plan further attacks on civilization.

Make no mistake: The enemy won't let us quit the fight and will come for us again if we let down our guard. We may get Osama bin

Laden one fine day, but his followers will continue their evil (and impossible) campaign to enslave the world of Islam and then the entire world. One can read their political/religious tracts such as "The Management of Savagery"[37] and know that ordinary Muslim would never subscribe to this wild-eyed nonsense. But they find sufficient numbers of naïve and disconnected younger people to carry out a tactical ground campaign. Al-Qaeda thinks it can exhaust the civilized world, starting with Muslim states, but in fact, they have no idea of how to manage, much less grow, a healthy political-economic state with vibrant markets that afford opportunity to individuals. Nor do they offer justice, dignity and liberty. They promise "Heaven on Earth" for the true believer but proffer only a Fascist Hell of absolute, mindless obedience.

The way forward then, is to continue to recruit, develop and promote creative and innovative thinkers in every officer and enlisted rank. We must *teach* people *How to Think*, and abandon the Cold War paradigm of *training* people *What to Think*.[38] Then, we must remain dedicated to our mission: defend the United States and to help other states wrestle with their problems of civil, social and economic development. But a world with increasingly powerful economic engines such as the US, Europe, Japan, South Korea, China and India affords opportunity for countries such as Iraq, Afghanistan and Pakistan to serve growing markets with their produce and products, as well as Iraq's vast energy resources.

I've learned that cultural knowledge is a decisive force multiplier in my experiences with Kadhim, in Iraq. As a Division, *The Screaming Eagles* of the 101st showed the way. Now, my former division commander, General David Petraeus, is in Iraq, leading the effort to complete stabilization operations in support of Iraq's constitutional government.

In Iraq, we learned quickly that we have to understand that anthropology, economics, civil infrastructure management and law are as important as the engineering and science skills that are more characteristic of our Cold War cadres in the services. These social science skills are vital force multipliers and we now have to teach that understanding at every level, including Congress and our executive branch departments and agencies.

CONCLUSION

I have written about my Army; as fine an army as ever took to the field of battle, along with its brother services, and about those who protect our country and extend the torch of liberty and justice to so many millions of oppressed peoples.

My time in Iraq was short compared to the tens of thousands who are there now and who have completed multiple tours in harm's way—accomplishing more, changing lives for the better, and serving their country far better than I. I only pray that this single account of what a soldier experienced and learned in Iraq will capture the experience of my soldiers, reflecting their courage, their belief in the US Constitution, and their undying dedication to their countrymen.

This book is to honor them and to educate those they selflessly serve: YOU.

"The Military is made up of the best and the brightest this country has to offer," is a phrase often quoted in the media and by our civilian leadership, but our society doesn't really believe those who serve are the best and brightest. Sure, we are good folks, but if we were the best and brightest we would be doing something more highly visible and financially lucrative in our lives. Success in this country is centered around financial gain and power, whereas success to the military means security, values, dedication and service without recognition: Silent professionals.

This book only provides a small glimpse into the United States military, and I harbor no illusion it will change the perceptions of those outside it. But I do hope Americans realize that those who decide to raise their right hand and pledge an oath are different and deserve America's thanks and support. Soldiers don't make policy, they only execute it. The US military will uphold and defend the Constitution of the United States to the last full measure, and all we ask of our countrymen is to do their part by actively participating in the democratic process. The military, according to the US Constitution, is subordinate to the civilian leaders of this great nation. On behalf of all those in uniform today and for those yet to raise their hand, I humbly request the people of this great nation to show the same passion, dedication, and loyalty to this country as their troops do and vote.

When the civilian leadership of this nation says we must fight, we will fight until the war is won. We only ask that you do the same and support your troops in the field.

Appendix I:
A STRATEGY FOR LEAVING IRAQ

DETAILS PER PHASE
This is not a timeline; it's an event-driven sequence of events that leads to a legitimate withdrawal of U.S. and Coalition forces in order to return Iraq to the international community of nations.

Phase 1: The Iraqi Sovereignty Council (ISC) is responsible for the development of a prioritized list of reconstruction projects that will include government, health, educational, judicial, police, border and military facilities in each of the provinces. Regional governmental leaders, sheiks, and other tribal leaders will vet the list and add or subtract within their provinces to ensure equitability and specificity for each population. Additionally, Islamic and other religious leaders will provide a list of religious, historical and administrative facilities that need assistance to ensure freedom of religion and access during the transition. During this process, it is crucial that the development of this list, and the involvement of local, tribal, military and religious leaders is publicly discussed and debated on local and international news and commentaries.

Phase 2: Once the ISC has compiled and publicly documented the list, it will present the plan to the Iraqi National Government (ING) for debate and approval. The public debate over this list is the main effort of this operation. The debate will include the conditions for implementing this list. Those conditions will include a mandate from the ING directed at the Coalition and the insurgency. The ING will place themselves between the perceived belligerents (the Coalition and the insurgents) in their country and levy demands on each. These demands will include reconstruction funds from the Coalition, a cessation of hostilities from the insurgents, a phased withdrawal of Coalition forces, and a peaceful integration of remaining insurgent organizations into the Iraqi political process. Although it is unlikely to get insurgent groups to step forward and engage in the debate at this point, the momentum of public opinion will begin to erode their legitimacy if they ignore the mandate and continue hostile action against the Iraqi people.

Phase 3: After approving the ISC plan, the ING will begin a nationwide information campaign, targeting the Iraqi people and showing them the details of the plan. This quid pro quo will help the ING to assert sovereign power by openly confronting the Coalition and the insurgency—in essence, speaking for the Iraqi people. This planned confrontation with the United States will help to dispel the premise that the ING is an American puppet, further legitimizing their authority when facing the insurgency and Arab community.

Phase 4: It is logical to assume that the insurgencies will remain silent during phases 1–3 to determine the ING's true resolve and overall Coalition intent. It's necessary for the Coalition to take the first step during phase four by executing a token withdrawal of forces from each of the primary provinces that have participated in the ISC planning process. These forces will withdrawal from two or three cities as a show of good faith in support of the ISC plan and ING. Once these moves are complete, the ING will begin a weekly progress report for the project list and detailed report on the level of hostilities in country by province.

Phase 5: This phase will be a continual process of quid pro quo as the key ING milestones are met in accordance with the plan. Reduction in hostilities + completed projects = phased withdrawal of Coalition forces.

Phase 6: When the reconstruction projects list is complete, and insurgent hostilities have leveled at acceptable levels to the ING, the Coalition will complete their withdrawal.

PHASED WITHDRAWAL MILESTONES
Examples of possible withdrawal milestones.

(Most of these have come to fruition and should be considered accomplished when the plan is first presented to the Iraqi people and the world.)

Strategic National:
- Iraqi Embassy in Washington DC staffed and operational
- American Embassy in Baghdad staffed and operational
- United Nations Embassy operational in Baghdad
- Iraqi Ambassador attends first UN Security Counsel meeting and General Assembly

Strategic:
- January 2008 National Elections complete
- UN validation of National Elections

Operational:
- 300,000 National Police staffed, equipped, trained and deployed
- 500,000 National Army Staffed, equipped, trained and deployed
- 100,000 Border Police staffed, equipped, trained and deployed
- 76 oil refineries operational
- 4.5M barrels of oil produced per day
- Infrastructure complete (list with specific facilities)
- Medical, education, power, government, religious, etc.
- National Salary System operational with ten year phase out plan as country develops free economic systems
- 12 radio stations operational
- 4 TV stations

Tactical:
- Insurgent violence less than or equal to one attack on Coalition and Iraqi forces per month
- Foreign fighters less than or equal to two attacks on Coalition and Iraqi forces per month
- Zero attacks against Iraqi citizens and foreign nationals

End State:
Operational Iraqi Government
Operational Iraqi Army, Police forces, and Border Guards
Informed Iraqi populace
Complete withdrawal of Coalition forces
American and Iraqi Embassies operational

Appendix II:
KNOWING YOUR ENEMY

By LTC Chris Hughes, Daniel H. French, Kevin McEnery

Know yourself, know your environment and know your enemy are words that have been the foundation for training effective application of our warfighting doctrine for years at our Combat Training Centers, and the focus of numerous After Action Reviews (AARs). It all seemed to fit so well with the doctrinally predictable Russians, became somewhat foggier with the less rigid Cubans, but was based on the specific threat of the 1970s and 1980s. The concepts of Know Yourself, Know Your Environment, Know your Enemy are valid and timeless; the question now is how we train these skills given our current enemy—one that does not rigidly follow a prescribed doctrine. In particular, how do leaders and units apply these concepts as they transition rapidly back and forth from Offensive to Defensive to Stability and Support Operations?

Arguably, we spend a great deal of time studying our environment and know temperature variants, weather patterns, key cities and key terrain. We know our unit and are comfortable with the unique capabilities we bring to the battlefield, and have a fairly good handle on requirements for various operations. But how well do we really know this new, thinking, yet still very human enemy? Do we understand what is important to them, or what they value and seek? Do we know what events or actions could possibly lead to violence? Do we understand how terrorist cells are put together and how we might be able to keep people from joining them? Do we understand the cultural and motivational differences between them and us? Most importantly, how do leaders at the tactical level develop a level of skill at doing this under pressure, often without the benefit of a dedicated advisor with regional expertise or deep cultural awareness? Let's take a look at these things, and hopefully better understand the

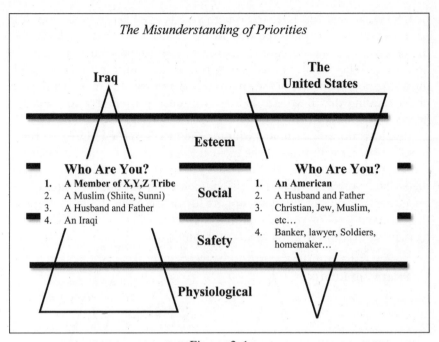

Figure 2-1

enemy we are facing, and see how we might be able to stabilize a very complex environment.

Let's begin with taking a look at the people in Iraq and what makes them tick. Figure 2-1 compares the people of Iraq with those of the United States. Notice what is important to the people of Iraq— being a member of a tribe, their religion etc., while in the United States we are proud to be an American, a husband, wife etc. Understanding these differences allows us to develop tactics, techniques and procedures targeting specific areas in order to stabilize the environment. We understand that the needs we believe to be so important to Americans are not so important to others.

In fact, the hierarchy in Figure 2-1 shows Iraq (and other distressed or developing states) responding to the standard Maslow hierarchical triangle, while that for the United States (and other more developed nations) is inverted, representing our high standards of living, which liberate us from apprehensions about the basic necessities of life.

Abraham Maslow developed a theory for establishing a hierarchy of needs, basically saying that human beings are motivated by needs and that certain lower needs need to be satisfied before higher needs can be satisfied. So what does this have to do with you as a Soldier? The Global War on Terrorism has changed the way we approach and plan for operations. In the past we focused on the "Spirit of the Bayonet" and taking the objective. Today we are placed in environments requiring an understanding of the people as part of the environment and we now must develop an understanding that if we are to win, we must also be able to "win the hearts and minds" of the people.

So, how do we go about "winning the hearts and minds" of populations in contact with units at the tactical level with a purpose of defeating those who are instigating the insurgency? Figure 2-2 uses Maslow's basic theory and portrays where a Division, Company or Platoon might apply resources to influence popular support for the insurgents. On the right is the expected level of violence and on the left is where a unit might place its main efforts to "win the hearts and minds."

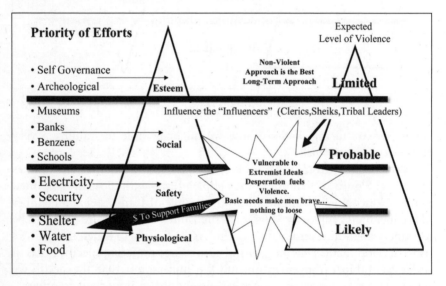

Figure 2-2

Notice how the threat of violence is greater when basic needs are not met. Take care of food, water, and shelter you can directly affect violence, and in fact lower its probability. The challenge takes time, requires great effort, and progress is difficult to measure. We have tried this before in places like Somalia where time and measurable successes became our enemy. As you go up the scale, where we might get a bigger bang for our buck, there is less probability for violence, but for the press and public, the results are visible and measurable. So where should we put our main effort? Why are young Iraqi men willing to risk death or detention by attacking much better armed, trained, and capable coalition forces?

Training for this type of war requires us to take advantage of the skills and training of other organizations. We might think about bringing in Civil Affairs or Special Forces Soldiers during training, allowing them to show you how to best organize in order to win the fight and the people.

We can also apply this theory to defeating Terrorist Cells as depicted in Figure 2-3.

Figure 2-3

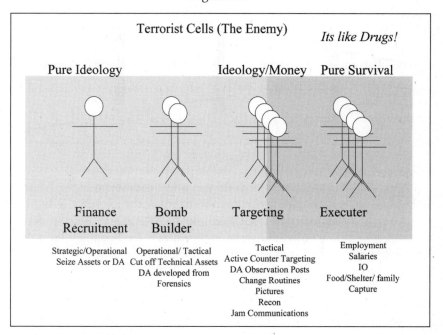

Above is a typical example of how a cell might be organized from the guy with the money right down to the person who executes the event. Notice where ideology (high end of Maslow's theory) fits in the Terrorist cell, and who is most concerned with survival. This becomes important because we now see if we begin to affect the basic needs of a population, we can also begin to affect the pool of persons who become executers for events. This is best done at the low end of Operational units and as you move to the higher echelons their focus should be on affecting the Financer. Figure 2-4 now overlays the principles of Maslow's Theory, showing what motivates the people within a specific cell, and who we might influence to most directly affect the cell.

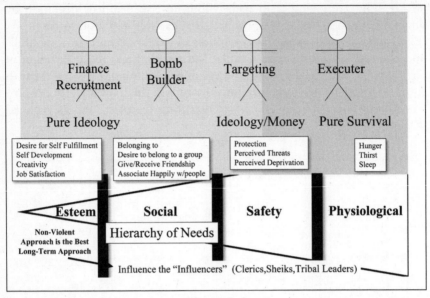

Figure 2-4

Your challenge becomes: How do you affect the esteem of the Finance Recruiter while also shaping the environment for the executer. What if a Company Commander had huge unemployment in his sector and decided to pay anyone who would assist in cleaning the city one dollar a day. Certainly only a small start to relieving unemployment, but it could be a huge step toward providing young Iraqi men—the primary "executors"—a viable alternative to support their families, without the risks associated with "collaborating."

Suppose then that this Company Commander's Battalion Commander took on the Sheiks, getting their assistance in rebuilding the city and offering a future with them having a role in running their city. Combine all of this with presence patrols and a secure environment and stability will follow. Before the war many, if not most, Iraqis depended directly or indirectly on the central government for income, jobs, and security. It is only natural that they would look for a new government to provide the same. Again, providing local leaders with a viable alternative to meeting their human need for prestige and importance in their community, and at the same time minimizing the cultural risks of being viewed as a collaborator can minimize the attraction of being a "resistance" member.

Figures 2-5 to 2-8 lay out "A Way" to identify the Center of Gravity and what might be some areas for you to target.

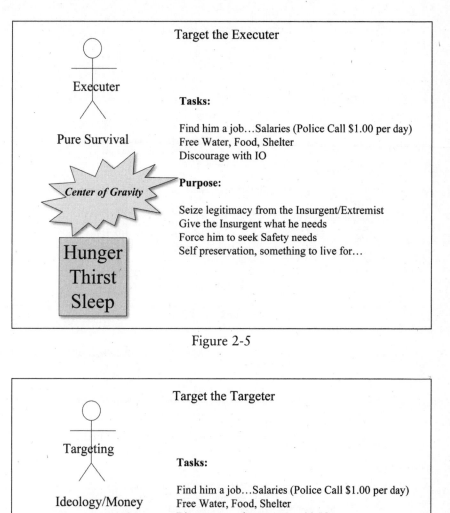

Target the Executer

Tasks:

Find him a job...Salaries (Police Call $1.00 per day)
Free Water, Food, Shelter
Discourage with IO

Purpose:

Seize legitimacy from the Insurgent/Extremist
Give the Insurgent what he needs
Force him to seek Safety needs
Self preservation, something to live for...

Executer

Pure Survival

Center of Gravity

Hunger
Thirst
Sleep

Figure 2-5

Target the Targeter

Tasks:

Find him a job...Salaries (Police Call $1.00 per day)
Free Water, Food, Shelter
Discourage and encourage with IO
Security of his neighborhood

Purpose:

Seize legitimacy from the Insurgent/Extremist
Give the Insurgent what he needs
Force him to seek Social Needs
Self preservation, something to live
for

Targeting

Ideology/Money

Center of Gravity

Protection
Perceived Threats
Perceived Deprivation

Figure 2-6

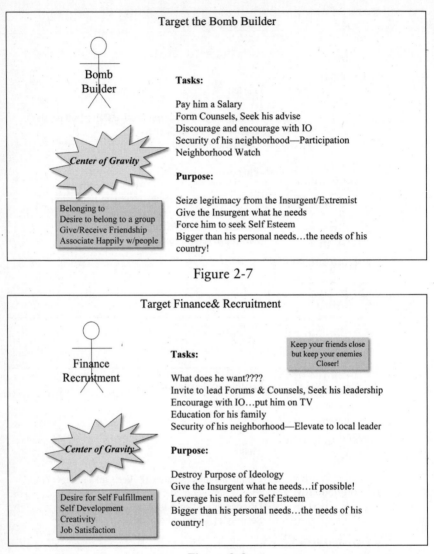

Figure 2-7

Figure 2-8

This is only a technique to Know Your Enemy and more importantly to develop a way to win in battles that looks nothing like the movement to contacts we practiced in the Combat Training Centers. One thing is clear, and that is the environment we face in the future will be unlike any we have trained for or faced in the past. Developing techniques and procedures to keep our soldiers alive is what all of us should be about.

ACKNOWLEDGMENTS

First, I would like to acknowledge four special people: My loving wife Marguerite, my incredible daughter Ashley and my friends Kadhim al-Waeli and Benjamin Works. Marguerite—my best friend— bore many burdens with good cheer, great love and keen sensitivity during the years covered in this book and in support of my writing.

As a high school and college student, Ashley spent hours and hours editing and helping refine the narrative, encouraging me time and again, to keep going, when I wanted to quit. She's a damned good writer in her own right and I hope she'll continue that.

Third, I want to acknowledge my most excellent friend and brother-in-arms, Mr. Kadhim al-Waeli, who served as my translator and cultural advisor while I was commanding *No Slack* in combat operations within Iraq. A native of An-Najaf, the first city we liberated in Iraq, Kadhim, time and again, gave great guidance as we occupied Iraqi cities and towns and then turned our work to restarting governments and public services. At this writing Kadhim continues that work as Senior Advisor-US Coalition Iraq for Lieutenant General Ray Odierno in Baghdad.

As to Ben Works, he is a reliable friend and coach. Ben edited this book carefully, formatting, catching typos, honing the prose and inserting passages that I couldn't find words to express, and then landed the publishing deal as my literary agent. I first met Ben through Kadhim and find him a wellspring of good ideas and insights into counterinsurgency and cultural affairs. Ben jokingly refers to himself as a "lightly decorated Vietnam veteran" and as a "recovering Yalie." He's been a nucleus for a lot of interesting little operations when I needed some help or some idea. No way Ben was going to let me give up on this book.

My profound thanks go to General "Commander" Richard Cody who put me to good use and who encouraged me to write this book; to Mr. Rick Atkinson of *The Washington Post*, who provided the foreword to this volume, and to Mr. Jim Lacey of *Time Magazine*, who contributed his articles and narrative inserts that pepper the chapters on our campaign in Iraq.

I also want to thank General Gordon Sullivan (former Chief of Staff, United States Army) for his encouragement and Mr. Wes Allison of the *St. Petersburg Times* for his contributions in this work. Also thanks to 1st Sergeant Ron Gregg for his notes on field sanitation and to Colonel Marcus De Oliveira (Above the Rest-Six) for his notes on the matter of the Iraqi national wheat harvest included in this book.

I also thank General David Petraeus, our division commander, who gave us the support we needed to tackle the tough problems of implementing peace in a traumatized land and collapsed state.

I want to thank "Major Bob" Bevalacqua for his work with Kadhim on the Cultural Advisory Task Force (IQATF). Thanks, too, to Hank Kinnison and his team at Wexford Group for their vital work on bringing to life the IED TF initiative.

Thanks to Dr. Lon Seglie, the man who inspired me to write when I worked at the Center for Army Lessons Learned (CALL). I further thank my instructors at the National War College: First, Dr. Janet Breslin-Smith, who encouraged several of us students to publish an anthology of lessons we learned in Iraq and Afghanistan. Also thanks to Dr. Theresa Sabonis-Helf, Dr. Chris Bassford, Colonel Gordon Bonham, Mr. Harvey Rishikof and Dr. Bard O'Neill.

Thanks, as well, to my South African "embeds," Mr. Garwin McLucky and Mr. Stewart Ramsey of SkyNews; to Mr. Dan Baum of *The New Yorker*, and to Lynne Rabinoff (a New York literary agent). These are the folks who read and reread to help and encourage me!

Thanks also to those who helped and kept me inspired: To Mrs. Marguerite Hughes (again—my best friend), Mrs. Karyn Elliot (NWC Classmate, CIA), Mrs. Connie Mellott (Red Oak, Iowa), LN1. Anna Nahulak USN, Mrs. Denise Leibold (Clarksville, Iowa), Captain Alysia

Harvey USAF, Mrs. Jessica New and Mrs. Jill Crider (*No Slack* spouses). Thanks also to Mr. Jay Harms (Platt City, Missouri), to Mr. John Emmerling (author), and to Steven Smith, my editor at Casemate.

Special thanks go to my many mentors: to Master Sergeant Dr. Patrick H. Hughes USAF-Ret. and Mrs. Donna J. Hughes (my parents), Lieutenant Colonel Albert Clark (AC) Welch USA-Ret., Mrs. Lacy Welch, Major Salome Carrasco USA-Ret., Mrs. Patricia Carrasco, General Thomas Hill USA-Ret., Lieutenant General James Campbell, MS Kathy Condon, Major General Jeffery Hammond, Major General Thomas Miller, Brigadier General James Terry, Brigadier General James Nuttall, Brigadier General E.J Sinclair USA-Ret., Colonel Art Negal USA-Ret., Colonel Thomas Schoenbeck USA-Ret., Colonel Larry Hollingsworth, Mr. Richard Simpson, Mr. Russell Benda and Mr. Donald Downs.

And thanks to all my comrades-in-arms: To Captain David Gonzalez, Major Tony New (Bayonet Six), Lieutenant Colonel Pete Rooks (No Slack-Five), Lieutenant Colonel James Crider (No Slack-Three); to my Brigade commander, Colonel Benjamin Hodges (Bastogne-Six) and to Command Sergeant Major Bart Womack (Bastogne-Seven), Lieutenant Colonel Patrick Frank (Bastogne-Three), Command Sergeant Major Richard Montcalm (No Slack-Seven), Major Matthew Konz (Cougar-Six), Major Alberto Garnica (Wolverine-Six), Major Thomas Ehrhart (Demon-Six), Major Steven Thomas (Gator-Six), Major Christopher Hennigan (No Slack-Two), Major Michael Avey (No Slack-Three/Alpha), Captain Eric Schnabel (Demon-Two/Six), Colonel Rickey Gibbs (Eagle-Three) and Colonel Edmund Palekas (Battle Force-Six).

Lastly, I wish to thank Mr. Thomas Christie (former Director of the Office of Testing and Evaluation in the Office of the Secretary of Defense), Major Anthony Milavic USMC-Ret., Lieutenant Colonel Greg Wilcox USA-Ret., former Captain Terron Sims and the rest of the gang who meet every Wednesday evening in The Old Guard Room at the Fort Myer Officers' Club (Patton Hall) to chew the fat. They're a helpful and interesting crew.

NOTES

[1] A low defensive earthen or sand wall built by bulldozers; a type of field fortification.

[2] These are army radio call-signs in a system or "net" that works thus at the battalion/brigade/division level: (designation)-1 is Personnel, -2 is Intelligence, -3 is Operations, -4 is Supply/Logistics, -5 is the Executive Officer (XO), -6 is the Commander and -7 is the senior NCO. The companies in the battalion have their own call signs and nets.

[3] Shorthand for the Russian Rocket Propelled Grenade series of shoulder fired anti-armor weapons, most commonly the RPG-7.

[4] On April 21, 2005 Akbar was found guilty of two counts of premeditated murder of Army Capt. Christopher Seifert, 27, who was shot in the back, and Air Force Major. Gregory Stone, 40, struck by shrapnel, and three counts of attempted premeditated murder.

[5] On April 28, 2005, after about seven hours of deliberation, Akbar was sentenced to death. The sentence was reviewed by a commanding officer and automatically appealed. On November 20, 2006 Lieutenant General John Vines, commander of the 18th Airborne Corps, affirmed the death sentence against Akbar. The case then went to the Army Court of Criminal Appeals under an automatic appeal.

[6] This classic movie could well serve as primer on Arab culture and campaigning for troops serving in Iraq, Afghanistan and elsewhere. Units could show the film, then discuss its many educational scenes.

[7] Colonel Perkins would later lead his brigade into Baghdad and directly to Saddam's central palace in the now-celebrated "Thunder Run." His decisive action was the final straw that broke the regime's back. At times, during his daring thrust, he was forced to use his pistol to shoot fanatical *Fedayeen* who were swarming around his tank.

[8] As a Sayyid, al-Sistani claims descent from the family of Mohammed and wears the black turban of the Prophet's descendents. Al-Sistani is the premiere

Ayatollah in the Shi'a faith and heads their College of Cardinals, the Hawza, located in an-Najaf. His website is www.sistani.org.

[9] Then Lt. Colonel Hal Moore observed the problem of the M-16's lack of "knockdown power" in his after action report for the battle of LZ X-Ray in the Ia Drang Valley, in late 1965. That battle is the basis for the book and film, *We Were Soldiers*. Supporting reports continue to come in from Afghanistan and Iraq.

[10] Revelation 18:21, The Christian Bible, King James Version (KJV).

[11] Daniel 2:46–48, KJV.

[12] Jeremiah 27:8, KJV.

[13] From Kadhim al-Waeli: The word Hajj means pilgrimage, Hajj is only when Muslims go to Mecca and Medina. The term for those who travel to shrines during Ashura and Arbaeen (40 days after Ashura) is *Zeyarah* or "the Visit." The people who go to Najaf and Karbala are called by the honorific *Za'areen*, the visitors.

[14] See Appendix II for a demonstration of that model and its application to counterinsurgency in Iraq and elsewhere.

[15] The nickname is taken from an early '70s rock group, "Commander Cody and the Lost Planet Airmen."

[16] General Schoomaker retired on 10 April 2007 and returned home in that truck, his honor intact.

[17] "To make war upon rebellion is messy and slow, like eating soup with a knife." —Seven Pillars of Wisdom; pp.163-64

[18] "Do not try to do too much with your own hands. *Better the Arabs do it tolerably than that you do it perfectly.* It is their war, and you are to help them, not to win it for them. Actually, also, under the very odd conditions of Arabia, your practical work will not be as good as, perhaps, you think it is." The Arab Bulletin, 20 August 1917.

[19] United States Department of State, National Security Strategy (Washington, DC: U.S. State Department, 2002), Overview, 1.

[20] Edwin Black, *Banking on Baghdad: A Saga 7,000 Years in the Making* (New Jersey, John Wiley & Sons, Inc, 2004), pp. 191–192.

[21] Edwin Black, *Banking on Baghdad*, p. 376.

[22] Daniel Benjamin and Steven Simon, *The Age of Sacred Terror*, (Random House Trade, 2003), pp. 39–40.

[23] Rand Corporation, The Operational Code of the Jihadists, (Army Brief; Brian Michael Jenkins, 2004), p. 4.

[24] Jim Lehrer, Bin Laden's *Fatwa*, PBS, News Hour. wpbs.org/newshour/terrorism/international/*fatwa*_1996.

[25] Benjamin and Simon, *The Age of Sacred Terror*, 46, pp. 158–159.

[26] Samuel B. Griffith, *The Art of War, Sun Tzu*, (Oxford, Oxford University Press, 1971), p. 9.

[27] Carl Von Clausewitz, *On War*, (New Jersey, Princeton University Press, 1984), p. 596.

[28] *Fatwa*-Online, Makkah Imam, "Nip Terror Groups in the Bud," 24 July 2004, News.

[29] Translation of Sahih Bukhari, M. Muhsin Khan, *Peacemaking*, Volume 3, Book 49, Number 857.

[30] Samuel B. Griffith, *The Art of War, Sun Tzu,* (Oxford, Oxford University Press, 1971), p. 84.

[31] Edwin Black, *Banking on Baghdad*, p. 10.

[32] Rand Corporation, "The Operational Code of the Jihadists" (Army Brief; Brian Michael Jenkins, 2004), p. 4.

[33] Infantry Officers Advance Course, Low Intensity Conflict Lecture, (Fort Benning GA, 1987).

34 http://www.redstate.com/stories/special_events/the_way_i_see_it_there_are_two_ways_to_rule_people

[35] Maxim derived from Adam Smith's *The Wealth of Nations*; and his followers.

[36] The Terrorists repeatedly strike at bus depots on the lines to the marketplace.

[37] Written by Abu Bakr Naji in 2006 and translated by William McCants, "Management of Savagery" is mostly an ideological rant about Al-Qaeda establishing interim governments in occupied territories to serve until the State is brought down. See: http://www.ctc.usma.edu/Management_of_Savagery.pdf

[38] See Major Donald Vandergriff's monograph *Raising the Bar*, and his book *Path To Victory*.

INDEX

27 Articles of Conduct, 245

Abdulla, Mohamed Lataf, 148
Abizaid, GEN John, 223–224, 275
Adams, CPT Cary, 53
Afghanistan, 191, 193, 208, 212, 222, 224, 227, 235, 248, 249; CIA, 246; IED Task Force, 215; national debate on, 252; Northern Alliance, 149; popular revolt, 150; Taliban, 268
AH-64 Apache Attack Helicopter, 38–39, 158
Air Assault School, 191
Air Force Joint Terminal Attack Controller, 68, 127
Akbar, SGT Hassan, 22–27, 33, 130
Al Hadar, Iraq, 192
Al Jazeera, 15, 107, 274
Allison, Wes, 105, 120, 286
Anbar Province, 38, 235–237, 269
Aristide, Jean-Bertrand, 15
Army Budget Office, 238
Army Initiatives Group, x, 207, 226, 229, 275
Army Operations Center, 232
Army Pre-Command Course, 206
Army Strategic Planning Board, 211, 219

Army War College, 207, 242, 244
Arnold, Gen. H.H., vii
Ash Shurah, Iraq, 166–171, 186, 192, 207
Asymmetric Regiment, 219
Atkinson, Rick, 88–89
Aviation Task Force, 226, 228–230

Ba'ath Party, 41, 53, 88, 94, 102, 111, 115, 130, 147, 150, 247, 273, 275
Babylon, Iraq, 123–124, 140–143, 147–148, 152–155, 263
Baghdad, Iraq, 47, 52, 137, 157–158, 184, 237, 245; 1918 occupation of, 257; 1st Marine Expeditionary Force, 155; 3rd Infantry Division march to, 76, 136; *Fedayeen* forces, 50, 54; fighters from, 133; invasion of, 19; Iraq Republican Guard, 45; Iraqi air defense network, 208; Iraqi resistance in, 166; joint headquarters in, 216, 219; Nashville zoning similar to, 41; occupation of, viii; open markets, 269; orders to move on, 115; "Tels," man-made hills, 56; "Thunder Run," 246

297

Bailey, COL Jeff, 250
The Balkans, 262
Barnes, CPT Jason, 140, 148
Bastogne Brigade Combat Team, 39, 113
Beamer, Todd, 10
Bevelacqua, Bob, 236–238
bin-Ali, Hussayn, 154
Black, Edwin, 257
Blue Force Tracker, 38, 40, 116, 135
Boeing Corporation, 227–228, 230
Bosnia, 227, 236, 268
Bosnia Training Program, 235–236
Bowers, SPC Ray, 37, 78–79, 99–100, 116, 135, 165
Bradley fighting vehicle, 52–53
Bratton, 1SG Steven, 6, 43–44
Bremer, Paul, 45, 247, 269, 276
Brown, CPT Scott, 42–43, 142, 152–153, 196
Bush, President George W., 37, 113–114, 206–207

Calculated Risk, vii
Camp Pennsylvania, Kuwait, viii, 10, 12, 14, 21–22, 25, 35
Carlisle Barracks, Pennsylvania, 207, 242
Carr, SPC Kim, 74–75, 102, 146, 172, 182–183
Carter, President Jimmy, 16
Cedras, Haitian LTG Raoul, 15–16
Center for Army Lessons Learned, 216
Central Intelligence Agency, 221, 243, 246
Central Iraqi Government, 149
chemical and biological weapons, 19
Chiarelli, MG Peter, 233–235, 237–240
China, 278

Christianity, 260
Civil Military Operations Center, 174
Clark, Gen. Mark W., vii
Clausewitz, Karl von, 46, 247–248
Clune, Christie, 12
CNN News, 25, 44, 131–232, 275
Coalition for Iraqi National Unity, 150,
Coalition Provisional Authority, 41, 44, 166, 184, 187, 237, 246, 264–265, 266, 268, 271–273, 276
Cody, LTG Richard, 245; cancellation of the Comanche, 226–231; G3, 207, 211–212; greets Hughes, 209–210; guidance for Hughes, 219; Hughes' NWC request, 244; Hughes' reports back to, 275–276; IED Task Force, 215, 217–218, 221–225; Iraqi Advisor Task Force, 236–238; Kadhim and, 232; senior aviator, 208
USS *Cole*, 257
USS *Cole* Commission, 214, 253
Comanche helicopter, 226–231
Combating Terrorism Directorate J34, 205, 214, 243
Combined Explosives Exploitation Cell, 217, 221
Combined Joint Task Force 7, 219, 239
Command and General Staff College, x, 244
Command Missions, vii
Condon, Ms. Kathy, 233, 235, 237
Crider, MAJ James, 18, 37–38, 48–49, 52, 63, 67, 71, 73, 124–125, 136, 160–162, 165, 169–170, 172
Crusade in Europe, vii

Crusader Artillery System, 228
CSPAN, 253

Damascus, Syria, 56
De Oliveira, LTC Marcus, 50–51,
    62, 177–180, 182
De-Ba'athification decree, 269
Defense Language Institute, 233
Department of Defense, x, 221, 223,
    226
Department of Homeland Security,
    214
Dermer, COL P.J., 250
Desert Shield, 17
Desert Storm, 17, 190
Director of Information, Army
    Operations Center, 217
Diwaniya, Iraq, 154
Dunlop, MAJ Kevin, 53
Al-Duri, Izzat Ibrahim, 166, 169

Easter Sunrise Services, Babylon,
    153–154
Egypt, 264
Ehrhart, CPT Tom, 61, 69, 73, 124–
    125
Eindhoven, Area of Operations, 166
USS *Eisenhower*, 15
Eisenbower, Dwight D., vii
Erbil, Iraq, 56
Euphrates River, 52–53, 76, 123,
    128, 141, 143, 157
Euphrates Valley, viii, 47
Evangelist, 1LT (-), 22, 74
Executive Agency for IED's, 226

Falluja, Iraq, 274–275
Family Readiness Group, 197
fatwa, bin-Laden's 1998, 255, 258;
    Sheikh Al-Sudais, 260; Ayatollah
    Sistani, 88, 112, 115
Fedayeen, 42, 44–45, 50–51, 53–54,

57, 60–61, 64–66, 75–77, 93,
    103, 112, 147, 212
Federal Bureau of Investigation,
    221, 243, 246
Federalist Papers, 270
Flight 93, 10
Fort Benning, Georgia, 191
Fort Bragg, North Carolina, 191
Fort Campbell, Kentucky, viii, 3, 8,
    15, 17, 40, 67, 120, 122, 190–
    191, 193–194, 199, 205,
    207–208
Fort Drum, New York, 8
Fort Hood, Texas, 238
Fort Leavenworth, Kansas, 206, 216
Fort McNair, Virginia, 244
Fort Polk, Louisiana, 63
Fox News, 236, 275
fragging incident, 19–24, 26–28, 30,
    32–36
Frank, MAJ Pat, 23, 48, 57–58, 62,
    158
Franks, GEN Tommy, 45
Freakley, GEN Benjamin, 54, 158,
    165, 180, 192
Free Iraqi Forces, 49, 145, 147
*Fresh from the Fight: The Invasion
    and Occupation of Iraq*, 252

Gade, COL Renn, 250
Garnica, CPT Albert, 100
Geneva Convention, 270
Gibbs, LTC Ricky, 163
Global Missions, vii
Global War on Terrorism, ix, 231,
    252, 255
Golden Age of Islam, 258, 260
Goldwater/Nichols Act of 1986,
    243, 253
Al Gomer, Dr. Majorid, 172
Gore, Albert, 206
Grand Mosque (in Mecca), 260

"Green Line," 159–160, 162, 164, 166, 177, 180
Gregg, SFC Ronald, 50, 80, 106, 108
Griffin, SPC (-), 20–21, 24
Griffith, Samuel, 40
Grill, 1LT Nick, 100–101, 117
Gulf War I, 150, 153, 207, 114
Gulf War II, 114
Gunther, 1LT Dave, 101

Hadith, Iraq, 258
Haiti, 45–46, 262, 270
The Hajj, 51, 154–155
al Hakim, Ayatollah, 270
Hall, Gregory, 28, 30, 32
Hamas, 214, 273
Hammam Al Alil, Iraq, 170–171, 185
Harris, COL Jeff, 248
Hassan Mussawi, 151
Hendrick, CPT Townly, 36
Hennigan, LTC Al, 11
Hennigan, CPT Chris, 11–12
Hezbollah, 214, 273
Hierarchy of Needs, Maslow's, 182, 234, 272–273
Hill, CSM (-), 192
Hillah, Iraq, 76, 82–83, 86, 89, 119, 124–128, 130–131, 135–136, 138, 140, 142, 144–149, 152–155, 157, 172, 231, 276
Hillah, Battle of, 123–127
Hodges, Col. Fredrick (Ben), 135, 169, 180, 192, 195; al-Hillah, Battle of, 123–124; An Najaf, 57–58, 115, 141; entering Iraq, 40; the fragging incident, 20–21, 23–27, 33–37; government in al-Hillah, 146, 148; Hughes' arrival in Kuwait, 13–14; movement to Najaf, 47; Najaf, Battle of,

61–63; names AO Eindhoven, 165; Objective Fox, 64
Honduras, 276
Hopkinsville, Kentucky, 12
House Armed Services Committee, 222
Hughes, Ashley, 3, 5–6, 285
Hughes, LTC Christopher P., vii, viii, 62, 179; Al Jazeera, 274; Hillah, Iraq, 82–84; Hillah, Battle of, 123–131; Hillah, government in, 140–155; al-Waeli, Kadhim, 48–49, 51–52, 55–56, 59–61, 65, 70–71, 75, 77–78, 90–92, 94, 96, 102–103, 107, 112, 139, 142–145, 161, 169, 231–235, 238–239, 245, 278; Army Initiatives Group, x; Army Strategic Planning Board, 210–211; arrival in Kuwait, 11–14, 18; arrives in Washington, DC, 199; assigned to Honduras, 276; assist from Cody, 244; Blue Force Tracker, 38, 40, 115–116, 135; Brown, CPT Scott, 42–44; cancellation of the Comanche, 226–231; change of command, 189–197; Cody, LTG Richard, 207–212; Command and General Staff College, x; Cougar's fight, 137–139; departure for Iraq, 3–10; Easter in Babylon, 152–154; embedded reporters, 14–17; finds Kadhim a job, 231–235; the fragging incident, 20–37; friendly fire incident, 117–122; Global War on Terrorism, ix, 255–266; grain harvest, 176–178, 180–183; Haiti, 15–16; Hammum Al Alil, 171–174; hot-wiring classes, 129; IED Task Force, 212–226, 235;

Iraq invasion, ix, 39; Iraqi Advisor Task Force, 235–240; Joint Qualified Officer, 243; Joint Staff Antiterrorism Directorate, 26; justice and freedom, 272; Kurdish situation, 158–165; mentioned in President Bush's speech, 113; Montcalm, CSM Richard, 5, 21, 23, 101, 116, 129; Mosque of Ali, 73–76, 86–93; Najaf, Battle of, 53–61; Najaf, movement to, 47, 49–50; National Salary System, 273; National War College, 241–254, 275; Objective Fox, 63–71; Operation Eindhoven, 165–170; Pentagon, 203–207; plan for end of Coalition occupation, 265–266; planned meeting with al-Sistani, 97–102; possible contaminated battlefield, 128; post war, xi; preparing for war, 19; promoted to Colonel, 275; returns home, 197–199; riot at Mosque of Ali, 103–115; Scud missiles, 18; six-phase operation, 266; solution to the Iraq War, 263; stitch and bitch, 7, 10; Tigris River Valley Commission, 184–185, 187; *USA Today* interview, 16; Warrior Combat Lunch Series, 249; Welch's advice, 46; Wilson, SFC, 106
Hughes, Marguerite, 3–9, 197–199, 242–243, 285, 286
Hughes, Michael, 3, 6, 197
Hughes, Patrick, 3, 5–6
Hurricane Katrina, 253
Hussein, Saddam, 169; alleged crimes against, 47; Babylon, 141–142; chemical Scuds, 18; chemical weapons, 128; controls the sheiks, 271; cycle of terror, 262; distupted trade routes, 237; dogma of his regime, 182–184, 187; his people condemn him, 114, 145, 147, 150–152; hold he has on his people, 91; know your customer/people/territory, 275; mission to destroy him, 71, 77, 88, 113–114; murdered senior al-Sadrs, 270; Najaf, 51, 56, 132; palace, 83, 140; portraits of, 93, 96; regime controls people, 172–174; socialistic dictatorship, 272

Idaho Air National Guard, 128
Improvised Explosive Device, 212–218, 220–221, 269
Improvised Explosive Device Task Force, 215, 219–224, 226, 235, 245, 275
India, 278
Ingram, LTC Jeffery, 52, 54, 56, 65, 126
Integrated Production Team, 226
Iran, 142
Iran/Iraq War, 142
Iraq, 185, 222, 235, 248–249, 262, 277, 185; Anbar Province, 38; debate on, 252; decapitated economy, 269; foreign insurgents, 264; ground assault, 39; invasion of, 19, 253; solution, 263; violence in, 261; what went wrong, 255
Iraqi Advisor Task Force, 235, 238–240, 275
Iraqi Dissident Force, 49
Iraqi Army, 264
Iraqi Army 5th Corps, 171
Iraqi National Congress, 49
Iraqi National Government, 264–266
Iraqi National Guard, 128

Iraqi Republican Guard, 47
Iraqi Sovereignty Council, 266
Iraqi Special Republican Guard,
 44–45
Irbil, Iraq, 166
Irish Republican Army, 214
Islamic Jihad, 214
Israeli Defense Force, 214

Japan, 278
Jawaheri, Ayatollah Hassan, 143
Jette, COL Bruce, 212
jihad, 259
Johnson, LTC James, 191–192,
 195–196
Joint College, 243
Joint Qualified Officer, 243
Joint Readiness Training Center, 98,
 194, 249
Joint Staff Antiterrorism Director-
 ate, 26
Joint Staff Operations Center, 214
Joint Task Force Bravo, 276
Jomini, Antoine Henri de, 248
Jones, CPT Tony, 36
Jordan, 264
Juad, Eskendar, 148
Al Jubari, Sheik Ahmed, 171, 199
Al Jubari, Marsham, 168–170
Al Jubari, Armer, 182, 195
Al Jubari, Sheik Athal, 195
Judaism, 260

Karbala Gap, 49, 116, 128, 135,
 154
Kass, Dr. Lani, 248
Keene, GEN Jack, 209
Kershaw, COL Mike, 250
al-Khoei, Ayatollah Abdul Majorid,
 98, 102, 106–107, 108–109, 143,
 270
Kidhir, Iraq, 154

King, Martin Luther, 119
Kinnison, COL Hank, 215, 218
Konz, CPT Matthew, 59, 69, 137–
 139, 167–173
Koran, 184, 256, 259–260
Kosovo, 208, 227, 268
Kumm, SFC (-), 22–23, 74
Kurdish situation, 158–165, 179–
 181
Kuurdish Democratic Party, 180
Kuwait, 10, 19, 39, 51, 62, 149

Lacey, Jim, 28, 32, 35, 43, 52, 77,
 89, 93, 108, 113, 131, 149, 252
Latin America, 270
Lawrence of Arabia, 47, 245
Lawrence, T.E., vii, 112, 245
Lebanon, 273
Linnington, COL Mike, 123–125

M1 Abrams tank, 52–53, 64, 87
M-249 Squad Automatic Weapon,
 119, 121
Macedonia, 176
Machiavelli, Nicolo, 248
Macintyre, Jamie, 232
Makhmour, Iraq, 180
Maloney, SFC Daniel, 50, 159–160,
 162, 164
al-Manshadawi, Ayatollah Amer,
 143
Maude, GEN Stanley, 257
McCaffrey, Barry, 209
McCoy, COL B.P., 250
McKnight, LTC (-), 249
McLucky, Garwin, 15–16
Mecca, 154
Mesopotamia, 41
Metz, LTG Thomas, 232, 234, 238–
 239
Middle East, 255
Military Units, United States, XVIII

Airborne Corps, 234; 1st
Armored Division, 220; 1st
Cavalry Division, 233; 1st
Marine Expeditionary Force, 37,
40, 155; 1st Battalion, 327th
Infantry Regiment, 40, 66, 112,
135, 177; 1st Battalion, 4th
Marines, 155; 1st Battalion, 8th
Infantry Regiment, 46; 10th
Mountain Division, 8, 15; 10th
Special Forces Group, 158; 2nd
Armored Cavalry Regiment, 63,
194; 2nd Battalion, 320th Field
Artillery, 127, 153; 2nd Battalion, 326th Engineers, 24; 1st
Battalion, 327th Infantry Regiment "No Slack," 26, 228, 247;
31st foreign army in An Najaf,
87; al-Hillah, Battle of, 123,
125–127, 130, 135–136, 143,
148, 155; An Najaf, viii; An
Najaf, Battle of, 37, 48, 50,
56–57, 60, 62, 64–65, 70, 89;
Easter Sunrise Services, 153;
embedded reporters, 17; fragging
incident, 23, 119–122; Hughes'
departure, 191–199; invading
Iraq, 39–41, 45; Iraqi demands
and complaints, 173–174, 185;
Mosque of Ali, 92, 103, 106,
109–116; No Slack, vii, x–xi;
Operation Eindhoven, 165–166;
preparing for deployment, 3, 6,
12, 42; Qayyah West Airfield,
158–159; return from Iraq, 205;
2nd Battalion, 70th Armor Regiment, 52, 54, 126; 3rd Corps,
232–234; 3rd Infantry Division,
14, 19, 33, 37, 39–40, 44–45,
47–48, 50, 52, 57, 66, 76, 123,
136, 149, 157; 3-101st Aviation
Battalion, 126; 3rd Battalion,

327th Infantry Regiment, 62,
112, 136; 4th Infantry Division,
46, 219; 5th Special Forces
Group, 65; 7th Cavalry Regiment, 53; 75th Ranger Regiment,
217, 249; 82nd Airborne Division, 128, 193; 101st Airborne
Division, vii, viii, 6, 8, 17, 28,
35–36, 38–39, 54, 57, 70–71,
88–89, 113–114, 120, 126, 130,
135, 150, 158–159, 161, 166,
168, 171, 178, 185, 195, 197,
207–208, 222, 231, 270,
276–278; 506th Parachute
Infantry Regiment, 179; Central
Command, 223, 246; Delta
Force, 215, 218; Special Forces,
215, 236
Mogadishu, Somalia, 249
Montcalm, CSM Richard, 5, 21, 23,
101, 116, 129
Moore, Sharon Tosi, 252
Mosque of Ali, The Grand, 51, 55–
56, 64, 70–71, 73, 75, 79, 87,
143; riot, 103–115
Mosul Area of Operations, 165
Mosul, Iraq, 155, 158–160, 166,
168, 171, 176, 187, 190, 196–
197, 222, 270
Multinational Force Corps, 239
Multi-National Force Iraq Cultural
Advisor, 234
Multinational Ground Force, 234
Muslim, 256–259, 277–278
Myers, GEN Richard B., 224

Najaf, Iraq, viii, 56, 71, 75–77, 79,
82, 87-89, 93-94, 97–101, 103,
107, 109, 111-113, 115– 118,
121, 123, 130–131, 133, 135–
136, 141, 143, 145–146,
149–152, 154, 157, 212, 231,

234, 276
Najaf, Battle of, 37, 47–48, 50,
    52–53, 55, 57–58, 60–68, 71,
    89–93, 131
Nashville, Tennessee, 41–42, 197
National Defense University, 243,
    253
National Public Radio, 260
National Review Online, 28, 131
National Salary System, 273
National Security Strategy, 256
National Training Center, 17
National War College, 241–250,
    252–254, 263, 275
Nebuchadnezzar, King, 141–142
New, CPT Anthony, 56, 58, 69, 99,
    110, 159, 170–171
Newbold, LTG (-), 246
Newsome, MSG (-), 19
Ninawa Province, 187, 270
"No Slack," see 2nd Battalion,
    327th Infantry Regiment under
    heading "Military Units, United
    States"
Northern Alliance, 149

Objective Fox, 63–64, 66, 69–70,
    89
Objective Lynx, 127
Odierno, LTG Ray, 234
Office of the Secretary of Defense,
    220
OH-58 helicopter, 70, 98
Operation Desert Shield, 78
Operation Desert Storm, 41, 78
Operation Eindhoven, 165, 170
Operation Iraqi Freedom, 28, 239,
    270
Operation Market Garden, 166
Origins of Terrorism, 40
Osama bin-Laden, 236, 255–261,
    275

Ottoman Empire, 238

Pace, GEN Peter, 224, 246
Pakistan, 278
Palace Mount, 153
Palekas, LTC Ed, 62, 136
Panama, 45
Patriot Missile System, 19, 24–26
The Pentagon, 199, 224, 235, 241;
    bureaucracy, 203; cancellation of
    the Comanche, 228; CNN team,
    232; Hughes arrives at, 204–205;
    IED Task Force, 222; institution-
    al culture collides with duty, 226;
    Iraqi Advisor Task Force, 235;
    Rumsfeld arrives, 206; Votel, Joe,
    217–218; Wolfowitz' comments
    about, 207
Pentagon Joint Staff, 205, 207, 215,
    220, 223, 243–244
Perkins, COL David, 50–52, 64
The Personal Memoirs of Gen. W.T.
    Sherman, vii
The Personal Memoirs of U.S.
    Grant, vii
Petraeus, Gen. David H., 108, 135,
    158; Hillah, 144, 146; CO, 101st
    Airborne Division, 88; commands
    in Iraq, 276, 278; decision to
    rotate commanders, 190, 207;
    forming a government in Iraq,
    176; Hughes' change of com-
    mand ceremony, 192, 197; lead-
    ers from Hammam, 171; Mosque
    of Ali, 92; note from, 168; "The
    Surge" of 2007, 269
Physical Security Equipment Action
    Group, 215
Port au Prince, Haiti, 79
Potts, SFC (-), 66, 68
Powell, GEN Colin, 46, 246
Prophet Mohammad, 64, 257–260

al-Qaeda, can exhaust civilized
world, 277; draws its strength
from, 257; foreign occupation of
Arabs, 256; God justifies jihad,
259; ignorance of Islam, 260;
radical Islamic fundamentalism,
264; tribal leaders murdered by,
268; war against, 261; winning a
limited war against, 258
al-Qaeda in Iraq, 269
al-Qaeda Security Strategy, 255, 258
Quayyarah (town and airfield), 84,
155, 158, 165, 166, 186, 192
Qum, Iran, 270

Ramsey, Stewart, 15–16, 59
Rapid Equipping Force, 212
Red Oak, Iowa, ix
Reed, SSG (-), 12, 196
Reeves, MAJ Blain, 180
Reich, Walter, 40
Richardson, LTC Jim, 126, 138–139
Rishikof, Harvey, 248
Rivera, SGT Reuben, 114
Roberts, CPT Mario, 34
Roche, James, 225–226
Roland Air Defense System, 127
Rooks, Major Peter, 5, 18, 20, 24,
35, 37–39, 62–63, 77, 86–87, 92,
96, 107, 117, 125–126, 136,
141, 146–147
Rumsfeld, Donald, 205–206
Rwanda, 262, 268

al-Sadr, Muqtada, 107, 270
al-Saedi, Ayatollah Saeed, 143
Samawah, Iraq, 154
Sayyid Awyah, Iraq, 166
Sayyid Ayatollahs, 270
Schnabel, 1LT Eric, 67–69, 108–109
Schoomaker, GEN Peter, 212–213,
222

Scud missile, 18–19, 24–26
Seifert, CPT Christopher, 33
Selleck, Tom, 182
Senate Armed Services Committee,
253
The Seven Pillars of Wisdom, vii,
245
Shanksville, Pennsylvania, 10
Shelton, GEN Henry H., 224
Shiites, Shi'a Islam, viii, 51, 56, 64,
77, 88, 107–108, 113, 147, 149–
150, 154–155, 260, 268, 270,
274
Shinseki, GEN Eric K., 206–207,
210, 213
Shurah District, Iraq, 195
Shuryrat, Iraq, 166
Sinclair, GEN (-), 192
al-Sistani, Grand Ayatollah Sayyid,
61, 88, 97–99, 101–103, 105–
110, 111–112, 115, 145, 210,
270, 275
Skynews, 15
Somalia, 42, 262
South Korea, 278
St. Petersburg Times, 105
Stability And Support Operations,
131
Stone, MAJ Gregory, 33–34
Strassman, Mark, 43, 108
Strategic Strategies Division, G3,
236
Al-Sudais, Sheikh Abdul Rahman,
260
Sun Tzu: *The Art of War*, 40, 44, 46
Sunni, 154, 166, 260, 268–269, 274
Supreme Council for an Islamic
Republic of Iraq, 270

*Takedown: The 3rd Infantry Divi-
sion's Twenty-One Day Assault
on Baghdad*, 28

Taliban, 149, 268
Task Force 160, 208
Task Force Hawk, 208
Technical Support Working Group, 215
Thomas, CPT Steve, 21, 38, 148
Thucydides, vii
Tigris River, 41, 157, 166, 171, 174, 179, 186, 192, 241
Tigris River Valley Commission, 184, 186–187
Tikrit, Iraq, 166
Time magazine, 28, 52, 108
Truscott Jr., Gen. Lucian K., vii
Tullahoma, Tennessee, 11
Tunnell, COL Harry, 250
Twitty, COL Stef, 250

United States Central Command, 223, 246
United States Department of Defense, 243, 247, 249, 252–253
United States Department of State, 243–244, 246
United States House of Representatives, 206
United States Supreme Court, 206
USA Today, 16

Veghel, Area of Operations, 166
Vines, LTG (-), 234
Votel, COL Joe, 217–225

al-Waeli, Kadhim, 52, 278; Al Hillah, 139, 143–144; arrives in

Washington, DC, 231; cultural advisor, 232, 238–239, 245; first meeting with Hughes, 48; Free Iraqi Fighters, 145; Hughes misses advice, 161, 169; in Najaf, 55, 61, 65, 71; meeting with GEN Metz, 232–235; Mosque of Ali, 56, 59–60, 70, 75, 77, 102–103, 107, 112; movement to Najaf, 51; translates Saddam's inscription, 142; volunteers to fight in Iraq, 49
Wahhabis, 273
Warren, MAJ Kyle, 23, 25–26, 36
Warrior Combat Lunch Series, 249
The Washington Post, 88
Weapons of Mass Destruction, 128
Welch, LTC Albert C., 46
West, COL Gary, 248
Wexford Grouup, 215, 219
Weyrauch, CPT Paul, 223
White, Thomas E., 210
Williams, Gary, 236
Wilson, SFC Pernell, 86–87, 92–93, 106, 161, 165
Wolff, COL Terry, 63–64
Wolfowitz, Paul, 207, 224, 226
Womack, CSM Bart, 13, 20, 192
World Trade Center bombing, 193, 224, 243, 257
Yugoslavia, 175

al-Zarqawi, Abu Mussa, 271, 274
Zeyarah, pilgrimage, 154